W9-CWA-549

TIPS FROM THE TOP

MICHAEL FEUER
EDITED BY DUSTIN S. KLEIN

Cover design by Sue Rahn
Layout and design by Andrea Jager
Edited by Dustin S. Klein

ISBN: 978-0-9911081-3-8 (hardback)
ISBN: 978-0-9911081-4-5 (soft cover)

Contents

Book Dedication

This book is dedicated to my two favorite editors. The first is my wife Ellen, my de facto editor who since the very beginning has been my first draft reviewer and proofreader. She reminds me not to fall in love with my turn of a phrase and instead to focus on what's in it for the readers.

The other is my official editor Dustin S. Klein, publisher and vice president of operations at *Smart Business*, who has been my collaborator and editor for more than a decade. He provides sagacious insight and prospective, helping me fill in any missing blanks. Dustin is also a supporter and gentleman who always says "Thank you."

I would be remiss if I didn't acknowledge my long-time trusted executive administrative assistant, known succinctly as "JP" (Joan Perchinske), who is my right-hand person and ally in just about everything I do.

This trio has made my writing especially fulfilling, knowing that they are always there holding my safety net.

Author's Note

Three years ago I wrote a best-selling book, "The Benevolent Dictator," published by Wiley and edited by Dustin S. Klein. This book focused on empowering employees, building businesses and outwitting the competition.

The content of my first book was based on my many years of experience building companies from scratch, including the international office products retail chain, OfficeMax, which started with one store and a then business partner, a handful of other investors and only $20,000 of my own money. During my 16 years as CEO, we built the company to more than $5 billion in sales and grew the chain to more than 1,000 stores. I was gratified by the national reviews that the book received and somewhat shocked by how many readers wrote to me stating that I helped them with a thorny problem or through a rough spot. Some said the book inspired them to go to the next step in fulfilling their business dreams, and for others it reaffirmed that they were either on the right or wrong track.

Universally, readers asked me when my next book would be published.

My journalistic experience chronicling my business victories and defeats, began a decade ago in September 2004 when my first column, Tips from the Top, was published by *Smart Business* in its, at that time, 20 some business journals around the country and posted on the Web at www.sbnonline.com. The genesis for the columns came about when my long-time friend Fred Koury, the founder and CEO of Smart Business Network Inc., approached me about writing a piece for his magazines. My initial thought was that he must be desperate to fill his pages, but he then explained that he had been reading a monthly newsletter I wrote to OfficeMax associates since the company was launched.

The OfficeMax narratives were an important communication tool because I wanted to ensure that my colleagues and associates heard the good, the bad and the ugly directly from me. They started in 1988 when the company was created. This was before the Internet became ubiquitous, so I began mailing my monthly thoughts to every employee. I wanted to guarantee they would see these newsletters and, accordingly, had them stuffed in their paychecks. I figured that in order to get to their money, they would have to get past my message whether they liked it or not. Perhaps many thought initially it was either a promotion announcement or a termination notice; therefore, it got read. After a while, I thought I should stop these newsletters because people may have considered them corny or a form of my own self-aggrandizing ways.

Again, much to my surprise, after stopping for only a few months I began receiving notes from employees asking: "What's wrong? Are you selling the company? Have you given up or are you just too busy now for a 'monthly conversation' with me?" The stronger messages came unsigned. I was flattered, and resumed writing. These newsletters then took on a life of their own as I expanded the distribution to business colleagues outside my company throughout the country and internationally.

When Fred invited me to write a guest piece I agreed to give it a shot. I'm not sure I was that great of a writer, but I certainly was fast. I dashed off those first published pieces in minutes. A couple months after the launch of my column Fred called me to say that the magazine was getting letters commenting on the quality of the columns and that the approach was unique. Full disclosure, I learned long before that one could do almost anything when writing except bore the reader, so I did try to spice up my column with a bit of humor and a sprinkling of iconoclastic comments.

After a short time, the column won its first national award followed by 10 more in the ensuing years. The truth is that initial recognition scared the heck out of me because I realized people were actually reading the columns and that I had better be careful and thoughtful about what I wrote.

As they say, the rest is history. More than 125 columns, and counting, have been published since I wrote that initial piece that launched with the headline: Don't shoot the messenger, unless it's delivered by email.

In this new book, "Tips from the Top," we have complied what readers have told us represents the best of the best columns I've written during my tenure with *Smart Business*. Some columns will give you a new idea while others will serve to underscore you're on the right track after questions have crept into your mind that you might be heading in the wrong direction. It is my hope that others will be inspired or, if nothing else, spur someone to discover new ways of achieving objectives.

Editor's Note

This book contains more than 100 columns written by Michael Feuer, spanning more than a decade. The columns are not presented chronologically in the order in which they were published, but instead have been organized into 10 distinct chapters. Starting with chapter one, Leadership, columns are grouped together within each specific category, ending with chapter 10, Competition. In between, eights chapters unlock proven techniques ranging from Overcoming Challenges to Negotiation. Also note that the columns appear as originally published, without editing. We reference at the beginning of every article the date each initially appeared. We believe this organizational format will enable readers to use the book not only for an enlightened read from beginning to end, but also as a fast reference on specific topics as listed in the table of contents.

TIPS FROM THE TOP

1

Leadership

Broken promises, missed opportunities

This column was originally published in October 2004

How many times in the course of a discussion has someone said to you, "I promise I'll get back to you," or "Let's get together and take it to the next step"? I'm sure you'd answer, hundreds of times. Next question, what percentage of the time have these people actually followed up and made the effort to close the loop? Worse, how many times have you made this type of promise and then failed to do what you said?

The truth is unfortunately, or fortunately if you're a hard core opportunist as I am, most people don't do what they say they are going to do. Are they bad people? Nah. Are they lazy? Not really. But, they are opportunity-missers. Reasons are varied and numerous why people don't do what they make commitments to do. However, the bottom line is these promise breakers miss huge opportunities to take an idea or concept and make something of it, or, to not take advantage of a new business relationship that could lead to something meaningful where you could actually even make a buck.

My awareness of lack of follow through and its dire and costly consequences more than likely stems back to my childhood. When I was a kid, no doubt I said a lot of things about what I'd do, but never did. Thanks to my parents, they broke me of this bad habit by holding me accountable. If I didn't do what I said, they'd take away privileges, like eating, for a few days. This might be somewhat of an exaggeration but you get the drift. When I went into business, I quickly learned that competitors and associates many times just didn't do what they said. They'd forget to provide the data requested, neglect to come back with a resolution or just ignore the opportunity or problem. Instead of taking away their food as I implied my parents did, I simply ate their lunch.

Early on in my career I developed follow-up tactics that were almost foolproof. Highly sophisticated and technical they weren't, such as writing myself a note and assigning a time and action due date. I became compulsive about doing this the minute I left the person with whom I was talking. I was even known to write it on the palm of my hand, the back of an envelope, or in dire circumstances, on the cuff of a white shirt, if the opportunity was cost justified with ruining the shirt. Next as soon as I was in safe territory, I would write or, most times, dictate a note on my ubiquitous trusty companion, an Olympus digital voice recorder. When transcribed, I'd then put the note in a tickler file. On the appointed date for follow-up, I simply launched my message. Almost every time, I got a response and many, no make that many, many times, those responses paved the way for a new deal of some sort or another or a stronger business relationship.

As I moved up the ladder in management and became a CEO of a *Fortune* 500 company, I used this tactic after every meeting and encounter, recording for posterity and follow-up what was to happen and by what date. Quickly I developed a reputation for having an iron-clad memory, a person who never forgot a detail, and for those naysayers who always look for the bad inside the good, some even called me a micro manager. I simply did it then and there and got the task off my plate. It can also make one feel very smug and virtuous like doing a term paper a week before it's due.

Some people feared me because of my obsession with follow-up and details; some undoubtedly disliked my style because they couldn't "blow" one by me, as I always held them accountable. But the good news is, many more learned from me. Some people even provided me with the best form of flattery by mimicking my technique after I shared my simple little secret with them. Most importantly, I seldom missed an opportunity, not because I was smart, or even pedantic for that matter. No, the real answer was since childhood I never wanted to run the risk of ever again missing a meal. As they say, the devil is in the details. Dealing with the details can become an art form that can lead to huge success not to mention an ever expanding waistline.

Us, them or for the love of the company

This column was originally published in December 2004

Every day in business we make decisions. Some because we want to, others because we have no alternative. If we decide to do one thing or go in a new direction, it may affect groups A, B, and sometimes even C or D. The reality is with every choice there are pluses and minuses. Some of the more thorny decisions will, no doubt, ruffle a few feathers. The higher up one goes in the organization, the more far reaching the decision's implications and the greater the degree of feather ruffling.

I learned a long time ago that, just as the lyrics in the once popular Bon Jovi song proclaim, "It's Lonely at the Top."

So, how do we make decisions that will stick and most likely work? How do we make them quickly, yet with thorough deliberation?

Soon after starting my company, the reality hit me like a ton of bricks: as the business continued to grow and I made the requisite hard decisions, some people would like them and others wouldn't, and many times I'd be second-guessed along the way. If one studies failed companies, it becomes evident that much of the failure, if not all, lies at the feet of the management team, and specifically the CEO, who couldn't pull the trigger and say yea or nay on critical strategic and financial matters. I also learned through, at times, bitter experience that procrastinating or taking half measures to solve problems were the worse possible choices. The winners in business today are those who can move from mind to market faster than the competition, and that means making decisions, not to mention taking calculated risks.

My method of making the difficult choices, which at times candidly to me seem to be of biblical proportion, was to follow the old time-tested formula of "ready, aim, fire." This means take emotion out of the equation, gather together the hard facts, decide where you want to go, and equally important, how you plan to get there. Secondly, don't fixate on trying to please everybody because that just "ain't" going to happen. Certainly, always take into consideration the effect of the decision on all of your constituents, starting with your customers, because without them you simply won't have a business. Get thoughtful input from your associates/employees, investors and advisors, but not necessarily always in that same order. Finally, and most significantly, don't make your decision on how it affects "Us" or "Them;" instead make the decision "for the love of the company" and the good of the entity. Through trial and error, I've learned that by putting the organization first, instead of special interest groups, you'll win many more times than you'll lose.

Beware, however, there are serious downsides to this Machiavellian, unemotional, fact-based decision-making process. First, expect to be by yourself more and more, as some will choose not to spend unnecessary time with you because they'll feel you made a choice that was adverse to them. On the other hand, there are some real upsides. One is, you'll spend much less time going out for lunch and, instead, can fulfill your mid-day sustenance requirements in about five minutes at your desk, which on the plus side gives you around 55 extra minutes to really think about your business and its future. Multiply five lunches a week times the 55 minutes, and that's serious quiet time. If you like cars as I do, there is another real positive. Since people won't want to be with you as much, there's no need to own a big SUV with a lot of seats or a long, ugly sedan. Instead, you can justify buying a svelte, two-seater sports car, knowing that the second seat, in all probability, will be occupied by a trusted companion, your briefcase. (I have three sports cars, which translates into a lot of tough decisions over the years).

Decisions are not supposed to be easy. Business is not a popularity contest. If you're a fan of mediocre grade B movies, watch "Wall Street" starring Michael Douglas as Gordon Gecko who exclaimed, "Want a friend, get a dog." I don't necessarily agree with Mr. G because he simply was a crook and definitely didn't love his company, plus dogs take a lot of extra work and time away from decision making.

To pull the trigger and make your move, listen and learn. Your wife, husband or significant other is another good source, as is your barber who you tend to listen to, particularly since he/she is normally wielding a very sharp razor. Next, study the consequences of your decision from a short, intermediate and long-term perspective. Finally, you've got to lead, follow or get out of the way — make your decision and then build consensus with anyone and everyone who will listen to you. Speak with passion and conviction, and always have your facts and figures at your fingertips.

Sure, some in the "us" camp will "dis" you, and the "thems" will talk behind your back. Others will even refer to you as, in the Harry Potter stories, "he who should not be named," refusing to utter your name, but instead referring to you as a pronoun. But, rest easy because you made your decision for a greater good — the love of the company. All things being equal, you will not only survive, but succeed. Lastly, remember, sometimes "it's lonely at the top," but the view is truly spectacular.

Do consultants borrow your watch to tell you what time it is?

Run your business with your head, heart and gut

This column was originally published in January 2005

Before jumping on a soapbox about consultants, I'm compelled to provide a true confession that, in the past as a *Fortune* 500 CEO, I've used them. Some are even good friends. Select groups are truly very competent, and although I hesitate to admit it, I've crossed over the line to the dark side a few times recently by acting as one of "them," trying to help a few companies.

At times, everyone in business and in life needs a second opinion, a sounding board or even an unbiased expert to help work through a problem, a strategy or an opportunity. Consultants, as third-party hired guns, are also effective at providing some heavy lifting in implementing systems, processes and the like.

However, what I've really learned over the years is that good managers, executives, and owners run their business with their head, their heart and their gut. On a very good day, all three of these sources come into play, and on a really bad day, any one will get you through.

Doing one's job is much like lifting weights or working out: no pain, no gain. What I've found is that most people don't spend enough time thinking and too much time just doing for the sake of doing. Why, I'm not sure. Maybe it's because it requires concentration and sometimes thinking can even hurt between your ears as you deliberate issues while trying to come up with a solution.

The lazy way out can be to simply say "let's call in the consultants and let them figure it out." This is a good thing for the consultants, but not necessarily so good for the company. Early in my career, I had a boss who used to say "mind your own troubles." There is a lot of truth in that phrase. One needs to take ownership and simply work through the issues before teeing up the project for outsiders.

Bringing in consultants sometimes, to me, is much like making friends with the toughest guy on the schoolyard playground and then starting to talk trash with someone bigger than you, all the while knowing that the tough guy will try to bail you and your big mouth out. That's much how many companies use consultants. Companies dump a load of garbage at their feet, telling them to "make it work." The consultants like it because this is good money. The company is the loser because it should be minding its own troubles and better controlling the process.

There may be a better way. Start with a legal pad, not because I used to sell them to make a living, but because it's a tool for a simple process to flush out issues. In the middle of a page on the pad, draw a vertical line from top to bottom. On the left side, list the issue or issues at hand, and on the right side start writing top-of-the-mind thoughts about possible solutions. Use your head by writing solutions that are close to being intellectually sound, fact based, learned or tested. For the heart portion, list those things that you hope, pray, fantasize that by some miraculous act, even divine intervention, might work. Finally, think with your gut. We've all had those situations where the answer that worked best came from some mysterious sources within. It might have had little to do with logic, but like love, when it happens, you know it's right.

Step two: take your legal pad firmly in hand and keep staring at the pages and scrubbing your list. Take off those things that have no chance of working, are simply ridiculous, and ideas that you would be embarrassed for a colleague to see, as he or she would know instantly that you are, at times, a closet flake with flakey thinking and ideas.

Step three: stop and hide the legal pad where no one will find it for a period of time you determine. Be it an hour, a day, a week, or even a month. Some call this a cooling off period. I call it a sanity check. At the self-appointed time for redemption, take out the legal pad again and give it a fresh read to see if your list comes close to passing the probability smell test. If it doesn't, quickly rush into the restroom and flush the pages down the john, knowing that you'll have total immunity from future embarrassment and the possibility of discovery of being a total flake. This is something none of us can do today with email or on a computer. However, if the list does make some sense and the solutions, albeit even slightly remote, might work, start fine tuning, tailoring and tweaking.

When you're all done, you then have a plan. At this point, you can now bring in your associates to help further flush out the idea. Finally, if you're so inclined, look at that time piece on your wrist, knowing that you've reached the bewitching hour to bring in the consultants and hand over your watch with a big, smug smile.

Persistence, perspiration and performance
A delicate combination

This column was originally published in March 2005

When I was CEO of a *Fortune* 500 company, I was always fond of saying, "We pay for performance, not perspiration." I evoked this curt comment when certain associates got on my nerves by constantly reminding me how hard they were working.

We all know that type. They're the first ones in the office in the morning but, more times than not, they're also the ones spending those extra minutes or hour reading the paper, checking the Internet or calling their kids who are not interested in talking to them anyway. These managers have an insatiable need for subtle self-promotion and the bragging rights of always being the last man or woman standing, or certainly the hardest working corporate person. They usually become legends in their own minds.

Don't get me wrong; there is a definite correlation between persistence, perspiration and performance. Some of the most successful and productive executives I know are also among the hardest workers. The difference, however, between these people and those who talk about how hard they work is that the former work smart and can demonstrate the fruits of their perspiration.

I'll always bet on the manager who knows when it's time to hunker down and pull an all-nighter to accomplish the big objective and then take a long weekend as a reward to re-charge his or her batteries, versus those who just put in the face time and don't ever seem to get done or don't quite reach the goal at hand.

My personal work style was to get to the office early, have a plan for the day which I usually prepared the night before, and then tackle the most difficult or unpleasant tasks first. It's a great system because the day gets easier hour by hour.

Sometimes I literally hit the ground running when I got out of my car as I psyched myself up for the challenges that awaited me down the hall and to the right when I entered my office. I didn't do this because I'm particularly gung-ho, but instead it was my way of marshaling my inner-strength to persevere or in some cases sucking it in and gathering the courage to "just do it." I progressed through the day with a fairly strict agenda and tightly structured calendar. However, I always left a little time for management by walking about. It was my way of taking a quick break and also at the same time, taking the temperature of the organization by engaging in very short conversations with a variety of people from clerks to vice presidents, as I traversed the corridors. It also served to let people know that I was paying attention, was accessible, and most importantly, that I cared.

Once I completed my rounds I'd get back at it until I was finished. After ticking-off everything from my 'Must-Do, To-Do List,' I then moved on to thinking time or meeting with colleagues to brainstorm, or sometimes just schmooze, bond or focus on new and better ways to get things done. The bottom line was that I found myself persevering on what I set out to do, and every once in a while, I'd even note a dignified few beads of perspiration either figuratively or literally forming on my forehead as the day progressed.

As my day ended, usually about 7:30 p.m., I'd pack up my briefcase hoping that my Three-P Formula (Persistence, Perspiration and Performance) enabled me to leave the place a little better than it was when I showed up in the morning.

Of course as I navigated my way down the hall at the end of the day, I always saw those same few people grinding away, with ties askew, shirts slightly damp and wrinkled, still probably thinking about all of the work they had to get done. I also suspected that some just hung in there so as to be seen milliseconds before they made their mad dash to the parking lot, as soon as my tail lights dimmed in the distance. Sometimes, just to satisfy my own curiosity, I'd walk to my car as if I was leaving for the day, get in, and then jump out and head back to my office, pretending I had forgotten something. I always loved passing those contenders for the Appearance Trophy on their way out of the building, thinking the boss was gone, and seeing that sinking expression on their faces when they realized they'd been busted!

There is certainly a lot of truth in the saying, "the harder you work, the luckier you get." However, just like the deodorant television commercial proclaims, "never let them see you sweat."

I would rather do it myself

Six words that can doom any manager

This column was originally published in February 2006

Every one of us wants to do ourselves the things we do best. Why delegate something that is satisfying, enjoyable and sure to produce meaningful results?

Psychologists call this operating in the comfort zone. I call it a zero-sum game. As the boss, we might add positives to the tasks we do ourselves, but we take away from the organization by never quite letting go and teaching others to do it well.

And some have a secret fear that someone else might even do it better.

Take the CEO who came up through the ranks from salesman to sales manager but who still insists on personally calling every shot with his former key customers. By "coincidence," each time the new salesman plans a visit to the CEO's big former customers, something comes up so that the salesman, at the last minute, has to do something else and so can't make the trip.

The CEO always gleefully says, "I'll pinch hit for you this time." Is the CEO afraid to let go because no one can do it better? Or, perhaps he is concerned that he will lose his safety net by letting his sales skills deteriorate.

Salespeople aren't the only ones hesitant to pass the baton. I know senior investment bankers who are managing directors but who still insist upon getting in the trenches with the junior guys during initial client drafting sessions.

Some accountants aren't any better. Even those running small and medium-sized firms still boast that they burn the midnight oil preparing income statements or tax returns while managing the place during daylight hours.

There is nothing wrong with new managers, department directors or CEOs getting down in the trenches and getting their hands dirty. There is something terribly wrong, however, when they turn around and finds themselves all alone in that very comfortable trench.

The toughest lesson new bosses have to learn is when to complete the handoff and when they, as a student of their particular specialty, must become the teacher. At the beginning, it might take twice as much time to have someone do something that the boss could have done alone.

Yes, some things will not only take more time, they won't get done exactly as the new boss would do it. In the short-term, this may result in missing a sale or making a mistake. As all experienced managers know, some of the best lessons learned are from mistakes made. Good managers, however, seldom make the same mistake twice, which is how they learned important lessons as they grew into the job.

When the new boss won't let go, subordinates pick up very quickly on unspoken messages and body language. If the new boss keeps telling the replacement, "I'll do this for you, it will only take me a few minutes," or "I'll call Mr. X or Ms. Y because I know them better," gradually the leader will "force morph" a subordinate into a worker who becomes dependent, deflated and loses motivation.

On the flip side, the new boss rapidly becomes overwhelmed trying to do two jobs. Consequently, the manager's new responsibilities, along with former ones, go unfulfilled or are completed halfway. This doesn't even take into account the fact that the new executive will never build a team if he or she does everything alone, won't let go or won't invest in training others.

This pingpong game of giving and then taking back is called yo-yo delegation. Employee spend way too much time looking over their shoulders waiting for the boss to step in and take over. The boss justifies the action by thinking that it is the most efficient way to get the task done right for the good of the organization.

The reality is that the boss is fostering ineffectiveness because the next time around, the employee won't know how to do it because he or she wasn't initially given an opportunity. Most of us learn by doing. The teacher's job is to keep students off the rocks and on track without constantly breathing down their necks.

Just like a good parent, sometimes one only need say, "I'm here for you if you need me." This engenders trust and holds the novice accountable.

In a yo-yo environment, morale goes in the dumper, a revolving door of good people becomes a vicious circle and the boss who said, "I would rather do it myself" is doomed to failure.

You can't have it both ways. You can be the chief, but it's almost impossible to be your own Indian, too. You can, however, have it your way when you learn to delegate, empower and gain satisfaction from the success of those you trained.

This gets to the bottom line of running anything and that is, "management is achieving objectives through others." In short, paraphrasing Paul Simon, "I'd rather be a hammer than a nail."

I say, "Once a hammer, always a hammer; once a nail is enough."

Do you use your time to your best advantage?

Stop worrying about wasting time and start increasing your productivity

This column was originally published in June 2006

When I was in elementary school on every report card there was a box that was checked either yes or no to indicate whether "student uses time to best advantage." Unfortunately as a ten year old I didn't appreciate the significance of this then seemingly benign measurement. Like most of us, I have spent much of my business career time-stressed and time-pressed. Over the years I have employed a bit of discipline, combined with a modicum of creativity, not only to overcome my impatience over wasted time, but also to become more productive.

I am one of those people who are always looking for an edge in saving time by trying to beat the system. The spectrum of my "dread of the ticking clock" ranges from always being the first person on and off airplanes, to being first out of the parking lot within three minutes after the winning run crosses home plate. I have dealt with this little personality flaw by concluding that impatience is probably hard-wired in one's DNA.

Thus, while recognizing that I can't cure this minor neurosis, I can certainly treat it.

Now, instead of complaining to anyone and everyone about things that waste my time, I've taken proactive steps to increase my productivity. As an added bonus of the techniques I'm about to explain, one can also ameliorate certain unpleasant experiences ranging from enduring a dentist appointment to sitting through a skull-numbing event.

What's my holy grail answer to unleash you from the trauma of lamenting the loss of every second of down time? It starts with a mental agenda which is launched almost as an out-of-body experience. Deeply stored in the recesses of the left side of the brain you create your own "my agenda folder" much like the folders we all use on our computers.

In this agenda, you mentally build a list of things that you must do (such as preparing a report or, in my case, writing my monthly column). You can also choose any subject on which you want to do to expand your learning. If at first you're not comfortable with this mental storage process, you can put your agenda written on an index card and keep it with you at all times.

Case in point: you're sitting in the dentist's chair as the invariably loquacious hygienist fires irrelevant questions at you in between the frequent one-word command of "RINSE!"

Given the natural apprehension of being at the dentist and having someone (who in my mind is an antagonist by training with sharp instruments always in hand) fussing in your mouth, you immediately launch your cerebral "to do list." Next click on the innerpersonal mental agenda you previously etched in your memory. Now choose one of the specific items you've efficiently stored away and organize the material in your head for the task at hand. Utilizing both visual imagery and an interior soliloquy you begin preparing your mental work product, much as you would do if at your computer or with pen in hand.

Before you know it, the unpleasantness of the event from which you have taken a mental hiatus has concluded. Instantly, after the hygienist removes that antiseptic-smelling, plastic bib and launches into the obligatory diatribe about advanced flossing techniques, you must move quickly to capture the fruits of your thought-processing session. I recommend, again, carrying index cards or dictating, as I do, into my constant companion, a digital recorder. In a pinch you can always download by writing on the palm of your hand, preferably in non-indelible ink.

Sometimes under dire straits, I have been known to write in a frenzy on my shirt cuff, but limit this only to my greatest ideas.

After disciplining yourself and overcoming a few false starts, this mental regimen will become a way of life. Beware, however, as there are some downsides if done incorrectly.

To the casual observer you may appear catatonic at times, and that can be disconcerting as well as disruptive to all around you, particularly in long lines such as at movies and the supermarket. Moving your lips while mentally dictating your thoughts is also risky for obvious reasons. (Visualize a muscular stranger standing next to you asking, "You talkin' to me?") On the plus side this technique can be employed virtually anywhere when you elect to tune out and turn on.

So what is the business application to what I have just recommended? Simple. Garden variety day-dreaming and fantasizing certainly have their time and place, but don't require a next step. However, this new productivity tool disciplines you to translate your thoughts and ideas into actionable realities that can accomplish objectives. Most of us today just don't have enough time, so something has to change.

By scrupulously managing unproductive downtime, you'll discover those precious extra few minutes each day that will have a significant cumulative effect while perhaps even lowering your blood pressure. After about six months of using these "mental gymnastics" you will have unleashed your creativity and dramatically expanded your capabilities. You'll become more productive, work fewer hours per week sitting behind a desk and extend your abilities as a true mobile executive. You'll think more and worry less about delays. Cerebrally your brain eventually will hard-code itself to go immediately from stand-by mode, at the time and place of your choosing, to real-time creating. Plus, you will be entitled to give yourself that positive "yes" report card checkmark, which may have eluded you in elementary school, signifying you now use your time to best advantage.

Oh yes, as a postscript, after this column is published, I plan to change dentists.

Beware of first impressions

Maintain objectivity and probe with open-ended questions

This column was originally published in September 2006

It happens to all of us. Sometime, somewhere we have fallen or will fall victim to one of the most deadly sins in business — making snap judgments on first impressions. It can occur when a person walks into your office for an interview or when you meet a client or customer for the first time. Take the highly anticipated interview that you have scheduled with the prayed for Mr. or Ms. Right. After months of scouring resumes and talking to head-hunters, you are certain you have found your "savior." Your fantasy is this person will join your company, initiate changes, fix what's broken, make you even more successful, and give you that elusive time to spend with your family. With much expectation, your assistant announces that the "water-walker" has arrived and you eagerly have the person ushered into your inner sanctum for the moment of reckoning.

You straighten your tie, pull down your jacket, prepare to flash your best smile, and extend your right hand as the hoped for miracle-worker crosses your threshold. In seconds you size up the candidate from head to toe. Instantly you feel a searing pain in your frontal lobe as your great expectations deflate like a cheap carnival balloon.

What happened? You have just succumbed to making an instant decision based on a mere initial visual scanning. Deep down inside you know by training and intellect that you shouldn't "judge a book by its cover," but nonetheless you feel as if you're in a Borders Book Store staring at the dust-covered book jacket of what must be the worst novel on the planet. In this case, something has "turned you off."

Okay, so the candidate's big, bold, very out of date glen-plaid suit with the wide-striped shirt and polka dot tie may not exactly go together. Besides the clothes, perhaps your would-be messiah grew up in a place where dentists and orthodontists were unavailable. You know in your heart of hearts, just as your parents taught you, that beauty is truly only skin deep.

So what do you do next after making this superficial decision: (1) salvage the interview and dig deep to find the person's inner strengths and capabilities? (2) if the applicant is from a competitor, at least take the time to gain an insight as to why the other guy seems to beat you? or, (3) try to figure out a way to make the session as professional as possible, doing so in the shortest amount of time that would be socially acceptable and without the risk of the candidate filing some kind of legal complaint for perceived discrimination? Although rudeness doesn't justify a lawsuit, it can lead to tarnishing the reputation of you and your company.

The best course of action at this point is force yourself to ask intelligent, insightful questions that may penetrate the candidate's negative aesthetic façade. Open-ended questions requiring him to respond in a cogent manner by at least stringing together a few intelligent sentences is a good first start. Never ask something that merely needs a "yes" or "no," but instead probe by framing your interrogatories in a manner that makes the candidate think. Ask the responder to walk you through how he or she salvaged a bad business situation or explain the steps taken to land the best business deal of the person's career. Try this for five or ten minutes and you may find that the candidate grows on you and may actually have unique redeeming qualities.

Bear in mind that if your issue with the individual is merely cosmetic, there are always fashion consultants, a variety of other types of coaches, and under the most severe circumstances for an otherwise superstar, minor cosmetic surgery might work, although this may be a stretch. Seriously, over the years, I have found that many of my first impressions have been proven totally inaccurate once I dug a little deeper and determined how someone thinks under fire, communicates, and translates concepts into actionable plans.

This same booby-trap of first impressions applies to negotiating deals when you underestimate an opponent perhaps because of their "oh shucks" mannerisms. I had a boss who once taught me an important lesson: "The dumbest farmers grow the biggest potatoes."

The most successful sales people have learned never to judge a customer who walks into the showroom based solely on his or her garb or physical appearance. The best true story I have ever heard occurred in a very toney NYC 5th Avenue jewelry store when an unshaven gentlemen in tattered jeans and a work shirt came through the door. The sales people on the floor, except for one, looked askance at this shopper. However, a young new saleslady decided to engage the potential customer, asking the basic qualifying questions before jumping to a "not going to waste my time" conclusion. The bottom line resulted in a fairy-tale come true for the saleslady, after the unkempt customer purchased a 70 carat diamond ring for his wife. The buyer turned out to be some high potentate from an exotic country, and this sales person earned the highest commission in the store's history.

Not all interviews or stories have happy endings. Sure, about 50 percent of the time that first gut reaction will probably be closer to the truth, but on the positive side the other 50 percent of the time you may have the opportunity to discover a diamond in the rough, pun intended. As they say, "beware of first impressions" and "strangers bearing gifts."

CEO superhero
Fate or fantasy?

This column was originally published in December 2006

As very young children we all have our fantasies. They can be as outrageous as saving the world from outer space invaders to meeting Prince Charming just before the stroke of midnight. When we progress to adolescence, the fantasies continue. Now they become more grounded by the world around us: being the high school quarterback who throws the "Hail Mary" pass in the final game of the season or the actress, discovered by a Hollywood agent while playing Juliet in the school play, who becomes an instant American idol. As we begin careers, our dreams most likely turn to those measured either economically or intellectually. We devise sometimes obscure ideas that will transform our companies or organizations into the new industry gold standard. Or some fantasize that they will become revered by their employees as they lead an egalitarian organization in which retirement is mandated at age 30 with full pay and benefits or when each employee reaches a net worth of $10 million through lucrative stock options, whichever comes first.

However, eventually for far too many, inertia sets in as dreams begin to flicker and then fade. What happened to those who envisioned themselves as the CEO Superhero, a great leader who could leap tall buildings with a single bound, move faster than a speeding bullet and be more powerful than a locomotive? What caused the disconnect? The "wanna be" leaders were certainly as smart as the next guy, just as educated and perhaps even better-looking. It probably began with a twinge of doubt about this or that, which was eventually followed by off-the-charts insecurity. Instead of innovating, many acquiesced and blended into the masses, driven by the all too common phenomenon, "F of F" or Fear of Failure. All of a sudden, instead of dreaming about leading, a previous "dare-to-be great" innovator looks forward to the tranquility, safety and obedience of merely following. So what makes one person a dynamic leader and the other a follower or laggard hanger-on? Is it a matter of fate, or a lack of fantasy? Everyone knows how to dream, but an incredibly small number know how to transform innovative dreams — fantasies — into an unprecedented smash hit. Is there magic in the metamorphosis of taking a germ of an idea to new meteoric heights? No, I firmly believe that true discovery is many times just a matter of follow-through, combined with the tedious and methodical amalgamation of forming a myriad of pieces into a grand mosaic — a completed puzzle that ultimately unlocks that elusive secret sauce.

In scenic Shaker Heights, Ohio, sits Laurel School, an independent girls' school where my wife happens to work. Every time I call her, the receptionist answers the phone with the proud assertion and challenge: "Dream, Dare, Do" immediately followed by the school's name. This motto underscores my personal philosophy about the integral ingredients for achievement. Laurel School has synthesized a complicated formula into three simple words.

Though most of us frequently dream, only a precious few have been taught to dare and do. Too many have learned that if they dare to think or act differently, it could be a very risky proposition, one that might even lead to failure or ridicule. Worse yet, that seemingly "great" idea might turn out to be the next grand dud, much like the infamous 1957 Edsel (by far the biggest car failure in automotive history) or the "New Coke" (which is the lesser known 1980s product/marketing catastrophe based on an ill-conceived concept with an ambiguous name that didn't resonate with the consumer). And if that were not enough, we ponder the sacrifices involved in "doing." After all, we live in a world of immediate gratification where most believe extra effort must have a guaranteed, iron-clad pay-off, or why bother? There are just too many reasons to live a safe life and not take any chances. This is a wonderful country where the ordinary person can still live the American dream with a house in the suburbs, a two-car garage, a big flat-screen plasma TV, and a combo cellphone/PDA with "Spell-Check."

No guts, no glory; no pain, no gain; the more difficult the struggle, the greater the victory. We've heard all these hackneyed phrases too many times, but they are true: to create something meaningful, very meaningful effort must be invested. We've been brainwashed through the years that great leaders are more likely than not just ordinary people in extraordinary situations. I believe the opposite to be true. It is extraordinary leaders who take the ordinary and find a better way. Just look at what's been done by dramatizing the attributes of the basics: bread, water and coffee, which are now marketed around the world in unique stores, or glitzy packaging and formulations that generate massive sales and profits. The streets are littered with peoples' potential great ideas — fantasies and dreams if you will — because when the authors of these concepts reached the proverbial fork in the road, they chose the path of least resistance. Instead of working through the issues and discovering improved alternatives, they succumbed to the comfort of inertia. But in the cases of those few, who did persevere, today you'll find them running their own businesses, leading major corporations as senior executives or making meaningful contributions in their chosen field, be it commerce, academia, health care or public service.

Remember, the problem with dreaming is that most of us wake up and cannot recall the outcome. However, when you combine Dreaming with Daring and Doing, your fantasy can become your fate.

Do as I say, not as I do
A new CEO mantra or a dyslexic PDA calendar?

This column was originally published in January 2007

Just count the number of well-known, and formerly well-respected, CEOs and other C-level types who have fallen on their swords after revelations that they have been involved with the now infamous practice of backdating stock options. The benefactors of their ignominious actions have been co-inhabitants of the Executive Wing. Misguided corporate titans have also seduced the best and brightest to join their companies with a lure of guaranteed fortune from "opportunistically" dated options. Worst of all, in too many cases, their motivations have been driven by egregious personal greed.

When the first few incidents of backdating options surfaced, some thought they were isolated cases, perhaps attributable to a CEO using a malfunctioning, Palm-type personal digital assistant (PDA) with a dyslexic calendar function that randomly transposed dates or dropped a digit or two here and there. Initially, apologists for corporate America donned their rose-colored glasses and said "no big deal, this too shall pass." But it did not! Instead it became painfully obvious that the practitioners of this new calendar math seemed to multiply exponentially to epidemic proportions.

How could this be? Aren't CEOs supposed to be the Captains of our free enterprise system, who not only inspire and innovate but also lead by example, disseminating their advice to subordinates while holding themselves to an even higher standard?

It may have started with a few high level executives justifying in their own minds that they were simply trying to find an economical way to hire or keep top performers. With the equivalent of getting a sneak peak at tomorrow's Wall Street Journal stock price pages today, they picked an option grant date that guaranteed new riches to the recipients. At first a misguided CEO thinks, "I'm doing this for the good of the company, so what if it is a little on the gray side? What counts are the end results."

There are dozens of similar scenarios that have no doubt been played out in the run amok executive's mind. However, at the end of the day, none would pass my longstanding "Mother Rule." Forget Sarbanes Oxley; if you wouldn't want your mother to know you did something then it's gotta be wrong.

The "crack-cocaine" addiction in corporate America doesn't always involve a white powder — sometimes just the stroke of a pen. How could reasonably intelligent executives get themselves into so much trouble? It has something to do with these CEO's super-sized sense of self, incessantly being fueled by the yes-men whose full-time job is to pave the way for the boss. Gradually the CEO starts to think he's omnipotent because he has the power to easily make things happen.

There are antidotes to stem these illusions and keep all managers on the straight and narrow. The most effective is a simple "reality check" that keeps you well-grounded and curbs rash impulses to take the first bite of forbidden fruit that leads to inappropriate behavior launching a career of deception.

One of the keys is, don't isolate yourself and hang out only with people who are (pardon the phrase) suck-ups. No matter if you're the CEO, small business owner or mid-level manager you must regularly talk one-on-one with those employees on the very lowest rung of the ladder. Get off your derrière and go into the cafeteria or snack room, sit down and break bread with the troops.

At first they may wonder what they did wrong to have you as a lunch partner. However, these sessions will be an eye-opener. Quickly you'll realize that your employee's problems are strikingly similar to yours. They just want to do their job right and take care of their families. Most importantly, you'll learn that they hold you and your abilities at a very lofty level. Although, it's a frequent favorite American pastime to criticize the boss, in truth most employees think their boss or bosses, particularly the CEO, are much better leaders than they really are.

Your "reality check" will kick in when you realize that bad actions always trickle down and can have devastating effects on every employee. If you make a bonehead decision, or are ever tempted to cross the line between right and maybe not so right or obviously wrong, think twice about the consequences not just for you, but for your people. At the end of the day, it's your duty as the boss to ensure that your employees and investors are first in line before you. Funny how these things work out, but if you follow this path you'll often wind up with a bigger payoff for yourself, be it economically or in other more esoteric forms such as personal gratification and/or the increased esteem of your associates.

The ubiquitous Wall Street saying describing the greedy is: "There are bears, bulls and pigs." For those with questionable motives or a dyslexic calendar, I would propose a change and say; "There are bears, bulls, and CROOKS."

CEOs who backdate stock options and commit other acts of malfeasance prove once again that so few can do so much damage to affect the perception of so many who always try and do it right. The good news is most executives follow their own words by doing themselves what they ask others to do, without ever taking a PDA out of their pocket.

What to do when the flame flickers
Knowing whether to reignite or to extinguish

This column was originally published in May 2007

The headline in this column is not an indication that the subject of my monthly column is moving from business matters to affairs of the heart. I have enough trouble with the free-enterprise system and navigating its various tributaries. I'll leave romance to philosophers, poets, pseudo-psychologists and Dear Abby.

What I am exploring is knowing what to watch for when a subordinate, associate or yes, even you — the C-level professional/entrepreneurial owner with ice running through your veins- starts to get a twitch, a notion that something "inside" has changed. It might start in the back of your mind as a little whisper and eventually build to a shout. For subordinates, and others, telltale signals of change are easy to spot. If it's you who is wavering from your norm the nuances are a bit more elusive.

Without warning it seems as if cold water has inexplicably doused that incessant burning in the belly that awakens over-achievers in the morning and gnaws at them at night, until they reluctantly let go and drift off to sleep. Fueling that constant internal flame is the search for a better way, a scheme about how to "one-up" the competition, or to "take one for the team" under the sometimes sophomoric assumption that to die figuratively for the company is to live forever.

Almost out of the blue, one day you realize something has changed. At first you probably think it's "that virus going around." You're a bit lethargic; your thinking just isn't as sharp as it has been in the past.

Your mind, for no apparent reason, wanders from ROIs, gross margins and the bottom line to abstract, granular thoughts as in white sandy beaches or the undulating grassy knolls of golf courses. Sometimes this affliction is manifested in thoughts of the next big vacation instead of the previously ubiquitous next big deal.

If this bug strikes you and you're an owner/entrepreneur or top C-level executive, at first you think you're "just tired." You rationalize that after a few days away from the office or a couple of good nights' sleep, you'll bounce back like the bull in the shop, kicking behinds and taking names. However, after several extra-long weekends off, you come back increasingly lethargic. In meetings, instead of using your steel-trap mind to capture every word, concept and nuance, your thoughts drift to unrelated matters, subjects that you previously dismissed as too trivial. You leave the meeting knowing that if someone put a 45 to your head and said "give me a one-minute synopsis of what was discussed, or you're toast," you'd reply "get the butter and jelly."

What gives?!! The answer is that the flame is flickering and, in the heat of battle, instead of your temperature rising, now that high thermostat reading just makes you sweat.

Welcome to "Burn Out City." It can happen to the best of us: your employees, your friends and even you. The good news is that there are steps you can take to refocus your people or yourself. You can first try to reignite, and if that doesn't work you can extinguish the flame, but do it your way. The truth is you can have it both ways, depending on where you are in your career, what you're doing and, most importantly, what remains undone.

In business the worst affliction you, your team members or a management member can have is the Mediocrity Malady. It happens when you, or a subordinate, subtly switches to autopilot and goes on cruise control. I call it "quit and stay." This is not fair to your company, your associates and, most of all, it's not fair to you.

When you spot the early warning signs in a subordinate who heretofore had been a "superstar," try giving him a new challenging assignment that just might get the juices flowing again. This can be anything from taking on the management of additional personnel to working on a highly confidential "what if scenario" for the future. Personally, I have never found that lightening the work load helps people reengage and bounce back. Instead, it just delays the inevitable. You will know if it's working when the "A Player" again begins arriving at work a little earlier and staying a lot later. Bags under the eyes are another good sign, since it probably means that the "born again" superstar has contracted the 3 a.m. syndrome. Instead of sleeping through the night, he or she is back to thinking in short-hand alphabet soup terms such as EBITDA, P&Ls and the like. If you are the one inflicted with this malaise, the same concept of taking on a new and energizing challenge is also an effective treatment and antidote.

Immediately begin delegating more, including the lofty aspects of your job that you once coveted, and start using your time to plan "the big one," be it a new concept, an acquisition, a merger or whatever. Make sure that it is challenging — the bigger the better — and that you have established tight deadlines.

If after this, you still find that the flame is almost out, it's time to take that alternative fork in the road and map an exit strategy that leaves the place a little better than when you got there. In business, as in love, it all comes down to dealing with alternatives and making choices. The end can sometimes be an exciting new beginning. Remember, your work is what you do, not who you are. Many a smoldering fire has reignited into a burning blaze; you just need to fan the flame a bit.

Eating an elephant and building a business...
What do they have in common?

This column was originally published in October 2007

And the answer is: You eat an elephant and build a business the same way, one bite at a time. Executives and leaders with a smidgen of common sense and the realization of their own vulnerability have all had that sinking feeling in the pit of the stomach, at least once, when the size and scope of a pending project or major undertaking suddenly becomes overwhelming. Be it starting with a blank piece of paper to create a plan for a new business, revitalizing a frumpy and tired product line, or figuring out how to climb any other mountain, the reality can run cold chills down the back of the most seasoned and stoic chieftains. Being charged with the responsibility to jump-start an inertia-ridden work group or division can also cause more than a few sleepless nights.

To get started with the "one of the bigger meals of a career," first one needs to have the idea and conjure up a big picture of what has to be done. As in photography, when you pull back to get the entire subject matter in the frame, it always looks bigger and more daunting than perhaps it really is. Once, however, you get the picture in focus and zoom in on the subject you start to crystallize the individual pieces and parts but not the entire, if you will, elephant. A close-up of each cross section or smaller piece launches the building process.

Certainly you always begin by including all the whistles and bells. From there you rationalize the project not only economically, but also in terms of the time and resources needed to get the job done. However, before you put pencil to paper this obligatory question must be answered: when the new initiative is up and running, will it produce as promised, satisfying the return on investment criterion, and also serving the customers or end-users by offering something special that they will want and need?

Simple enough so far but what do you do once you have the big picture, know the returns and have satisfied yourself that it is worth the unavoidable and inevitable pain and strain you and your team will have to endure to complete the effort?

The next step is where our "one bite at a time proverb" really comes into play. If you pull back and look only at the big picture you are likely to be so riddled with second thoughts and possibly overcome with fear of failure that you will put this well-conceived effort on the back burner or, worse yet, scuttle it altogether.

The trick is what piece to start on first. Initially, logic would suggest starting at the bottom with the foundation and then building step by step. Makes sense, but sometimes taking the traditional route is not the most efficient, nor most effective. Creating is not always a linear process. Many times you can start eating that elephant simultaneously from the top, bottom and the middle with different teams focusing on various tasks. Many movies are shot out of sequence, meaning that it is not unusual to film the end or the middle of a movie before the opening scenes. The same strategy can apply to building a business. It just may be more economical to begin with the middle or end parts for a variety of good reasons, such as the immediate availability of specialized resources or materials.

Here is an example. In opening retail stores there are teams and or individuals assigned specific aspects of the project such as designing the building, laying out the interior, buying the merchandise, creating the grand opening ad campaign — with each doing his own thing concurrently. In the final stages, it takes only a few days or weeks depending on the size of the store for all of the fixtures, merchandise, and signing and marketing dots to be connected. When it all comes together the doors are unlocked and management prays that, since it was built, they will come.

It's mandatory that you decide, up front, who is responsible for what. Make sure everyone involved has seen the picture of the entire elephant and understands what it is supposed to look like at the end. Include all of the objectives, the financials, and other parameters. Set up checks and balances to be sure no one goes off the reservation, by having continuous communications with predetermined check points along the way and formally scheduled all-hands meetings.

Don't have any illusions. While eating your elephant, I guarantee you'll have some indigestion. No worries, though, that's why Rolaids were invented. A final point to remember, always keep in mind that if you're in charge you are also the one who is responsible to walk behind that elephant with the broom and shovel. It's just biological with animals and projects that there are always things that need to be cleaned up and kept tidy.

Life is sometimes one big puzzle and so is creating a business, and/or managing a process. At that magical moment when all of pieces fit together you'll have that "Aha!" sensation knowing that your dream has become a reality. If you follow these steps, the dessert will be sweet success.

Dying a thousand deaths
Why errors of omission can
be fatal to your business

This column was originally published in May 2008

It's been said, "Life isn't always fair," when it comes to how we're judged. Very profound words but no great revelation for anyone in business. Even the glory of unique innovation and head-turning results is ephemeral, evaporating all too quickly as it becomes yesterday's news. The public's mindset today is, "What have you done for me lately?"

Thomas Edison invented electricity but when was the last time you acknowledged this life-altering discovery? Have you ever exclaimed, "Let there be light" as you entered a darkened room and flipped the wall switch, while giving thanks to this holder of over 1,093 patents? Conversely, when you flip that same light switch and night does not instantly turn into day you're likely to mutter expletives about the unreliability of this basic utility.

Then there's the example of the company that paid 200 consecutive quarterly dividends with the precision of a fine Swiss watch. One day out of the blue, that company has a shortfall and the dividend is reduced or eliminated. The morning paper will plaster this "omission" in a banner headline followed by predictions of gloom and doom for the offending company. No one cares that for the previous 50 years the dividend was barely noted with a one-line notice hidden in the back pages of the paper. Worse yet, when each dividend check was received by the shareholder, it probably rated a big yawn if any reaction at all.

We're constantly being measured by what we don't do or neglect to do. Companies spend billions of dollars devising programs simply to meet customers' expectations. Some of the most successful businesses really don't deliver anything very astonishing. Instead, they provide consistency, be it a good hot cup of coffee or a safe, clean hotel room in every location around the corner or around the world. When these companies miss one time, the customer goes bananas. Vitriolic correspondences are launched accusing the company of incompetence and apathy.

How can your business minimize the risk of being chastised for what it doesn't do? First, you need to set standards below which the company cannot fall — no way no how. Secondly, promulgate these goals as the holy grail of your company's entire reason for existing. Make it part of your mission statement ensuring that everyone from the janitor to the CEO knows what is expected and, more importantly, what role they play in delivering on the promise, all the while knowing that being taken for granted is the price of admission. Fail once and you will die 1,000 deaths for what you neglected to do. Harsh reality is if you do it right 99.9 percent of the time, no one gives it a second thought. Do it wrong once and your customers will indelibly etch the transgression in their memories.

Organizations can improve their odds of survival and success by paying attention to basics and dealing with details. Example: as a salesperson, you make a prospecting call on a potential new client and the next day you send a thank-you note. You won't get much credit for doing this. It is a zero sum game. You'll be remembered only for the note or call you didn't make when your competitor does indeed send the thank-you letter or follows up verbally. Here's another scenario; a subordinate's 90-year-old great-grandmother passes away and your company forgets to send flowers. If you send the flowers, they'll blend in with the others, but if you neglect to do so, your missing bouquet will be conspicuous by its absence.

This same discipline applies to your personal life, as well. Have you ever missed sending a lousy $2 valentine card to your spouse or significant other? If you do participate in this cupid's ritual and you're lucky, you might get a peck on the cheek. If you don't, be assured it's the start of World War III, and your partner will never let you forget it.

Make your own list of must dos and have your employees do the same. Sometimes the big winner can be the company that doesn't stand out for the wrong reasons.

Many great businesses have been built on reliability, and too many companies have ultimately failed for errors of omission. Being invisible at the right times can be a strategic advantage.

Putting lightning back in the bottle

Entrepreneurs have done it before, but why do they want to do it again?

This column was originally published in November 2009

Pick up the paper, turn on the TV or scan the Internet and, on any given day, it is a pretty good bet that you will learn about some superstar who is making a comeback — sometimes for the second or third time. Those that comprise this unique breed of cats could be rock or movie stars, athletes or politicians and, yes, even corporate entrepreneurs or executive whiz kids who have all but faded into the sunset.

The bigger question is: They may have done it once, but can these mere mortals do it again? There are numerous theories about why former stars who have made their mark on the world would want to risk reputation, money and self-esteem to grab for that elusive brass ring one more time.

Second chances at fame and fortune can require defying Mother Nature and the aging process, which is dicey. Periodically, sports overachievers seize the headlines with their resurrections. In business, which does not necessarily require as many physical attributes, the odds of a successful curtain call and standing ovation at the end of the day are somewhat improved over those for a super jock. That is because mental dexterity is required in commerce, rather than sheer physical skills and endurance.

Company founders and CEOs, or a combination thereof, can more easily pull off a second hit by following a disciplined straightforward process. It is not unheard of for an executive to do it right once and then repeat the success somewhere else. Within a year or two of a comeback attempt, the world knows if the business maestro did it or was a flop. Talk about putting a spotlight on one's achievements or failure, and it does not get any better or worse than this.

Some businesspeople do it for the money. Nevertheless, I would bet that most do it because they strongly believe they can and are classic, calculating, risk-taking, type-A overachievers who want to show the world they aren't one-act wonders.

My experience is that the best executives always have something to prove to themselves or somebody close to them. This provides the encore performer a strong incentive to jump back into the fray.

While building anything, one always makes mistakes. However, the biggest mistake is to repeat the previous error of omission or commission in an existing or new undertaking. There are numerous serial entrepreneurs who keep creating a growing string of successes. You can find them on Wall Street, in technology, retailing, manufacturing and the nonprofit world. Best known perhaps is Steve Jobs of Apple fame, who was also incredibly successful with Pixar, the animation geniuses, and NeXt, the higher education workstation developers. Entrepreneurs not nearly as famous as Steve Jobs have brought us multitechnology corporations and companies such as the original MCI followed by AirFone.

Each seem to have a common gene in their DNA that provides the ultimate high when they create/build a better mousetrap that fuels jobs, opportunities and financial security for themselves as well as their employees, supporters, investors and suppliers. The other common ingredients of serial achievers are that they need the bright lights, a stage and a fair amount of control. Very few are gun-slinger, hip-shooter types who come up with an idea and just follow their gut feelings.

Instead, the successful second-act players have honed their instinct and skills and created a series of methodical steps that they follow, each of which keeps them off the rocks. They understand the basics of how to get from A to Z while minimizing pain and wasted motions and maximizing available capital. Past experience teaches them where to put the time and effort and to ensure that they obtain the expected return.

This reincarnation is not limited to just CEOs and entrepreneurs. It is also prevalent among super salespeople and specialists of all sizes, shapes and types.

There is a rhythm to success and a maze to navigate. However, if they have done it before, there is a better than even chance that they can put the lightning back in the bottle once more. The much-celebrated crooner, Frank Sinatra, summarized it well when he sang "the best is yet to come."

Do you work to live or live to work?

Have it your way — there's a time and place for both

This column was originally published in December 2009

Is your work the means to an end or the epicenter of your life? Most businesspeople, on a conscious or subconscious level, want superiors, peers and other constituents to believe they are one of those unselfish corporate types who do whatever it takes for the good of the company. Everything comes in second place: family, friends and one's very existence, including creature comforts such as adequate sleep and eating three square meals at a table, not a desk. If that is you, then you have checked the "live to work" box.

But wait a second, does this really make a modicum of sense?

When I interview management candidates after I have determined the interviewee might be a fit I always ask: "What comes first, your family or your job?"

Those who immediately respond "my job" move down multiple notches on my scale of suitability if, in fact, I believe this is their permanent sentiment.

For a chance to play in the big leagues, most wannabe executives will do whatever it takes to make the lineup. The smart ones, however, know that just like a good novel, a business career has a beginning, middle and, hopefully, an abundance of exciting last chapters.

When aspiring managers begin ascending the corporate ladder, many work as if the clock has no hands. Toiling away at their desks from early morning to the wee hours of the night is an investment in the future to gain experience, a means to accomplishing meaningful objectives and, yes, to a certain degree, an opportunity to obtain face time, sometimes even vying for the coveted corporate appearance trophy. Those who go for appearance alone, without the meat on the bones of accomplishment, are easily unmasked as having a "big hat but no cattle."

However, hitting the trifecta of experience, accomplishment and the ability to showcase a "get it done" work ethic makes for the complete package.

Once a manager reaches a certain midpoint in a career and has a few good people working for him, he moves from the role of solo doer to that of teacher and navigator who can successfully direct others along a process from point A to point B. Appearances are secondary at this point, as the key is what is in the package, not the wrapper.

During this stage, the middle manager should have that "aha" moment recognizing that business is not an all-or-nothing proposition and he can get a life. I admired any employee working for me who without equivocation would state he could not meet with me at a time that I requested because of another important commitment, which could be attending a kid's ballgame or a first school play. This communicated volumes to me about the manager's character and ability to balance priorities and make appropriate choices that fit the circumstances.

On other days, however, I would see this same manager looking like death warmed the next morning because he just pulled an all-nighter to get the needed task done.

A real game-changer occurs when one reaches the ranks of senior executive with a team of players in the anteroom who are more than ready, willing and able to answer the bell. This gives the leader the opportunity to plan rather than just do, calling the signals instead of responding to them. Priorities change as the executive becomes a dreamer — a visionary who can look beyond today to tomorrow, identifying the future challenges and opportunities, and positioning the organization to respond to them.

In many respects, this is both the best of times and the worst of times. The best is that the leader has others to do the heavy lifting. This provides the executive the time to make other contributions, not just to the company but to his family and community, as well. The worst-of-times component is that the buck stops at the leader's door. Important decisions have to be made daily, and that pressure can take a toll both mentally and physically. At this point in a career, the need to balance becomes something that is just not nice but necessary to endure the pressures at the top.

An all-time best fast-food jingle positively asserted, "Hold the pickle; hold the lettuce. Special orders don't upset us," with the payoff line of "Have it your way." The secret of having it your way in business is learning when and how to balance a career with a fulfilling personal life.

Common business sense
There still isn't an app for that

This column was originally published in December 2010

Unless you've been living under a rock for the last three years, you know that the term "app" is shorthand for software application, made famous by the technology geniuses at Apple. It came into vogue with the iPhone and now with the iPad. Following Apple's remarkable success, just about every other manufacturer has figured out how to put microchips in a cheap plastic case and call it a personal digital system or PDA, which does all kinds of incredible stuff.

Innovation spawns accelerated innovation, and today, there are more than 30,000 apps from how to find romance in all the wrong places to creating a voodoo doll with a photo of your least favorite person imposed on a deformed body, all for the purpose of poking it with pins with one click when circumstances dictate. These know-all, do-all digital marvels can be downloaded to miniature handheld devices that only a few years ago were a mere glimmer in a few computer geeks' eyes. Even more astounding is that there are more than 100 new applications being created every day. Based on these numbers, it's only logical to wonder what's next. Will there come a time when at the flick of a finger we will know the answers before we even know the questions?

At least to date, however, I have not found an app for common sense. It would be great to click on an icon to avoid stupid mistakes that can lose a customer, really get you in hot water with a boss, bank or investor, or result in hurling unintentional epithets.

Even with all of these new electronic tools we have at our fingertips today, management must still train employees not to rely solely on pseudo- or quasi-artificial intelligence to make the right decision but instead use their noggins. There are dozens of very effective and simple rules to ensure that your people think before they act. Most of them were taught to us by our parents, third-grade teachers and, for advanced learners, a few mentors that we have all met along our career paths.

Here are five common-sense rules that have saved many careers, a transaction or improved business. You've heard them all before but they bear repeating. I suggest at the risk of insulting everyone on your team, you pass this column on to them and make me the bad guy for insulting their tech-savvy intelligence by stating what should be obvious.

1. Always, count to 10 before hitting the send key and firing off an incendiary email. Unlike many relationships, jobs and even wealth, email is really forever and can come back to haunt you.

2. Ask yourself before finalizing a deal, "Are you doing it so you can say you won or because it really will provide benefit to the business?" Too many deals get down to proving who's the better deal-maker or salesperson, rather than who's the more effective businessperson.

3. As Abraham Lincoln said, "It is better to remain silent and be thought a fool than to speak and remove all doubt." All too frequently people talk themselves out of a transaction because they provide, as the kids say today, "TMI," or too much information. Translation, when you have made your point, zip it.

4. If it's too good to be true, it's almost a guarantee that it will prove to be too good to be true. Just ask any of the clients of convicted conman extraordinaire Bernie Madoff, many of whom are now probably holding second jobs flipping burgers to make ends meet.

5. Although it's nice to give the other guy the benefit of the doubt, trust, but always verify, too. Just count how many times in every U.S. president's term an appointment is suddenly withdrawn when Congress starts digging into a candidate's background.

Unquestionably, we're all becoming more efficient and effective because of technology. However, at least for now, there isn't an app for common sense and clear thinking. Nevertheless, the good news is that there are many apps to help you find at least 10 excuses for any bonehead mistake that caused irreparable damage, in at least as many languages.

Are your strengths also your biggest weaknesses?
How to maximize what you do best, while minimizing your shortcomings

This column was originally published in July 2012

Most of us sincerely want to be a better person, manager, spouse, significant other, parent, child or Indian chief. Certainly, good intentions and desire are the first steps in self-improvement. The second step is an introspective discovery process combined with a bit of discipline in order to make meaningful progress.

To get started, ask yourself several pointed questions. Has anyone ever made suggestions to you about your management or communication style? Maybe it was a boss or mentor, a good friend or an associate earnestly trying to give you a few constructive tips on how to improve. Best yet, it might have been self-discovery after you did something that did not quite measure up to your own expectations.

Reality is, for most of us, our strengths can also be our biggest weaknesses. As an example, if you're a type A, anal-retentive person who is detail-oriented to a fault and always crosses every T and dots every I, possibly this strength has morphed you into becoming a micromanager of others. Or, maybe you consider yourself a disciple of the great communicator, the late President Ronald Reagan, because you are a terrific speaker who can captivate the other person in one-on-one conversation or every individual in a large audience. The downside of this is maybe you're not a great listener because you fall in love with the sound of your voice and your words. This could translate into you talking too much and unintentionally giving the wrong impression of not being receptive to another person's point of view.

The list can go on and on. The trick, however, is to recognize what you are and what you're not, and then tweak your style for the greater good, helping not only yourself but also those with whom you interface by making yourself more effective and perhaps even a little easier to take.

Try this. Create two columns on a legal pad or spreadsheet and list all of the attributes you think you possess in terms of your management capabilities/style. Keep the list short and focus on what's important, as this is not an inventory of everything you've done or learned since the third grade. Once you've captured two, three or four key characteristics, in the next column record a corresponding set of those things you know don't help your cause.

Next, re-read this personal inventory of pros and cons and look for patterns. If you note, as an example, that you are incredibly disciplined and seldom give yourself any slack, see if you also jotted down on the detractor side of the ledger that people tend to think you push subordinates too hard without differentiating between what is mission-critical versus basic tasks. If you spot this corresponding weakness, it doesn't necessarily mean that you suffer from obsessive compulsive disorder, but you might just need to recalibrate your standards when dealing with others, recognizing that your subordinates don't have to become your clone to be successful.

Once you've drilled down on the most important characteristics that you want to change, it's time to develop a game plan. For illustrative purposes, let's again assume you're that great communicator, but you sometimes go over the top and incessantly interrupt others, which leads to missing out on their ideas, not to mention becoming a bore. If this is your Achilles' heel, you must focus on the triggers that cause you to behave in this manner in order to strive for improvement.

Maybe you're really not self-consumed, but instead, your mind races ahead to follow-up thoughts that you want to make without allowing enough time for others to absorb and comment on your initial words of wisdom. This suggests you need to put a mental circuit breaker on your lips after you make your first major point, allowing for a long pregnant pause to let others amplify on your point or introduce an opposing or complementary thought. By doing this, you'll help make the conversation or presentation more interactive, which may lead to better resolutions or open the door to new unexplored concepts or opportunities.

Armed with this newly created self-assessment, you'll become a more productive and better leader who has learned to make your strengths stronger and reduce the negative effects of your weaknesses.

Success does not create character; it exposes it...

...and, contrary to some beliefs, money is not the root of all evil

This column was originally published in June 2014

We've all heard the terms, "The rich get richer," "It's not the money, it's the money" and "Wealth doesn't buy happiness." The latter possibly was spoken by some rich guy who may have never worked a day in his life.

That aside, the bigger question is, "What are we made of?" No two people are exactly alike, and the important thing is not where we start, but rather what we do along the way and how we finish.

Success and money mean different things to each of us. To some they equate to freedom, to others they're badges of accomplishment or a way of keeping score.

For the majority of business people who have "made it," wealth further enables them to do the right thing charitably, and to make the best decisions for the greater good of others, including their customers, associates, investors, families and the public.

It can also unleash the pursuit of lofty goals such as furthering medical discovery and treatment, providing for the less fortunate or establishing a vehicle to promote education for those who might not have the necessary resources.

Why attack success?

It's confounding to business leaders why so many, particularly politicians and pundits of various ilk, seem to publicly bash success at every turn, almost to the point of creating a Scarlet Letter imagery for notables who have beaten the odds to create wealth.

Perhaps it's pure jealousy, but likely it's because these types need a battle cry to divert attention from themselves and turn others against a select group.

This isn't much different from what has been done repeatedly since the beginning of time by the naïve, disingenuous or nefarious to further myriad ulterior motives.

Certainly, there are some who achieve success at any cost or take inappropriate shortcuts. And yes, those who cross the line deserve everything they ultimately get, and then some.

Give back in some way

Consistently doing the right thing is not exclusively measured economically. Whether rich, poor or in-between, giving back can also take on many noneconomic forms. This can include generously committing one's time and devotion to a cause or simply helping a friend, neighbor or even a stranger accomplish something they can't do themselves.

Granted, many times it is difficult for someone who is toiling long hours just to get by to devote the time and effort to helping others in traditional ways.

These same people, however, give back in other ways, including how they treat those with whom they work, their families and friends and by how they conduct themselves day in and day out.

It's been said by many that "our character is what determines how we live our lives."

Being fortunate enough to be in the right place at the right time, combined with a little skill and some luck can lead to extraordinary opportunities and affect one's character.

Success and money, however, don't necessarily enhance good character, but instead many times serve to expose it.

Who you know can trump what you know

Being a know-it-all can be self-defeating

This column was originally published in August 2014

Sometimes who you know is much more important than what you know. As an example, although it's not always fair, being acquainted with a CEO of a non-related company to get your kid a scarce summer job trumps his or her being a genius. Knowing someone who has previously solved a thorny problem also beats having to start from scratch to do the exact same thing.

Executives are measured by what they achieve rather than by the specific knowledge they might personally contribute to a major undertaking. A business leader is much like an orchestra conductor who must direct the virtuosos on stage to produce just the right tone that resonates with the audience.

Can a maestro play each of the instruments in the ensemble to perfection — becoming, if you will, a one-man band? Most probably can't. Instead, the leader of the company or an orchestra must have a great ear, a sense of timing and the ability to modulate the tone of each piece, bringing the entire organization or orchestra to the desired crescendo.

Improve upon the basic skills
Most executives weren't endowed with finely honed skills when they began their careers. Instead, most started with basic skills and eventually became competent through a series of experiences. Along the way they also made invaluable contacts through networking. This is all about becoming the catalyst and big thinker, asking others who they know to fill in the blanks or to provide the integral missing piece.

It's certainly gratifying to be the innovator who can be a soloist. But at what cost? And, just because the leader might not know who to ask at the moment doesn't mean he or she can't identify and motivate someone who has done it before to provide the critical piece to complete the puzzle. Frequently, it's just a matter of knowing someone who knows someone else.

Being a leader is all about understanding how to get something rolling and moving forward without always recreating a completely new masterpiece. An incubator product, concept or way of doing something frequently includes components of what previously was or now is.

Borrowing the "know how" elements from the original creator and making your nascent innovation better or simply incorporating pieces from the past can produce a breakthrough. Look at Alexander Graham Bell's first phone and today's smartphones. How about today's Ferrari spawned from Henry Ford's Model T?

Serve the new unique needs

With the phone and the car, the new disrupters and innovators improved upon something that already existed. They likely got started by determining where to look first for answers to serve their new unique needs. They didn't necessarily have to be the specialist.

The mentality that every piece and part must be "invented here" many times results in wasting valuable time, effort and money.

A great conductor learns how to make beautiful music by combining what he or she knows with the talents of others to create an encore performance.

2

Communication

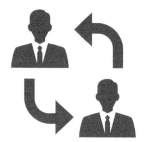

Communications etiquette

Don't shoot the messenger, unless the message is delivered by email

This column was originally published in September 2004

I have two simple email rules for people who report to me. First, if someone has bad news, it must be delivered in person or, if that's not possible, by telephone. Email is not an acceptable substitute.

I want to the hear the bad tidings in person so I can look the individual in the eye and gauge how bad the bad really is by the amount of perspiration on his or her upper lip and how many times the person's voice cracks. This also works on the phone. I just substitute my perspiration barometer for the number of hushed whispers and intermittent, indecipherable mumblings I detect per minute.

Am I a masochist, some kind of voyeur, or do I really enjoy watching and hearing people squirm? Absolutely not.

Instead, mano-a-mano communication helps me help the person solve the problem at hand. My issue with bad news via email is that it's just too easy for people to log on and then log out by dumping the issue in the inbox, then emotionally abdicating by feeling that since they've spilled the beans about the problem, it becomes the recipient's issue to solve. One-on-one delivery also forces the deliverer to come up with an idea or two about how to save what's left to be saved.

Rule Two is that one may deliver good news by email, but this means of conveyance usually tells me that the person sending the message can't accept success or really doesn't deserve the credit.

I've found that when something truly good has happened, the person responsible will do whatever it takes to deliver the news up close and personal. Probably, the person is thinking he or she can look me in the eye and see if I break out in perspiration caused by excitement or whether my voice shrills, hitting new high notes when I hear each tidbit — all of which can give that person courage and fuel to ask for a bigger raise at salary review time.

Good communication techniques are a two-way street. I've had people wait for me in the parking lot, most likely having slept in a lawn chair since midnight, just to be the first to deliver the positive message. Others of my same gender have even followed me into the washroom, where I'm captive at least for a minute or so while they blurt out their success story.

Coming to my office door and sticking one's head in is just as effective, but does lack a bit of the drama of the above-mentioned intercept venues and tactics.

Don't get me wrong. I really love email, and use it more than most. I have the latest and greatest email toys and tools that ensure I'm always connected, even in the most unusual and intimate locations. Email is great for a quick update, detailed reports, fast-breaking news or even snide remarks about a competitor's shortcomings, particularly unexpected earnings misses, which always bring a perverse smile to my face.

But unless you can see the whites of their eyes and combine the body language with their words, you'll never get the full story and what the implications really mean.

New corporate malady:
Squinting eyes-flying thumbs syndrome

This column was originally published in April 2005

J ust when we thought we've seen it all … just when everyone
thought: what else could happen to corporate America? Could
there still be more after insider trading revelations, Sarbanes-Oxley
legislation, audit committee troubles, re-stated financial statements?
Stop holding your breath for the next shoe to fall. It's already
happened.

Now there is yet another malady afflicting businesses, both big and
small. And worse, it's spreading everywhere: academia, government
bureaucracies, the judicial system, you name it.

What is this new scourge sweeping the country and threatening the
free enterprise system? We've all seen it before our very eyes. Many
of us do it and I, sadly, admit I'm right there at the top of the list. I'd
call this problem the Squinting Eyes-Flying Thumbs Syndrome. We
encounter it every day whenever people meet, be it in the corporate
boardroom or the office cubicle. It's pervasive on Wall Street and
from prestigious Ivy League campuses to urban community colleges
to major medical centers. Enter a room, anywhere, where there are
two, five, or more than 10 people meeting, and at first you will think
you're being greeted with outstretched arms from those present. But,
these people aren't gesturing to you; instead, they're pointing their
arms to their respective laps. In their hot, little hands, slightly below
the table's edge, where they think it's out of sight, you catch the first
glimpse of some surreptitious activity in progress.

What is causing this diversion? It is the plague of the PDA —
not a new acronym for a physical disease, even though it's just as
insidious. No, it's the Personal Digital Assistant, now equipped with
on-line Email, text messaging, calendar and Internet access, all neatly

packaged in a sleek, metallic, clamshell with a full keyboard, flashing lights and who knows what else.

You can't sit in any meeting without apprehending participants sneaking a peek at their 2-inch-by-2-inch screen. There they sit with arms outstretched to the lap, eyes squinting and thumbs flying. What's even more troubling and down right distracting, are those who sit there moving their lips without emitting any audible sounds, as they scroll through their messages.

I've even been in meetings where, at first glance, I thought a person going through this process was praying silently for divine guidance to solve the problem at hand, only to realize quickly that person never really learned to read without moving his or her lips. There have been other occasions when I spotted a person in a meeting who I thought was experiencing a medical emergency — eyes glazed, thumbs and fingers out of control, veins on either side of the neck bulging. As I prepared to rush to provide aid, trying to recall the ABCs of CPR, I rapidly determined that the would-be victim must have been reading a disturbing message that caused this manifestation of angst.

What can we do to stem this ubiquitous, raging exhibition of self-absorption and lack of focus? Here are three suggestions:

1. Post signs on meeting rooms that state, 'All PDAs must be checked at the door.' This is no different from government buildings, schools, and offices that post signs stating, 'No Firearms Allowed.' Certainly an effective solution;

2. Hire part-time, off-duty TSA personnel to search or wand meeting participants. When conclusive evidence is found, conduct pat-downs and, if necessary, full cavity body searches. Unlike air travelers, though, those entering the room will not have to take off their shoes;

3. If your organization does not wish to use these draconian methods, politely ask people to remove their PDA batteries and leave chargers at the door. You may also want to consider using metal detectors, assuming you can find some real bargains on the market from failed retailers or airports that have upgraded to the next generation of equipment.

Seriously, we can all reap many benefits if we curtail the tide of PDA usages in meetings. These benefits include having meetings in which participants actually pay attention to what others are saying and seriously ponder the problems and opportunities presented, rather than search for the latest stock quote. Thinking and responding could even come back into vogue at corporate and institutional gatherings. Try to fathom, for a moment, the productivity gains that are possible with everyone actually participating in the session.

Finally, the best news of all is that none of these remedies to the Squinting Eyes-Flying Thumbs Syndrome will have to be rationed, as we recently experienced with the flu vaccine. Instead, we'll all get more done, solve more problems and probably wind up working less because we'll be more focused, not to mention more polite, to our fellow meeting participants. As an added bonus, our behavior will revert to a more, civil time when listening was expected and conversation was an art.

Every one of us gets our time in the box
But what is really important is how much damage is done and how fast we get out

This column was originally published in August 2005

I don't care who you are or what you do: CEO, owner, mid-level manager or politician, someday, somehow you will find yourself in a predicament from which a skillful or graceful escape is, to say the least, challenging. Those who have been there know of what I write, those who haven't are in for a character-building experience.

That proverbial place is called the "hot box" when, for some inexplicable reason, you say or do something that doesn't make sense, may even offend, and undeniably defies good business and common sense. In a split second you realize that the old World War II adage "loose lips sink ships" is painfully true. At that very instant, you also realize you are the one on the ship, and worse yet, you are the captain.

How or why it happens in most cases is probably irrelevant. Sure, you will think to yourself "I said what?," "I did huh?" Self-recrimination, second guessing, or logic at this point of realization is an exercise in futility — instead, welcome to the world of damage control.

If it makes you feel any better, it is not only business people who periodically step into this dark hole. Just look at the infamous comment by our own George W. when he said in a May 2005 Washington speech, "It's in our country's interests to find those who would do harm to us and get them out of harm's way." Or worse yet, just south of the border our neighbor's President made an utterance this past May about Mexicans accepting jobs in the U.S. that minority American citizens wouldn't even do. Before the CNN crawl chronicling this tasteless comment finished crossing the bottom of our TV screens, Mr. Fox and his advisors were on their bikes back-peddling at speeds that rivaled the forward motion of Lance Armstrong.

The streets are littered with people who could not move fast enough or were not smart enough to recognize that they had arrived at a critical intersection where they either had to retract, retrace, in some cases apologize, or take the low road and deny, deny, deny. They could say that people did not understand them: "I was misquoted," or bury their head in the sand and pretend it never happened. These latter courses of action, while ethically questionable, as history has proved hundreds of times over and over, are a sure-fired path to oblivion, if not complete ruination.

In reality, however, most of the time in business, our missteps or statements won't sink the ship. The important thing to remember is how to correct the wrong and move forward. Going on the defensive can be useless and create even more angst and damage. Plus, it is a lot easier to come clean expeditiously and admit your transgression of promulgating a bad policy, making a bad judgment, or simply allowing the tongue to engage before the brain kicks in.

When you find yourself in an unenviable position, stop, reassess, and then take the high road even if it means admitting that you had a temporary mental lapse that is beyond explanation. I am a big believer in "your first loss most always is your best loss."

The good news is everybody loves a mea culpa. In the back of their minds, people are thinking, but for the grace of G-d it was someone else who stumbled and then fumbled.

I have even seen instances where the perpetrator of a huge misstep becomes the underdog hero by standing up and taking it like the proverbial man. In my career I have retracted a few policies that affected thousands after realizing they didn't quite work or weren't received with open arms as I thought. I have also been shocked by the many times I received glowing comments, especially from those most adversely affected, calling me a clear thinker with humility. It is amazing how quick and forgiving our constituents can be when we are wrong. The bigger the faux pas, the greater the forgiveness.

After your bruised ego heals from the lapse in judgment and you take off the hair shirt, you will learn from the experience. Remember nobody bats a thousand, no bowler rolls 300 games every time and Tiger Woods has only had a precious few hole-in-ones. The perennial saying, "it's not if you win or lose, but how you play the game" is really true when you find yourself in the hot box.

When you ask your employees what time it is do they tell you how to build the watch?

Training people to cut to the chase

This column was originally published in April 2006

All executives and managers need timely information delivered succinctly to make decisions, solve problems, and seize opportunities. The old adage "time is money" is amplified in today's "real- time" corporate America environment when many decisions must be made measured in minutes and hours, rather than days and weeks.

How many of us have had this problem? We ask a subordinate a basic question and it can take 15 minutes to get what should have been a 15 second answer. Why do some people have an incessant compulsion to provide minute detailed responses embellished with irrelevant "he said, she said" type anecdotes? I think the answer lies in the need for everyone to be perceived as a subject matter expert on something. Some subordinates, peers and even superiors provide so much detail in the hope that you will recognize them as the ultimate be- all, end-, all authority on even the most obscure topics.

Ask a simple question: "What time is it?," and the answer can turn into a rambling monologue on how the watch was built, complete with a side bar editorial about the precision artisans who built it. Who cares? This analogy, unfortunately, applies many times to business questions asked in a one-on-one session, by phone, in writing or via email. When you expect a one sentence reply you get five paragraphs of painful detail. Certainly details have a time and place and can be valuable in a thorough analysis, but details are superfluous when all you need is a data point or sanity check to proceed in crafting a plan or make a decision.

How can you break someone of the torturous habit of providing "too much information?" There are a number of effective methods that can help accomplish this objective, much like getting someone to kick the cigarette habit or stop using annoying phrases. Beware, however, that applying these principles to personal relationships can be hazardous to peaceful coexistence. And, of course, customers/clients almost always get dispensation.

Here are a couple of methods that have worked for me over the years. The easiest technique is the straightforward approach, but remember one size doesn't always fit. Sometimes you need a lighter, humorous approach, particularly when you're dealing with sensitive types prone to tears or pouting. The worst case scenario is when no matter what you say they just don't get the hint. This may call for, as a last resort, the ton of bricks methodology.

The straightforward approach: When someone begins to answer your question with voluminous information, politely interrupt them, at least the first time, and state that you recognize them as the expert possessing the intricate details surrounding the subject at hand. Positively assert that it's a given they know their stuff, but what you need now is a capsulated sound bite that is on point. With any luck this explanation will quickly lead your associates to giving you one or two sentences summaries, allowing everyone to get on with their lives.

For competent, yet chronically verbose, people humor can effectively get a person to provide you the *Reader's Digest* version rather than a tedious, unabridged response. One effective way to train the loquacious is to invest about $3 in a one-minute egg timer similar to an hourglass. Have the timer on your desk and when the person begins to respond, and you quickly sense you're in for a marathon answer, flip over the egg timer and pensively stare at this device as the sand drops through the glass. Usually the person, although occasionally aghast, rapidly takes the hint that you don't have time to make this discussion a career. This nonverbal communication is enhanced if you don't smile, or interrupt the speaker. Pulling a stop watch out of your desk is equally effective, and for those who want to go over the top, a digital timer on your computer screen that counts down the seconds can be very instructive, particularly for tech savvy windbags. If all else fails try holding your breath while the other person speaks. This, too, is sure to make your point quickly.

The ton of bricks method lacks the subtly of the above training processes, but sometime you don't have another alternative. For these hard core cases use your imagination knowing that for a while the person might think you're a trifle insensitive, but they always get over it.

News media reporters are the best trained to get to the point while making the response lively and informative. Journalism 101 teaches the "inverted pyramid" of the five Ws style of writing. This technique calls for always providing the key information in the first paragraph which includes the Who, What, Where, When, Why and sometimes even How of the story. This is done so that an editor can very rapidly reduce a news story as space/time limitations occur, pruning from the narrative non-essential facts or background, while knowing that the first few lines of the piece will basically give the reader or listener the most needed information.

You'll know that your people are on track when they adopt your techniques of training their own subordinates and associates to simply "spit it out" and get to the point while sermonizing on the virtues of "time is money." These time-efficiency converts then spawn new time-saver disciples. In a short time you will have created a new legion of one minute messengers who spend more time thinking and working than talking.

There's nothing wrong with a little self-promotion

But if you don't do it right, it's like flirting in the dark

This column was originally published in February 2007

There is a corollary to the old adage that the shoemaker's children go barefoot with otherwise productive and creative executives who are dismal at "marketing" their own ideas or accomplishments. These business pros can do a credible marketing job for others but not for their team or themselves. Reality is many executives' communications, self-marketing and "spins," if you will, often miss the mark and do not connect with their intended audience. It's much akin to flirting in the dark. If the other person doesn't see you, then you're not flirting.

Let's set the record straight. There is nothing insidious, egomaniacal, or in any way inappropriate about letting others know what you do well, perhaps how you do it, and why you're doing it. I am not talking about shameless self-promotion or shallow "boast and brag" assertions that only a mother would care about (and even that's iffy). Instead, substantive communications are the cornerstones of our free enterprise system. I don't have to give readers a lengthy tutorial on the proven positive effects that advertising, marketing and communications have on not only educating consumers, but also ultimately improving goods and services. As more people become aware of something, that awareness breeds competition and forces the originator to continue to make it better, which leads to all kinds of improved efficiencies, including lower prices.

Henry Ford knew the drill well when he launched the first Model T in any color as long as it was black. Shortly thereafter the spectrum of colors available covered the rainbow. The creators of the likes of the iPod or today's smartphones, to name just two examples, have improved on this lesson, fine-tuning these products through further innovation, combined with communicating their increased attributes and creating unprecedented demand. This has resulted in these items, which a generation ago would have been considered pure science fiction, now being used across all age and economic boundaries.

But what about marketing your own ideas to improve perception or sell a point of view? The streets are littered with good concepts created by clever people that never got out of the starting block because the promoters didn't have a clue how to get attention focused on their undertaking or how to enhance their credibility.

There are some simple basics to creating a buzz, garnering attention and getting things moving in the right direction. Whether you want to raise money for a business idea, get the well-deserved credit for something your team has achieved, or simply make sure your boss knows you're the next best thing since sliced bread, the process is essentially the same.

First, whatever it is you want to promote, including yourself, has to have substance, be fact-based, and deliver on whatever promise you're proposing, from a solution that solves a basic problem all the way to that great "whatever" that the world just can't live without any longer. In other words, it has to be credible and it has to be true. Once you get past that little hurdle, the next step is to make sure that others know about it. In real estate the three principles for success are: "location, location, location." Similarly, in marketing there are three key elements: "communicate, communicate and communicate."

Communication can take many forms and avenues, and you're limited only by your own imagination. It can include simply telling someone of influence something that no one else knows about yet. It's probably not a bad idea to tell the person to keep this "news" quiet, which will almost always ensure that the very next person he or she encounters down the hall will immediately be told your story, followed by the exclamation, "this is very confidential so don't say a word."

This technique applies to communicating what you've done or discovered with one person, or a group of your closest friends and associates, all the way to wearing a sandwich board sign while standing at a freeway exit. It's all about communication that starts with a whisper and builds to a shout.

Soon, much like a little snowball that begins rolling down the hill, it gains momentum, size, and scope with each revolution and quickly becomes the makings of a huge snowman. Two important caveats in crafting your communications are: you can't bore people and you have to make whatever you're saying new — it must be NEWS.

The holy grail of effective communications is creating: (1) Attention, (2) Interest, (3) Desire and (4) Action. This formula and sequence are pretty much self-explanatory but few follow this tried and true methodology. If you don't get someone's attention, you'll never get them interested. If they're not interested, how will they ever have desire? Finally, without successfully crossing these first three hurdles they'll never take any action, thus you'll be flirting in the dark.

Another word of caution. Don't get carried away, and never, and I mean never, fall in love with your own spin. Just like many things in life, a little can go a long way. Creating new news about "moi" cannot occur on a daily basis. Pick your spot before you communicate and make sure the subject matter will further your cause.

Never forget, if you want to be recognized as a subject matter expert, improve your credibility, or get backing for a new idea you must stop doing business in the dark, lest your ideas will never see the light of day. Nor, for that matter, will you ever find that special someone.

How to manage rumors and use them to your advantage

False information can become a WMD (weapon of mass destruction), seriously damaging a company

This column was originally published in April 2007

Since the beginning of time there have been rumors. Some are based on fact, many predicated on fantasy that are cobbled together with a smattering of relevant information combined with doses of the unsubstantiated.

Politicians are frequently masters at using rumors to float "trial balloons" to test reactions, running ideas "up the flag pole" to see if voters salute. Corporate executives run a close second to elected servants with this type of "opinion research."

Many times initiators and perpetrators of rumors launch them knowing they have a safety net to prevent a boomerang effect by maintaining plausible deniability. Just like in the TV and movie series Mission Impossible, when the mysterious voice on the tape gives his orders, he concludes by stating: "If you are discovered, the secretary of this secret team will disavow knowledge of your actions." The voice then asserts that this tape will self-destruct followed by a boom and a cloud of smoke.

Fact is, rumors can be very nefarious, equivalent to a WMD (weapon of mass destruction) used against the naive or unprepared. Stock touts and short sellers have used rumors since trading began to entice others into buying or selling a stock in hopes its price will move to benefit the perpetrator. Others are mere gossip mongers that take information out of context and weave a tale that can rival the storyline of a Harry Potter novel.

Every company or organization, at one point or another, will have to deal with rumors. These can range from the benign or annoying to the cataclysmic, threatening the very foundation and credibility of the entity.

A big problem with rumors is that it's usually difficult to determine their origin. As an example, participants at a trade show might hear a rumor about a competitor and then they're "off to the races," repeating it to industry suppliers. The next competitor down the line who hears the story embellishes it for his or her own benefit at the expense of the rumor's target.

If you are the subject of negative rumors it's much more important to launch your damage control than to immediately unearth the source. These harmful tales can take on a life of their own as they gain momentum and mutate, spawning other sub plots.

Rumors can strike out of the blue. Here's a typical scenario. You're sitting in your office looking at results for the past week, which for once, might hit plan. You're now breathing a little more easily and your perennial chest palpitations are actually gone. You're thinking "life is good," and your worst fears of a few weeks ago that the ship would sink on your watch are fading.

But then, your bubble bursts when the phone rings and it's your biggest customer asking if there is anything to the "word on the street" that the bank is calling your loan and you won't be able to meet customers' production requirements. Instantly, the palpitations are back with a vengeance, as perspiration starts dripping down the back of your neck. Your first response is to say, "Where did you hear this idiotic story?" But the customer cuts you short and says that's not the issue, he just wants to know if it's true and, if it's not, how you can give him the assurance he needs to continue to do business with your company.

It's time for action. You ask Mr. Big Customer to hold on the phone for a minute while you get your banker on the other line. You give the banker the *Reader's Digest* version of what you were just told, then conference together Mr. Banker and your "can't afford to lose or you're out of business Customer." After a two-second introduction, you restate the rumor and ask the banker to confirm, to Big, that the bank has no issues with your company. Instantly, the customer thanks you for providing the reassurance so expeditiously. The customer hangs up, and then you request that Mr. Banker be prepared to allay other negative inquiries that may surface.

Next, you summon your senior team and explain what just transpired so everyone is on the same page. Simultaneously you dictate a short note to all of your sales people outlining this issue and how to handle inquiries if they arise. You also provide an accompanying short list of possible customer questions, along with the answers.

If you think there is a reasonable chance your other large customers might hear this same story, you quickly get each on the phone, taking the initiative to tell them what happened, and offer to have your banker call them directly.

Your customers will appreciate your decisiveness, candor, and the respect you gave them by bringing them into the loop. You also showed them leadership and that you are in control.

The only real rule for handling rumors is: don't put your head in the sand and hope the problem goes away. Instead, deal with the issue head-on and get your pertinent players involved from the get-go. Always place yourself in the other guy's shoes by trying to understand what he needs to know to assuage his concerns. When you do it right, with a ferocious sense of urgency, you'll have managed the rumor and possibly even turned it into an advantage by solidifying your credibility with your customers.

Recent history has shown that WMDs can do huge damage, either literally or figuratively, depending if they are real or only imagined. Rumors can have the same effect unless you know how to react and manage the process.

Too much information
Everything you didn't want to know, but were afraid you'd be told

B asic communications supposedly started with the caveman about 130,000 years ago. Those succinct Neanderthal dudes really knew how to "cut to the chase" and get their message across. Using symbols and markings they communicated what needed to be known: "Where's the food, fire and danger?" When friend or foe happened to come across the message it was immediately understood. The human race progressed and took a giant communications leap in 1876, when Alexander Graham Bell, inventor of the telephone, spoke through this instrument to a companion device in the next room and said: "Mr. Watson, come here. I need you." It was artful in its simplicity (the message, not the phone).

Since those early times there have been huge changes in communications for the better, but with innovation comes excess. Today business people often provide "TMI" — too much information.

In examining a sampling of email messages that have been returned to me because the recipient was out of the office, I have been struck by how much people will tell you about where they are, what they're doing and why. On top of emails, just think about some of the out-of-office voice mail messages you get when you call someone for simple information.

Some of the more outrageous I have heard include this one from an employee who obviously decided to stop working but continue to collect a pay check. "I'm sorry I cannot read your email today because I am out of the office. Actually, my boss thinks I'm taking my sick grandmother to the doctor, but instead I'm on an interview that will hopefully lead to a better job so I can not only take my grandmother to the doctor, but make enough to even pay the bill for her exam." Here is another all too frequent example of TMI: "I'm not in today because I seem to have the bug that's going around. I spent all night in the bathroom, but by tomorrow I'll have this beat. Leave your message after the beep and I'll try to get around to you one of these days."

We've all experienced the same frustration of listening to and reading this type of drivel when we're simply trying to get a basic question answered. Just think about the dollars that are wasted in corporate America, including your organization, because people have the misguided sense that others want to know miniscule details, but were afraid to ask. Telling people what he thought they wanted to know certainly worked for Dr. David Reuben, the author of Everything You Always Wanted To Know About Sex, but Were Afraid to Ask. No doubt this doctor made millions giving people information they didn't ask for, but he was a notable exception and his subject matter was a bit more compelling than most.

The newest TMI phenomenons are blogs, many of which have evolved from the traditional intimate diary with a running account of the author's life. It used to be that a diary entry was a catharsis for average teenagers dealing with everything from peer pressure to raging hormones. The safety net for the writer was the security of knowing that what was inscribed in this chronicle would stay in this chronicle and never be read by another living soul.

Today, modern blogs which are open to the public on the internet and transcend all age boundaries many times include the scribe's innermost secrets. Some blogs have the added dimension of accompanying graphics that simply provide too much visual information, leaving little to the imagination.

Since this is a business column I will stick to offering up a few suggestions as to how you can manage your employees' voice mail messages and "out-of-office" email replies for the greater good. I am a proponent of establishing your own email/voice mail police, whose job it is to "protect and serve" — protect your organization's image and serve your customers' needs. Some might think this is a form of censorship and a violation of the Constitutional right to free speech. I prefer to think of it as an extension of marketing to enhance an organization's perception.

Start with surveying your employees' current message responses for their business email/voice mail messages. Warning: this is not a task for the faint of heart. Be prepared to be shocked by both the content and length.

Next, have your HR or PR professionals or some other capable associate put together brief scripts that get the desired message across. Each message should be tailored to the person's job function and provide an alternative contact when there is an immediate need.

Establish standards of what is appropriate and what is a no-no. Explain to your employees the rationale of why you are doing this and that it is, in effect, another communication technique to demonstrate how your organization is better than your competition. Consider ending all of the voice messages with the same tag line emphasizing your best attribute … such as "Prompt service is our No. 1 priority" or "Getting to the point makes us better." This sure beats gratuitous endings such as: "Have a stupendous day or a super great life."

Most employees will appreciate the scripted assistance because it gives them one less thing to do themselves. For those who don't like this new protocol, buy them a diary in which they can continue to record their personalized messages as long as they promise to keep them to themselves and never share them with your customers.

More we and less me
Changing one letter in a two-letter word is an easy first step

This column was originally published in September 2007

We often overuse the French phrase "esprit de corps," which literally means: "the common spirit existing in the members of a group." Today it is most commonly used to express a sense of enthusiasm, solidarity and loyalty for a shared purpose or goal. So far so good, but when managers try to develop this atmosphere, most fail woefully short simply because just saying the words won't make it so.

Virtually every corporation, organization or entity that is comprised of two or more people claims that its very foundation is built on teamwork. The reality, however, is that teamwork must be nurtured day in and day out, in the way a group undertakes every meaningful task. This applies whether the undertaking is building a huge bridge over a river or running a corner grocery store. The sports world has taught us a lot about winning and losing. The great New York Yankees Manager Casey Stengel said it best: "it is easy to get good players; the hardest part is getting them to play together." Ain't it the truth, Casey.

The streets are littered with companies whose wheels fell off the wagon because everyone had his or her own agenda, instead of focusing on the common cause for the greater good. Many of the leaders of these failed companies may have had their own playbook for self-enrichment and gratification. Others have simply failed to communicate with their own team on how to get from point A to point B. They never fully shared their strategy, the big picture vision, tactics and objectives, plus equally important what to look forward to when "the fat lady finally sings."

What are the best methods for well-intentioned leaders who want to build esprit de corps for their company of thousands ... or for their work group of just two or three? The number of participants may vary, but the techniques in building teamwork are the same.

First, the leader must set the direction of what is to be accomplished. Sounds pretty simple, but it's amazing how many top executives and even midlevel managers play their cards so close to the vest that the people who have to do the work don't have a clue as to why. One method of establishing direction and goals is to make it a multifaceted process broken down into simple time frames. An effective and easy way to communicate and measure is to use six months for initial startup objectives, a year to 18 months for intermediate goals and everything after that becomes longer term. Of course, the time frame you use depends on what has to be accomplished. Fire fighters measure objectives in minutes while the successful completion of a major highway construction project spans years. Team members can be motivated when they can see the finish line, rather than being told that there is one out there somewhere around the curve.

Next, get your team to buy-in to why it is they are doing what you want done. Make sure that everyone knows how you will keep score of wins and losses, and I strongly suggest that some of the initial goals be more easily attainable than those that are longer term.

Once your players know they can win, it will spur them on and give them the strength to get to the next step. There is nothing wrong if, along the way as the wins start piling up more quickly than originally expected, you raise the bar as your team becomes fueled by the thrill of victory.

As the "coach," you need to have daily, weekly or monthly pep-rallies. It is also critical that you identify and then empower team captains/cheerleaders who will help propel the mission and perpetuate the message.

We all know, however, from bitter experience that there are many pitfalls in building an organization and instilling a sense of pride and purpose. The biggest destroyer of creating esprit de corps is the indiscriminate use of the first person pronoun. It is nearly impossible to motivate a team to work together if you as the leader continually overuse the pronouns — I, me, mine — instead of we, us and ours. We have all heard statements, particularly in speeches and formal announcements, from otherwise very bright people, who almost smugly assert "I did this" or "my company/organization did that" instead of employing the royal "we" or "our." When a leader boasts about a recent accomplishment by stating, "I am pleased to announce ..." he is sure to deflate the most zealous team player who will think to himself, "What am I on this team ... chopped liver?"

It has been written and said many times that it's amazing how much people can get done if they don't worry about who gets the credit. We have all heard the statement that there is no letter "I" in the word teamwork. Highly successful leaders obtain the most satisfaction in knowing that they pulled everyone together to go in the same direction at the same time to accomplish a shared goal. There is a big payoff for the leader who knows how and when to use the correct pronouns, starting with less use of "me" and more emphasis on "we."

Enough is enough
Stop with all of the doom and gloom and celebrate the good

This column was originally published in June 2009

Since last fall, businesses, both big and small, at times, have been flying blind, trying to avoid the unprecedented proliferation of economic hazards. Solutions that worked in the past to counter disruptions proved to be ineffective. The first reaction was to hunker down and prepare for the next wave of troubles, not knowing whether it was going to get uglier and uglier before it got better.

Executives in most cases did what it took to prepare, preserve market share, serve customers and save money like never before. Furloughs and outright permanent reductions in force were the actions du jour in this new era of dealing with the unknown.

A natural part of this survival mode was for management to remind employees how bad it was, how it could get even worse, and why everybody must pull together and do whatever it takes to fight another day. These battle cries included dire prognostications, some subtle and some not so subtle, that there could be more bad news on the horizon.

At this point, every employee on the planet, unless he or she has been working alone in a cave, gets it. They understand all too well that they should be thankful to have a job. People now know that the true definition of a recession is when their neighbor is out of work; a depression is when they are out of work. Today, everybody is worried about his or her job, future and economic well-being.

Enough is enough! It is time to take a break and count your organization's blessings. It is time to tell your employees about what is good and what is working in the company. It's time to recount the remembrances/milestones that contributed to your past successes — people that made a difference, events that changed your destiny.

Pick a day in the coming weeks and announce that your company is celebrating "good news day." The objective is to commemorate the positives and recognize the successes. Remember, in the worst of the worst situations, there's always something encouraging, even if it is only the fact that the company has still kept the lights on. Most organizations, however, have much to be optimistic about — be it a roster of clients (so what if they pay a little slowly), a proprietary process or technology, or a brand that people know and occasionally even buy.

Make your own list — and speed counts. Your team needs to hear the sunnier side from top management now. For your good news day, plan a lunch, an afternoon session with refreshments or, if your business is on the critical list economically, simply gather everybody together in a room and start talking, sans the goodies. Put up some posters listing the top 10 things that are good or could turn positive in the future. This is the time for showmanship, some theatrics — and a bit of humor can't hurt either.

Speak from the heart and the gut. Tell your people what they do better than anyone else does. If you need help in your presentation, all you need do is turn on cable TV in the middle of the night and watch the evangelists do their thing. (You probably cannot sleep anyway with all your problems, so put your time to good use.) These silver-tongued proselytizers make the best salesperson look like a clerk in a flea market.

It's not practical to promise your people that there will be no more pain, be no more layoffs and that the good times are ready to roll. However, you can promise them that you will communicate with them often, always reporting the good, along with the bad and the ugly.

Most employees can deal with anything, as long as they get the facts and the company treats them like adults, rather than feeding them a lot of corporate mumbo jumbo that raises more questions than answers.

Your employees need to know that there is always hope and good stuff to come even in the darkest times. What they want to hear from you is, "this too shall pass," be it next year or in the years ahead.

A brief hiatus from the doom and gloom will go a long way in breaking the seemingly never-ending chain of despair. More than ever before, your employees and associates need something to celebrate that accentuates the positive and temporarily eliminates the negative.

Sometimes it's not what you say but how you say it
How to get your message across using a little honey

This column was originally published in July 2009

What would your first reaction be to this statement: "Keep your blankety-blank off the grass!"

Wait, don't answer yet. What would you think about this one? "We want everyone to enjoy our beautiful lawn, so let's work together to keep it that way." Unless you are a bully or just itching for a fight, the latter is clearly more preferable.

As our grandmothers taught us, you can catch more bees with honey. If we agree with this premise, then why does management so often begin with the negatives and go downhill from there?

Think about the communications in your organization and how many assertions start with a negative followed by a litany of unpleasant consequences. Many leaders think it's more forceful and expedient to say it like it is and simply cut to the chase. They fall into the bad habit of starting with, for example: "If we don't increase sales in the next month, we might have to lay off many of you," or, "We either save money on expenses, or we go down the tubes." Sure, these get the point across, but they also set a pugnacious tone that (1) confirms that management is a bunch of knuckleheads who think they are above everyone else, (2) triggers an action-reaction almost taunting the recipient to do exactly the opposite, or (3) results in the entire message being tuned out.

The key to effective management is accomplishing objectives through others. To do so, however, managers must effectively communicate what must be accomplished. A good initial step is to treat people as participants/partners in the process as a part of the solution, not the cause of the problem.

If your people aren't responding to your messages look in the mirror. Instead of blaming your employees, determine if your directives are providing clarity and the appropriate motivation.

Ask yourself how you would want to be told something important. You surely won't want to be told to do something or face dire consequences without an explanation. Frequently, management does not give employees enough credit for having the ability to grasp the obvious. Fact is, you can jump-start acceptance by explaining the issue and the anticipated fix using a logical, positive tone, focusing on the good, rather than the bad.

However, and there are always howevers, if the first communiqué does not elicit the expected action then put the honey in the cupboard and move to plan B. If the first sweet-laced mandate was ignored by some, then home in on those who might need a trip to the woodshed to understand what you really meant. Target your second message to the noncompliant laggards with the old-school, stronger-style message, as in "What part of no didn't you understand?" Unless these tardy adopters are dumber than a stump, the light bulb between their ears, with a little nudge, will flash, and they'll likely fall in line.

It's also very important to understand in most cases that the medium is the message. This means that the vehicle or venue you select to deliver your directive is just as important as the message itself. Delivering a serious concern about sales would be inappropriate as a part of your presentation at, say, a company awards event. Good news should be presented in an upbeat setting, while subjects that are more serious should be delivered in an environment that conveys the message as strictly business.

For instance, send an important message in an email with a grabber subject line that reads "Immediate Attention Required, Confidential Information About Our Company's Future." Alternatively, a statement of consequence could be presented verbally by senior management to a small or even larger group after which attendees would be handed an envelope bearing their name with a reprint of the points delivered verbally. This adds credibility and significance to the message. However, remember a serious message can still be delivered in a positive tone.

Finally, if all else fails, you can always revert to the no-holds-barred technique of starting out with "Keep your blankety-blank of the grass or there won't be any grass for you to walk on." Most times, the honey will work and your employees will respect you for being positive, yet forthright. If it comes to the stick and the woodshed, at least you will get credit for trying, and the good people will appreciate your follow-through and know that you are not merely a paper tiger.

In the heat of battle, learn to count to 10

A way to have your cake and eat it, too

This column was originally published in October 2009

No matter your job title, from file clerk to CEO, you have most likely at one time or another had the urge to take an action that would be immediately gratifying — making you feel good for at least a minute anyway. However, deep down inside you knew that you had better count to 10 before acting with your gut instead of your head.

What can make a grown businessperson want to act spontaneously without thinking of the consequences? The list is likely endless. Example: A customer calls you and wants a better price — for the fifth time in the same month. While listening to this utterly insulting request, a little voice in your head is saying, "Tell this numskull to take his or her business and put it somewhere a professional should never suggest."

How about this one? An employee walks into your office and makes a demand, which you think is inane and utterly overreaching — be it a promotion, a raise or a threat to walk out the door unless a specific requirement is instantly met. Your first thought is to tell the employee to go buy a tall three-legged stool so that he or she does not get too tired standing in the long unemployment lines.

In a verbal confrontation, time is your best weapon. By continuing to listen without interrupting, you accomplish two things. First, just like a child throwing a temper tantrum, your confronter will quickly run out of steam if you don't jump in. Remember, it takes two to have an argument. Secondly, if you listen closely, you'll get a clearer idea of what the real issue is. Most people don't say what they really mean or can't articulate their position — especially when they are slobbering as they rant. Therefore, you must be an effective interpreter. While maintaining your self-imposed vow of silence, contemplate if what is being asserted warrants a response or if doing so at that moment will just further inflame this unwelcome encounter. Once you figure that out you can construct a more thoughtful rebuttal — but on your timetable.

I bet many executives have fantasized about simply walking out on this type of intruder just for the pure enjoyment of doing so. Turning off the lights and slamming the door would be an appropriate exclamation point to the episode. Most leaders, however, have built-in "circuit breakers" that safeguard against seeking impetuous retribution.

Unpleasant emails present a different challenge. Here is an easy and fulfilling technique to handle a particularly nasty cyberspace message without doing permanent damage. As a bonus, this exercise can even prove to be therapeutic, as well. When an email sets you off, instead of precipitously retaliating, try this. Step one: Click on the "forward" button. Step two: Craft your response — the more vitriolic, the better. Say it from your heart without regret. There are 26 letters in the English alphabet so use them creatively by typing things you have only dreamed of writing. When your keyboard frenzy ends, this cathartic experience will provide a feeling of serenity, albeit too short-lived.

You're thinking does this technique make sense. Read on.

Because you hit "forward" instead of "reply," your email isn't going anywhere because the "to" field is empty. Voilà, your "get even" but never sent email didn't do any irreparable harm that spontaneous responses can inflict. Certainly save your draft email for reconsideration or future self-indulgence. However, in the meantime, you'll gain time to think of a more rational "censored" reply. Sometimes after deliberation, the same as in a one-sided verbal argument, you'll conclude that no response is the best response. The real message to the sender is you're not dignifying absurd comments with a return volley. Talk about revenge; this subtle form gets the job done in spades.

Instant communications is a part of today's business culture. However, learning to creatively stop and count to 10 may ensure that you're not the one who goes down for the 10 count. By putting a lid on your feelings, you can many times gain control of an incendiary situation. A short pause could give you the opportunity to find a solution that allows you to have your cake and eat it, too, without suffering any indigestion.

When you lose respect, you lose your authority

Business lessons learned under extreme stress and from unlikely sources

This column was originally published in November 2010

Important business lessons can be learned from observing how others in unrelated professions make decisions under stress. I have co-piloted planes and helicopters in the second seat next to experienced aviators, trained to race sports cars and ride motorcycles, scrubbed in to watch hospital surgeries, and even did a stint in an emergency room just to get an up-close look at how the highly skilled function under pressure. Recently, I added a police patrol ride-along to my repertoire in order to see what else it takes to have the right stuff.

The police are trained to make decisions with limited information. When a car is dispatched to unknown trouble, the officer often has limited information about what may be encountered. It could be a man with a gun or merely a barking dog.

In business, every day, executives must make decisions that can be life-altering. These include hiring and firing as well as dealing with serious issues that could affect a business's well-being. During my ride-along, I asked numerous questions. Topping the list of good advice from my new temporary partner was his response to my question of, "How do you get control in a difficult situation?"

My mentor for the evening stated, "When you lose respect, you lose your authority, and bad things can happen."

He went on to explain that, when he arrives on the scene, the first thing he must do is gain respect from everyone involved. Respect, he added, is achieved by first giving respect and not by muscling your way in and pushing people around.

Respect also comes from looking the part. That's why officers wear uniforms, have badges, and carry scary-looking guns and handcuffs. That is also why I'm not a huge fan of everyday "business casual." When one is attempting to wield power, if nothing else, he or she must look the part, either sitting in a squad car or at business meeting.

Most civilians think that when a police officer's radio crackles "211 in progress" (code for armed robbery), the officer hits the siren and lights, does a U-turn with tires smoking and speeds off to save the day. I learned on my ride-along that "fast is not really always fast." Instead, speed is about "being smooth," and first thinking through the proper way to proceed.

In business, how many times do executives react to a situation with lightning speed but without first weighing all of the possible ramifications? The streets are littered with the resumes of executives who acted before they assessed.

Once on the scene, an officer has to size up the situation and set priorities. If the bad guy has a gun to someone's head, the cop doesn't walk around asking a female witness, "Just the facts ma'am." The same applies with a corporate problem. When it occurs, the manager must triage the issue to mitigate the damage. It is equally critical in crime scene investigations and in finding a business solution to assess the situation and to do what is most important first before determining who is at fault.

Police officers depend on concise communications and teamwork when lives hang in the balance. Most times in business, lives are not at stake, but the need to ask for assistance is no different from a cop shouting over the radio "Officer needs help." Not every patrol person is a SWAT expert, but every officer is trained to know when to seek help. Too many managers wait too long to recognize that they lack the specific skill set to fix a portion of the problem. In both professions, those involved need to know when to call for reinforcements.

As I concluded my ride-along, I asked my new cop buddy his opinion of what it will take to reduce crime. His one word response: "Consequences." The perpetrators must know that if they do the crime, they'll do the time. This is no different from setting guidelines for employees, contractors and suppliers. A leader must make clear what is expected and what the consequences are if someone doesn't deliver.

I learned a lot on this ride-along, including that preparation and thinking before reacting go a long way in keeping the peace on the "mean streets," as well as in the corporate boardroom.

Finally, in case you're wondering ... no, we didn't stop for doughnuts.

What have we learned today?

Ask this question after your next meeting and be prepared for a few surprises

This column was originally published in January 2011

One of my favorite cable news shows is MSNBC's "Morning Joe," featuring co-anchors Joe Scarborough and Mika Brzezinski. At the conclusion of each broadcast these anchors, along with all of the day's guests, stand up and answer the question, "What have we learned today?"

Everyone who chairs a business meeting should ask participants this same question at the conclusion of the session. One word of warning: be prepared for some surprising responses. Too many meetings are simply an exercise in futility with nothing of substance accomplished because nobody learned anything new. While the presenter thinks the information is relevant and revealing the participants are left hanging in a fog. When you ask be, prepared for responses such as:

- The passive participant states: "I understand the purpose of the meeting was sort of, kind of about, oh, you know ..."
- The politically astute replies: "Boss, this was the best meeting ever, I got it and I know what to do," as he or she thinks, "Oh my God, I have to find someone who can figure out what we're supposed to do"
- The secure realist mumbles a few unintelligible words, while rolling his or her eyes. Translation: another waste of valuable time.

The difference between success and failure frequently hinges on the clarity of the goals, and who has to do what by when.

I've never met anyone who gets up in the morning, gets out of bed and says to him or herself, "I can't wait to get to work so I can screw up." It just doesn't happen. Unfortunately, what does happen frequently is that employees don't understand the objective at hand or what direction should they take in achieving it.

Most company goals and objectives are first introduced in a meeting where reasonably intelligent people gather to combine their thoughts and craft a plan. If in the meeting the goals are not appropriately communicated then it's a very good bet that either what was discussed never gets off the ground or, if it does, the undertaking will crash and burn in short order.

There are a few basics that can make all of us better communicators, particularly when chairing meetings. Of course, everyone knows they need an agenda for the meeting, but few follow their own outline. Out of the blue someone will bring up a point and then suddenly the meeting turns into a free-for-all and ends as a pointless exercise in how not to do it. I have fantasized that most meetings should be conducted standing up. This would force participants to get to the point before their backs begin to ache, knees get wobbly and feet turn numb.

There's an old adage: "Chance favors those who prepare." After preparing an agenda for your meetings, are you spending enough time flushing out what you want to really convey and what action, reaction you want to evoke? For this to occur you just can't throw a topic against the wall and hope it sticks. People need to be guided down the path. Another major pitfall of most sessions is that executives try to stuff 10 pounds of topics into a 5-pound bag. Keep the agenda manageable, covering the most important topics first, and stay on track while watching the clock as if you're playing in a college basketball game and you must score "the points you need" before the final buzzer sounds.

Always appoint an active participant in the meeting, not an administrative assistant, as the scribe. Rotate the responsibility among those who attend reoccurring sessions. It's amazing how people will stay alert and think before they talk when they know their utterances may be indelibly recorded. Also, the notes from every meeting must be published for all attendees by the next morning.

Finally, assign accountability to the individuals with a due date for each task. After a completion date is assigned the person responsible can say if they can't make the deadline, "I need more time, I don't want to do it because it's a bad idea, I don't know how to do it or I need more help." What they can't do is ignore the assignment and pretend it never happened.

At the conclusion of your next meeting go around the table and ask "What have you learned today?" If you don't ask, they won't tell and, more importantly, you'll never know.

Why are the simplest words sometimes the hardest to say?

Is love really never having to say you're sorry?

This column was originally published in June 2012

There's a classic line from the 1970 movie "Love Story" that has become a part of our popular culture. In the drama, the dying heroine played by Ali MacGraw says to her husband, played by actor Ryan O'Neal, "Love means never having to say you're sorry" as he apologizes for his anger. It is certainly a memorable and tear-jerking line, but is saying, "You're sorry" all that bad if it can soothe a wound caused by someone speaking or acting out before thinking?

Disagreements and anger are a reality in the workplace and in life in general. Various people react in different ways when under pressure. Some lose their cool completely and say things they instantly regret, while others launch into tormenting the perceived offender with the silent treatment. No matter the technique used to punish, all of these methods quickly become tiresome and, more importantly, adversely affect the workplace.

Too frequently in the work environment, many people just can't suck it up and utter the two simple words, "I'm sorry," even when they know they're dead wrong. It's not a macho thing either, as women don't behave much differently when they feel put upon. What's a boss to do when this stubbornness becomes problematic?

In a word: intervene. When not controlled, these unreasonable, obstinate antics can become time-consuming and disruptive. It could all start with an impetuous negative email or a less-than-mature voice

93

mail left in the heat of battle that cascades into a futile distraction, as otherwise effective and seemingly sensible employees act out as if they're in a 20- or 30-year time warp, behaving as if they're back in the third grade rather than adults in the workplace.

The most expeditious method that works with either the protagonist or antagonist in an office drama is to call a spade a spade, so to speak, and get the feuding parties together and cut to the chase, making each person agree to bury the hatchet but preferably not in each other's skull. If employees' anger management issues are left to fester, they can easily result in other people in the same work environment taking sides, and in short order, you will find yourself in the midst of a Civil War. The only thing guaranteed when this occurs is that there will be casualties. It is incumbent on the ruling manager to make sure that the company doesn't wind up as the victim, incurring a loss of productivity and causing everyone around the two factions to feel as if they're walking on pins and needles.

While many times it would be easier for the boss to ask one of the warring participants to approach the other to work out their differences, this tactic just takes too much time and the outcome can be iffy. It really doesn't matter who is right or wrong but that the nonsense is stopped dead in its tracks. The best way to accomplish this is to make it more than abundantly clear that anger in the workplace is a nonstarter and could be a career-inhibitor.

Allowing employees to exhibit a lack of civility will cause a domino effect that will lead to no good. Civility does not just apply to peers. Instead, it's applicable to all who must work together, including superiors, subordinates and even fellow board members. Don't confuse civility with agreeing or disagreeing with someone. It also doesn't mean one has to believe that someone is effective in his or her role. Instead, what must be required is that those within an organization, no matter what level, simply take the higher road and respect not necessarily the person but the role and make the assumption that everyone has a part in working toward shared goals, until it is proven otherwise.

Once everybody knows the rules of engagement, many times the negative engagement suddenly ends and it's back to business as usual. When that doesn't happen, it's time for offenders to be forced to go to their respective corners so as not to do each other or the company any more harm.

To promote coexistence when no one wants to take the first step and say, "I'm sorry," it's up to the adult in the room — and that would be you, the boss — to step into the fray with your whistle to call a permanent timeout to these types of disruptive shenanigans.

How to run your business in a fishbowl

A simple way to help protect some of your most important assets

This column was originally published in November 2012

It seems that every other week there's a major story in the media about a company claiming that one of its competitors has purloined a cherished secret that provided an unfair competitive advantage. This is all part of running a business in today's fishbowl environment, where sensitive information is too abundant and can be obtained by almost anyone and everyone who is so inclined.

In this era of heightened visibility, some of the best companies, especially high-tech firms, play everything incredibly close to the vest, particularly when it comes to providing information about current sales trends, new products and projects that they are exploring or developing. This is because such information is a coveted company asset. In today's "victory at almost any cost" world, too many are looking for that edge to leverage whatever they can to stack the odds in their favor.

We also read too frequently about how easily these secrets have somehow wound up in the wrong hands. Sometimes a loose-lipped employee simply talks too much to too many people in the wrong places. Occasionally, someone simply leaves a briefcase or smartphone, jam-packed with confidential information, in a bar, at a restaurant or on a plane.

What's not talked about much is the frequent practice of competitors simply asking what appear to be innocuous questions of lower-level personnel in a company in order to garner nuggets of "inside information" usually without risking the perils of violating any legal statutes. It's also common practice for Wall Street security analysts to simply walk into a retail store, as an example, and begin asking questions about trends, what products are selling and which aren't. It all gets down to the reality that it never hurts to ask a question because one never knows when a valuable tidbit will be revealed.

Like it or not, this is just the way it is, and there will always be people who ask and others who tell. What can you do to protect your coveted information? The answer is basic: Mandate that providing revealing responses to specific questions is a violation of company policy and could result in draconian consequences for anyone who spills the beans, no matter if well-intended. Once your employees and suppliers know the ground rules and the consequences, you're one step closer to closing the possibility of vital information inadvertently slipping through the sieve.

The best way to accomplish this is to establish, enforce and continually reiterate a "one voice, one company" policy. This translates into all hands within your organization knowing what can be told to outsiders and, more importantly, what can't. This policy must be in writing and must state what types of questions are off limits. It must also explain how the questioner is to be handled when the interrogatory is posed. In my retail chain experience, we often had competitors, vendors and industry analysts visit stores and ask all types of questions. Candidly, I don't blame them, but with a clearly understood policy, employees know how to respond by referring the questions to headquarters and a specific department or individual. Ninety-nine percent of the time, the person asking the question never follows up with the corporate office because he or she knows the desired answers will not be forthcoming.

Most employees want to please their employer and most want others to think they are in the know. When you create an ironclad policy, it takes the pressure off of your people and adds another layer of security about things no outsider needs to know. For your suppliers, require that each sign a confidentiality agreement and specify that you have a simple "one strike and you're out" policy. Also use your own secret shoppers to test your vulnerability by having them ask the forbidden, just to verify that the company veil is not being lifted by the unauthorized.

This protocol is certainly not foolproof, and periodically, there will be lapses — the most frightening of which are the ones you'll never learn about. It all gets down to a numbers game. Confidential information, just like the cash, equipment and other assets on your balance sheet, can never be taken for granted and must be protected. Anyone can look in your fishbowl in this day and age, but it is your job to make sure that what they think they might find is not what they get.

What to do if you're under a public, verbal attack
Deny, deny, deny; fall, tuck and roll; or put your head in the sand?

This column was originally published in November 2013

The quick answer to this headline is none of the above. A leader, by definition, must do exactly that — lead, which means being in front of a variety of audiences, including employees, investors and customers. Not everyone is going to be a gung-ho supporter. Sooner or later you'll encounter a naysayer who either has a point to prove or is on a mission to make you and your company look bad.

Many of these verbal confrontations come out of nowhere and when least expected. As the representative of your organization, it is your responsibility to manage these situations and recognize that sometimes a "win" can be simply minimizing the damage.

When under siege, it's human instinct to fight, flee or freeze. Typically these behavioral responses aren't particularly productive in a war of words. Engaging in verbal fisticuffs could simply escalate the encounter, giving more credence to the matter than deserved.

If you flee by ignoring the negative assertions, you'll immediately be presumed guilty as charged. It's hard to make your side of the story known if you put your head in the sand.

By freezing, you'll appear intellectually impotent. Worse yet, pooh-poohing a question will only fuel the aggressor's determination to disrupt the proceedings. You could use a SWAT-type police and military technique to elude a confronter by falling, tucking and rolling to safety, but that usually only works on the silver screen.

Perhaps the best method to manage unwelcome adversaries is to be prepared prior to taking center stage. This applies to live audiences or a virtual gathering when you're speaking to multiple participants, which is common practice for public company CEOs during quarterly analyst conference calls.

Most gatherings of this nature include a Q&A segment where the tables are turned on the speaker who must be prepared to respond to inquiries both positive and negative.

Before any such meeting, it is critical to contemplate and rehearse how you would respond to thorny or adverse statements or questions.

A good practice is to put the possible questions in writing and then craft your responses, hoping of course that they won't be needed. This is no different from what the President of the United States or the head of any city council does prior to a press conference or presentation. The advantage of this exercise is that it tends to sharpen your thinking and causes you to explore issues from the other perspective.

In some cases you'll find yourself in an awkward or difficult situation where there is no suitable yes or no answer, or when the subject of the interrogatory is so specific it is applicable to only a very few.

The one-off question is easiest to handle by stating that you or your representative will answer the question following the session rather than squander the remaining time on something that does not interest or affect the majority.

The more difficult question is one that will take further investigation and deliberation, in which case the best course of action is to say exactly that. Answer by asserting that rather than giving a less-than-thoughtful response to a question that deserves more research, you or your vicar will get back with the appropriate response in short order. This helps to protect you from shooting from the hip only to later regret something that can come back to haunt you.

Effective speakers and leaders have learned that the best way to counter antagonism is through diplomacy. It's much more difficult for the antagonist to continue to fight with a polite, unwilling opponent.

Finally, when being challenged, never personalize your response against your questioner; always control your temper; and don't linger on a negative. Keep the proceedings moving forward and at the conclusion keep your promise to follow up with an answer. This will build your credibility and allow you to do what you do best, lead.

F.U. or else!

Tie a string around your finger, before someone ties a noose around your neck

This column was originally published in September 2013

Calm down … those two letters in the headline are not what you might be thinking. However, it got your attention, for this leads to an important subject.

When you, or those with whom you work, don't follow the principles of these two letters, problems occur. Not doing what these initials represent can be the difference between success and failure, cost big money, create disappointment and actually ruin relationships.

Hopefully by now you've figured out that F.U. stands for Follow Up. This skill is central to achieving objectives, supporting your people or customers, and maintaining your credibility. Too many people just don't get it and consistently fail to make F.U. a part of their business regimen.

Words are cheap, but it's action that makes the difference. Many promises are made every day such as: "I'll get the answer and return your call soon," or "My person will call your person so that we can get together." Good intentions aside, if one does not make note of it, the call just might never happen.

Fortunately, only a relatively few get hit by locomotives because trains are big and people see them coming, but many are stung by bees. That's the same with following up. Virtually no one would forget to pick up the big order, or neglect to attend a huge meeting, but too many let the smaller, yet important, matters slip through the cracks. This not only affects the person who didn't receive what was promised, but also could significantly impede productivity.

As an example, an associate is to provide needed information first thing in the morning. Breakfast comes and goes and as the lunch hour approaches people along the line are sitting on their hands waiting. Do the math; count up what that could cost your business day in and day out. Frantically, and with a high degree of disgust, you track down the tardy offender and are appalled by the response, "Oh, sorry, it just slipped my mind. I forgot to write it down." Sure, this can happen once but by the second or third time it becomes a pattern and the credibility of the perpetrator can be lost.

Following up is a reflection of respect. When people don't have the courtesy of doing what they say, you begin to wonder if they can ever do it. In my companies, all those with whom I work quickly become aware of my sacrosanct F.U. policy.

Essentially after every meeting, whether a one-on-one or with a group, I assign a date for my own purposes of when what was discussed is to take place. If it was a task of significance, the date would be agreed upon with those who had to do the work.

When new employees receive a memo from me, with the unexpected "F.U." initials in the bottom left-hand corner, many are initially stunned, thinking I'm giving them a crude ultimatum or don't think much of their work. Fortunately, those with a modicum of common sense quickly realize that these two letters are not a pejorative as they are always followed by a numeric string that even a newbie can figure out represents a date.

I remind my team that I do not want to be their father or their baby sitter. Instead, when I ask that something be done by a certain date, and everyone involved agrees, it must happen.

Alternatively, the person assigned the task could always come back and say he or she can't meet the deadline, don't know how to do what was being asked, need help with the issue, or had figured out a better alternative. What could not happen is for the person assigned the task to pretend that no follow-up was required, or worse, that the covenant was never agreed upon.

Because so few follow up as promised, this presents your business with an outstanding opportunity to rise above others and create a rock-solid reputation for saying what you'll do and then doing what you say. All it takes is a little discipline and respect for those with whom you work. It's better to carry around a little string for your finger than run the risk of finding the proverbial rope around your neck as a result of errors of omission.

It's not complicated...

Close counts in more than horseshoes, hand grenades and slow dancing

This column was originally published in February 2014

Maybe you've seen the popular AT&T television commercials promoting the theme, "It's not complicated," for high-speed Internet services. In these vignettes, a moderator sits at a child's table in a playroom with some of the cutest kids on the planet and poses an innocent question, such as, "How high is up?" And then, out of the mouth of babes, come the humorous and insightful morsels of an answer that are smack on target.

Too many times in business and government, "Mountains are made out of molehills." Ask a simple question and frequently we get an obscure answer that simply raises more questions. The problem is most people either over-think the issue, are too concerned about responding without in-depth analysis, or fear they might appear shallow by speaking the obvious.

Equally unproductive is that a simple question can too frequently evoke the most bizarre meaningless answer. At the top of my list is the now infamous question that contains the verb "is" in a sentence that was posed to an otherwise articulate, silver-tongued politician about a touchy subject. His response was, "It all depends on what the meaning of the word 'is' is." This should have made him consider entering a monastery and taking a vow of silence, among other things.

I've often found that in brainstorming and kicking around ideas with others the first comment ultimately proves to be the best and most meaningful answer. It's been said that close only counts in horseshoes, hand grenades and slow dancing. I would add to this list that a speedy answer also, many times, gets the job done.

Certainly an off-the-top-of-the-head response might not be 100 percent correct, but in most situations 70 percent or so right is much better than the completely unequivocal, unabridged data points that might take a day or two, maybe even longer, to obtain. One does, however, need to weigh the ramifications of not being able to provide complete commentary, but typically zero variance is meaningful only in reading brain X-rays or perhaps calculating coordinates for a drone strike.

As a leader, you must communicate parameters for quick responses and assert a standing caveat that if the responder later determines that more information came to mind or was discovered, he or she must provide that amplification to those involved.

You must also create an environment that fosters team members to venture further out on the proverbial limb in order to keep a discussion moving forward. Most times when people are reluctant to give it their best shot, it's your fault because you've not communicated the value of, and your appreciation for, the practicality of providing relevant information that serves the purpose at hand. When a particular team member or members consistently hesitate in responding extemporaneously, it's time for you to reset the ground rules that will give them the comfort they need to become effective contributors and communicators.

Analysis paralysis can become the scourge of any organization, as it breeds indecisiveness, and hampers innovation and quick solutions to the most common problems and opportunities. For good or bad, success today is often measured in hours, days or weeks, instead of months and years, based on speed to market. In many respects, this is due to living and working in the digital age where immediate gratification is expected.

It's not complicated, and simpler and faster is usually better. Thanks, Ma Bell, for the entertaining reminder.

3

Managing People

Managing
high maintenance
prima donnas
Can't live with 'em,
can't live without 'em

This column was originally published in January 2006

Life is a lot easier when you have an employee who is very high maintenance, has an inflated sense of his or her own self-importance, and is a poor performer. In this case the answer for this prima donna is simple: take a page out of Donald Trump's playbook by looking the laggard right in the eye and uttering those two infamous words, "y-o-u-'r-e f-i-r-e-d!"

The bigger dilemma, however, is what you do when you have an employee who is without question high maintenance, a prima donna, believes he or she walks on water, but happens to be really terrific, getting the job done and then some? Worst yet, the person thinks they are truly irreplaceable and, even worse everybody else does, too, including you.

So here is the problem: either pull the plug and jettison this emotionally exhausting albatross, or find a way for peaceful co-existence without spending the rest of your career running the gauntlet every time this perennial malcontent gets bent out of shape or wakes up on the wrong side of the bed. Typically, a prima donna is deep-down inside probably an okay person. Somewhere, however, along the way, either their ego was stoked to the point of reaching biblical proportions, or they suffer from such an inferiority complex they have to tell you and everybody else, at every opportunity, how good they are. Some might think this description is of a borderline psycho, but the difference between a prima donna and a psycho is this prima donna gets results.

The trick in managing high maintenance people is to crack their DNA code and identify their individual hot buttons. What is the "Rosetta Stone" that deflates this person's ego to a manageable level, while maintaining their confidence? Is it their need to be the center of attention; or do they thrive on causing chaos, always claiming to be right, starting arguments just for sport? Could they sincerely think they are the next best thing to sliced bread? Once you ascertain what pushes their buttons, you are more then halfway home in discovering the silver bullet to neutralize their annoyance factor, but preserving their productivity.

Case in point: your number two guy is in fact a rainmaker who can woo customers, charm their socks off, while solving problems with little or no direction. The downside, however, is that everything with them is a cause celebre. They cause you personal grief, sleepless nights, disturb day-to-day operations and adversely affect morale and productivity.

The simple and easiest solution to this thorny issue is to call the person into your office and put your cards on the table. Tell them that they are great, you love them for their good work, but they are a real pain with which to deal and have reached the point of not only being tedious, but also approaching the crossroads leading to a place neither of you want to go.

During your heart-to-heart, ask them what you can do to avoid future problems that are unproductive and distracting to the mission. Promise, however, that when they have something to say to you, they can always come in, sit down and vent. Remind them that just like in Las Vegas, what is said there stays there. Make them a part of the solution by putting the onus on them to come up with a fix for a peaceful and productive coexistence. Allow them to win, on your terms, not theirs.

Let's say the person wants to announce the big idea he or she has been working on with you to the entire organization. Their number one motivation is once again to prove they are the best. Instead of you presenting the big plan yourself, let the star performer take center stage this time. You introduce the concept, but let the star tell the story from the idea's incubation to fruition. A word of caution: you must control this egomaniac's presentation by having a rehearsal so as not to alienate others with uncensored comments.

In reality, this is not much different then how one manages a six-year old, giving the child two alternatives from which to choose, of course, the right answer is obvious, but you let the runny-nose kid "decide" which fork in the road to take. All of a sudden the child is making the decision and takes ownership of the solution, even though you "managed them" to the right answer without giving up ground.

The worst thing a boss can do is let them see you sweat. Most of the bullies in this world become bullies because they know they get under somebody's skin. Be sincere, forceful, yet non-confrontational, keep an open mind, sucking it in and not making it personal even though you are tempted to do so. Never deny to yourself there is not a problem, while you and everybody else knows it is a big issue.

Prima donnas take more time and attention, but at the end of the day, the alternative of losing a high performer can result in lost productivity and anxiety. Don't ever forget the Prima Donna who produces is a recognized commodity for good or bad — they are the devil you know.

The dreaded annual performance review
Not a time for retribution, but a road map for the future

This column was originally published in May 2006

No matter if you're the CEO or janitor, we all report to someone and that someone typically annually assesses our performance in a formal or pseudo-formal manner. The words review, assessment, and grade can strike fear in the hearts of even the most competent, stoic and pragmatic, conjuring up flash-backs to elementary school when, on occasion, many of us had to take home that report card which was not as positive as our parents might have expected.

So, how do we make this annual rite of passage a productive and useful tool leading to improved performance? It starts with having the right attitude and recognizing that the review is just one more "dashboard gauge" to be used by both superior and subordinate along with myriad other indicators as to how we performed in the past year and how we're going to improve in the future.

If you're giving the review and the recipient is shocked with what you're presenting, then you've probably done a pretty lousy job during the preceding 52 weeks of keeping your subordinate informed as to your view of how he or she is producing.

An annual review should reveal very few surprises for either side, but instead solidify all of those things each party knew or had a very strong inkling as to the other's point of view. On a day-to-day basis there can be no substitute for open and candid communications, during which both parties share negatives including shortfalls, attitudinal issues, and equally important, positives sprinkled with a generous amount of "attaboy — attagirl" be it spontaneously delivered as you pass in the hall, or in an update. For special accomplishments, a written note of congratulations to the subordinate with a copy to corporate/institutional big- wigs can be as big a motivator as a raise, although granted, a letter plus the raise would be classified as the "real deal."

What's the best way to prepare for a substantive annual review? I have always started the next review on the first day immediately following the most recent review. Throughout the ensuing year I make random notes as circumstances warrant about the employee's progress or lack thereof. I keep these notes for each direct report, in a manila folder under lock and key. I have found that it is very difficult to sit down the day before an individual's annual review and try to recollect from memory what transpired during the prior 364 days. Maintaining notes on the individual's negative actions is not only effective in keeping a running score, but also a way of internally venting on matters of perceived importance without immediately blowing my cool and calling the person in on the carpet because at that moment the transgression seems monumental. This provides a cathartic effect as well when you commit your thoughts to writing, even though you put them away for awhile without making a federal case out of the issue at the time it occurred. It's another way of counting to 10 before engaging your tongue prior to having your brain kick in, during the heat of battle. Many times when I begin to prepare a review at the end of the employment year and read my earlier notes, I decide that in retrospect, that error of omission or commission was not as horrific as I thought at the time.

My next step is to formalize the entire review in writing, recognizing that I am going to give a hard copy to the recipient when the review is concluded. This disciplines me to ensure that what I put in writing is what I really mean. I am always aware that the recipient will most likely re-read the review at some point in the year ahead, and might even show it to a third party who could have another motivation in mind. My attorney friends call this a paper trail.

Always keep in mind that a review is not the time for retribution, retaliation, deflation or humiliation. Instead it is an important road map for the future. If you have a chip on your shoulder and intend to make the meeting an ugly payback session, then be benevolent and tell the employee to go to the Human Resources Department and bring his or her coat.

A review should be peppered and balanced with positive accomplishments not only with what went wrong or needs improvement. Stay away from descending into too much detail about any one specific incident, less you run the risk of engaging in a "he said, she said" finger-pointing session which will transcend into an exercise in futility.

Another must-do portion of the review is to wrap up with a series of agreed upon goals for the new year and methods of how both of you will keep score. People need clarity and direction.

Finally, be prepared to take constructive criticism from the employee, be it comments about your communication style or the lack thereof to failure to listen or be consistent by changing directions at a whim. This type of feed back can be valuable and I strongly recommend you commit to writing what you were told and keep it in your own personal good job/bad job file.

I have always concluded every review by asking the person "what can I do to help you be more successful?" As the employee disappears down the hall after the review, I immediately jot down my notes from the session. I then periodically open the person's folder during the year and continue the process of preparing for the next performance assessment, all the while recognizing that this process never ends because it is one of the key building blocks in the ongoing development of a productive, focused and successful team.

Professionalism combined with passion
A two-step process requiring time and nurturing

This column was originally published in July 2006

Every business owner, executive, manager, supervisor or Indian Chief whom I have ever met always wanted his or her team members/employees not only to be consummate professionals but also to have that incessant, nagging "burning in the belly," driven by a deep-rooted passion for the company or organization. I knew one over-the-top executive who attempted to accelerate the motivation process by distributing t-shirts emblazoned with such mottos as: "To Die for the Company Cause Is to Live Forever!" or, "Losing is Never an Option."

The reality is that professionalism comes from training and personal values, engendered by a sense of pride. Raw passion, however, comes from the soul and is an acquired emotion instilled over time by one's thorough commitment to the mission. An employee being involved with positive results serves to couple the organization's goals with the individual's personal objectives about life, living, and the opportunity to really make a difference. These positive outcomes can range from better serving the customer, rewarding stakeholders, or simply creating a better mouse trap with product and service innovations. Everyone has their own hot buttons; the trick is to align them with the company's modus operandi and goals.

It is naïve to expect a new person to come on board and instantaneously become imbued with passion. Unfortunately passion cannot be administered intravenously or mandated by others. It is the job of a leader to nurture the neophyte over time through education, action and example, allowing the new person to engage and be recognized for contributing.

Don't be fooled by the self-promoter who always seems to say the "right thing," sophomorically expecting the boss will be seduced into believing he or she has become an overnight convert just waiting to be the first to volunteer to drink the company's "Kool-Aid." Signs of "passion impersonators" who only want to expedite their career path include being the first to offer to work the weekend, nonchalantly stating "No problem, I'll just miss my son's jr. high school graduation, after all, he'll do it again in four years." Or, "I don't need to go to my best friend's wedding, after all, statistically there's a 50-50 chance she'll have another in a few years." A bit of an exaggeration, but people do say the strangest things and actually think they're believable.

When these types of off-the-wall assertions of devotion are uttered you must immediately recognize that you have a chameleon on your team who changes directions based on political circumstances as many times a day as Imelda Marcos changed her shoes. The passion litmus test is when the associate does the right thing consistently for the company, the customer, the stakeholder, always putting his own agenda well behind those whom he serves. Don't become disillusioned if your new employee doesn't immediately internalize your organization's mantra. Always remember that this process, like a fine wine, must ferment over time. Sure, it's easier when the goals are clearly compelling, such as finding a cure to a dreaded malady, or when the product or service produced generates heart-warming results.

Professionals come in all shapes and sizes and have a variety of job titles. Again, it is not a prerequisite that the professional buy into every aspect of the entity's various long-term goals, provided that he or she is not opposed to the tasks at hand. Just look at criminal attorneys who are charged with providing the best possible defense without making personal judgments as to the guilt or innocence of the defendant.

So how do you as an executive motivate your new team member to hit the ground running and start producing before the passion ingredient kicks in? The first step is to be sure you hire the right person for the right reasons. At the top of my "must possess" list is a sense of professionalism and the need for the candidate to recognize from within the obligation that comes with taking on a job or assignment and giving it one's all. France's Emperor Napoleon Bonaparte wrote: "Your own resolution to succeed is more important than any other." True professionals, whether they intellectualize it or not, are many times "hired guns" brought in to accomplish specific objectives. I have found that the one common thread, as corny as it sounds, is that the real professional was raised to understand the simple obligation of "giving an honest day's work for a day's pay." It's as basic as that. I have been associated with many talented people over the years who held themselves to this standard and I was seldom disappointed by the quality and quantity of their work. Apathy is the killer in any business, organization, or relationship, for that matter. Whenever someone responds to your request with an indifferent shrug, mumbling "whatever" under their breath, it's a sure signal that the person is just going through the motions without any regard to pride of doing the job right for either the company or, equally important, their own self esteem.

The best of the best always have their own internal barometer to measure success, and when you give them the appropriate direction, that barometer will work 99 percent of the time.

When they first begin the job they may go home at night and be able to "turn it off" more easily than one who is emotionally committed. However, if you provide the proper orientation and guidance, lo and behold one day the new hire's training and know-how will intersect with their emotions. This will be the magical point you've worked towards, when your student achieves the delicate balance of combining professionalism with passion which will make doing the work as fulfilling as reaching the goal.

Encourage your team to talk behind your back
They'll do it anyway, so give them your blessings

This column was originally published in December 2007

Just about everybody, after entering kindergarten, will at some point become involved in talking about another person behind his or her back. Sometimes comments can be hurtful, sometimes innocuous. However, if correctly framed, "behind the back venting" can also be constructive, not to mention therapeutic.

It's a national pastime for everyone to think that that he or she is smarter than the boss is. Many times an employee can and certainly should outshine the superior on specific subjects. As a boss, you can be sure your people will compare their abilities and creativity with yours and second-guess your strategies and practices. Therefore, I suggest that you facilitate the process so that talking behind your back can occur more regularly on your terms and be productive to boot.

There are some very simple and effective methods to provide "employee back-talk time." As CEO of my *Fortune* 500 company, I discovered that I could control this process by structuring a means where all my direct reports could have an open forum to take their best shot at me for good or bad. Early on, I created what I refer to as an "Operating Committee," which was comprised of my direct reports and other key corporate managers and executives who had to carry out company mandates, including many of mine, and run the place day in and day out. There was a distinction between this group and the Executive Committee, charged with creating policy and strategy that I chaired.

I attended only one Operating Committee meeting and made a statement that took less than a minute. I simply said that this would be my first and last appearance at "your" weekly committee meetings and that going forward the group would set its own agenda without me. I emphasized, however, that on every agenda there should be "back-talk" time during which participants could vent their frustrations and talk about any traditional unspeakables even if they reflected negatively on my leadership, decisions or capabilities. I stated that the only thing I asked was that once something was put on the table and the committee thought I was making some big mistakes, someone must be appointed to come and tell me (with my promise of immunity from prosecution). I made it clear to them that their job was to make me better and, to facilitate that, they could talk about my shortcomings, real or perceived, behind my back.

Now, I didn't just fall off a turnip truck, and I knew that not all of the comments about my charming personality and velvety soft glove style would be complimentary. I approached the process in a very Machiavellian manner, knowing that if I could get past the bruised ego I could become a more effective CEO and ultimately deliver better results for all constituents.

Weekly, my people were able to identify my errors of omission or commission, which were often plentiful. At times, I observed the folks leaving these Operating Committee meetings with a very satisfied smirk on their faces. Why? Because they got whatever was bugging them off their chests. They were able to compare notes with their peers; and I think in many cases, after the airing, they realized that what might have been festering as a big problem was, in the overall scheme of things, not particularly significant.

Another ancillary benefit of "back-talking" is that it tends to diffuse situations that might otherwise grow to biblical proportions. This release enables the team to move on to issues of greater importance. Just as relieving the pressure in a boiler that builds up, once diffused it is no longer a problem.

There are a number of other practical ways to foster venting in your organization. During particularly tense times, it is appropriate to excuse yourself from a planned dinner after a day of meetings with the team because your gut tells you they need to have download time among themselves. It takes a certain confidence, including a healthy ego, for the leader to foster this process. Most of the time when I bowed out of a dinner with subordinates, I knew that my team's ensuing collective catharsis would give them satisfaction and refocus their efforts. I admit occasionally that I felt a strange sensation, as in my ears burning, but this was a small price to pay.

In the public arena, our country's leaders have all experienced a not so behind-their-back venting particularly by the media within minutes after making a statement or promulgation. Pundits would dissect five ways to Sunday what was said that was right, wrong or irrelevant. This ongoing safety valve has served citizens well and provides an effective method for public officials to gauge acceptance of their actions and plan their next steps.

You as a leader can use similar "back-talk" techniques to maintain equilibrium in your company and reduce both petty and serious deep-seated distractions that impede progress. Being a good manager means accomplishing objectives through others. Being a great leader means keeping the team focused, on track, and communicating not only with you but also with each other.

Politics in business and talking behind the boss's back aren't always necessarily negatives, as long as you manage the process and encourage it with your blessings.

Make the journey as good as the destination

Dream as you go; don't wait for tomorrow

This column was originally published in November 2008

We all know top-level executives down to hourly employees who endure their jobs, thinking that if they can hang in there long enough, they can leave with the carrot for which they have suffered. It could be a retirement pension, a stay bonus, health care benefits, a gold watch, a golden parachute or any combination of the above.

This mindset makes for a miserable journey, and when one gets to the destination the payoff is seldom as fulfilling as imagined. Worse yet are those people who have muddled through their entire careers doing jobs they despise all the while dreaming of the "thereafter." When the end finally does come, their life could suddenly turn into a premature "hereafter," as in pushing up daisies.

Think about the wasted effort and frustration of waiting to realize a dream only to find out in the end it is really a nightmare. Maybe this sounds a bit draconian, but there are too many people who say they'll put in their 20, 30 or 40 years and then go do something "worthwhile." Imagine the dismal quality of their lives when their workday feels like a week and weeks seem to pass like years. This makes for disgruntled workers who inhibit productivity and pull the good people down with them.

Create enjoyment in the workplace.

Ask your employees what their favorite and least favorite days of the week are, and it's almost guaranteed that Friday is at the top of the list and Monday is at the bottom. Now that is not terrible, but if your people are more concerned about getting through the week than pursuing the challenges with which they deal every day, your business is or surely will suffer from inertia.

Management's job is to make sure that employees can gain a sense of enjoyment and satisfaction from doing their job efficiently and effectively. Leadership must set measurable benchmarks so that everyone can keep his or her own personal scorecard and recognize his or her own self-worth. Measurements can be just about anything from reaching a sales goal, completing a project or solving customers' problems in a way that meets or exceeds their expectations.

Sometimes, it is the simple things that count the most. As an example, in many major call centers when customer reps make a sale or solve a caller's thorny problem, they walk over and ring a bell in recognition of their accomplishment of the moment. Workplaces such as this, where performance is continually recognized, can be highly fulfilling. These same techniques can be translated into any environment. Sometimes the more outrageous the action, the more satisfying the recognition. Of course financial rewards are important and a meaningful reflection of good performance, but, as they say, "man does not live by bread alone."

Show appreciation to get appreciation.

Most companies pay "market rate" for employees in any given category. So why is it that one company has terrific employee satisfaction while others, whose pay is comparable, have dismal scores? It is not just about money. The best organizations figured out long ago that they must engage their employees and make them part of the process, not just spectators.

Most people don't get up in the morning and say, "I'm going to do a mediocre or bad job today." When that happens in your company, ask yourself if management is communicating with employees about the progress of the business, including the good news as well as the challenges. Equally important, has management told employees "thanks" recently and underscored to them that their efforts are not only just appreciated but also have enabled the company to succeed? Find the hot buttons that invigorate your people and start pushing them not just when you think of it or feel like it but on a regular and sustained basis. Also, don't be afraid to share periodic setbacks or bad news. This, too, sends an important signal that every employee is a part of the team, and it's the employees who define the company.

By doing all of this, don't be surprised at 5 p.m. on some Friday afternoon when you wish your people a good weekend and they respond with sincere enthusiasm, "Look forward to seeing you Monday." When this happens, you'll know that you're making the journey as rewarding as reaching the destination.

Respect: You gotta earn it, before you get it

Just because you're the boss doesn't mean you deserve respect

This column was originally published in February 2010

The late comedian Rodney Dangerfield's signature line, "I don't get no respect," always garnered a few good chuckles. As a leader, however, if you find yourself in this same predicament, it's no laughing matter.

Most executives usually try to do the right thing. They carry out their responsibilities, weighing the pros and cons of their actions and decisions.

Way too many executives think that their people will somehow recognize the angst they endure before gaveling an action into effect.

People cannot, however, understand why you do something simply through osmosis. This is where communication comes into play. How many times have you made an important decision and just filtered it down with what I call the "so be it" method? Sure, sometimes mandates are a part of being a leader and some are popular and others aren't.

Throughout my career, I've learned a number of lessons about respect. The most important one is that respect can be earned in many ways, and most times, it's simply a reflection of your attitude and actions, rather than what you actually say.

When I was a young CEO of my retail, publicly held, *Fortune* 500 company, I participated in what are known as Wall Street security analyst field trips, in which an underwriter organizes an excursion that takes portfolio investment professionals on the road with CEOs of similar businesses. One such trip was a bus tour of retail stores in Providence, Rhode Island, visiting each respective CEO's store along the way. The tour included a 45-minute walkthrough, led by the CEO of the chain explaining why his or her operation was the best on the planet.

On this particular tour, everything was running late and my store was the last stop. As the bus arrived, my watch told me there was a huge time problem because participants had planes to catch.

As we entered the store, it was spotless. All of the employees were wearing their "Sunday best" and you could literally eat off of the floor. The leader of the tour whispered in my ear that I had 10 minutes to get the message out. As I rushed 20 portfolio managers through the store, talking faster than the pitchman on the classic FedEx commercial years ago, the dejected looks on the employees' faces were apparent. My tour ended almost faster than it began as I walked backward out of the store continuing my pitch.

As we boarded the bus to the airport, I felt lousy. I knew the employees most likely had suffered acute gastrointestinal distress while preparing their store for "show time." As the bus barreled down the freeway, I realized this was a defining moment for me. Using my cellphone I called the store manager and told him to get in his car, catch up to my bus and quickly get me back to the store. Instinctively I knew that I had to show this store team that I respected them and their work.

When I returned to the store, the employees gawked at me with eyes bigger than saucers. I then spent about two hours walking the store, aisle by aisle, with all of the employees in tow, asking for their input on everything they do. I missed my plane, had to stay overnight and ruined my schedule, but it was worth it.

Word of this encore visit spread through our 1,000 stores faster than Grant took Richmond. In no time, this infamous visit turned into a celebrated success and became a part of the company's history.

You, too, can pick your own time and place to recreate a "respect event" that will speak volumes about how you do business. This can be achieved by arriving at meetings on time and ending the meetings as scheduled. It can also be reflected by not piling on the work just because you decided you needed something on your timetable without consideration of what else is currently on someone else's plate.

Respect is contagious and can start a cascading trickle-down effect. Your direct reports will begin to increase their respect for subordinates — and even you, if you're lucky. It's not only the right thing to do, it is the right way to build a business and create a positive culture.

If you feel you just "don't get no respect," you can improve your business persona by following this golden rule — "To get respect, you first have to give it."

People, people, people
The three biggest factors that determine success or failure

This column was originally published in July 2010

We've all heard the overused refrain that the three factors that matter most in the success of a business are location, location, location. However, at the top of my list, I would substitute people, people, people.

The problem is that, at some point, you have made or will make people mistakes. Either you selected the wrong person or you went awry in providing the employee direction and guidance. What must you do when you discover your misjudgment? It gets down to two choices. First, try to fix the problem or, secondly, when all else fails, eliminate the problem.

One of the most costly issues facing all organizations is turnover, but it can be even more costly to keep the wrong person in the wrong job. As much as you hope that, miraculously, the situation will improve, it seldom does. When all else fails, you'll have to correct your error because the Good Fairy won't.

Most smart companies today have numerous checkpoints to minimize bad hires. These include multiple interviews by various executives in the organization, psychological and work-style assessments to improve the odds, and a thorough vetting of the candidate's historical performance elsewhere, knowing that a tiger doesn't change its stripes.

Even after taking all of these precautions, sometimes the union between employer and employee just doesn't click. This results in having the wrong person in the wrong job or having the right person with the wrong attitude. When this occurs, the savior you thought would almost walk on water will start sinking faster than the Titanic did after hitting that humongous iceberg. The worst and most damaging action, or lack thereof, is to let inertia set in, while continuing to hope that there will be some form of divine intervention that will improve the performance of your fallen superstar.

The only logical course of action is to do a double-check and take a sobering look at yourself in the mirror to make sure the problem is not you. Ask yourself these simple questions: Am I giving the appropriate direction, setting realistic expectations and providing the necessary support? If you checked the "yes" box for all three of these, then it is time to solve your problem.

Start by having a heart-to-heart sit-down with the employee and ask him or her some tough questions. Among them: Do you have a clue that you are not getting the job done? Do you realize you are doing more damage than good, and what on Earth is the problem? This is no time to mince words because, just like the Titanic, the person is sinking more deeply by the minute.

If you get very lucky, the employee will have that aha moment and say, "I had no idea." Then there's still some slim hope, anyway, that you can create a road map to get this underperformer back on the reservation. If you pursue this course, make sure that you set a specific timetable as to what has to be done by when and what measurement you will use to judge improvements. This type of open communication can work and the laggard might just do a 180 and get back in the game.

Most times, no matter how much both sides try, it just won't work. When you realize that you are no Mother Theresa, it is time to move to plan B. Under this scenario, it gets down to damage control and plugging the gaping hole in your hull. This means bringing together other members of the team and figuring out who will do what until you find the next Mr. or Ms. Right. Don't be surprised to discover that once you air the problem with your associates, you'll learn that the underperformer's deficiencies were the company's worst kept secret. Typically, once you decide enough is enough, your team's reaction will be, "What took you so long?"

No leader likes to make people mistakes. However, when it happens — and you can be guaranteed that at some point it will — you cannot afford to prolong the problem. Never forget that the three keys to your success are: people, people, people — who consistently get it right and deliver on their promises.

How can a teaspoon improve your training?

Manageable doses and a little sugar can produce meaningful results

This column was originally published in October 2010

The song "A Spoonful of Sugar" holds the key to training your employees. As the lyrics explain, "In every job that must be done, there is an element of fun." Add a bit of sugar and the teaching becomes a bit more palatable.

Billions of dollars are spent every year on training, and although executives don't like to admit it, much of these efforts are for naught.

How many times have you sat through a session and walked away with barely having retained more than a few key points? Today, we live in a society of immediate gratification, combined with the fact that many people are afflicted with attention span deficiencies. Either we get it in a few minutes or lose interest and move on to something else or forget the material entirely.

Smartphones are the biggest distraction in business training. Rather than listeners being riveted on every word a trainer utters, too many times minds wander as attendees divert their focus to emailing on PDAs not so subtly hidden in their laps.

The problem is too many companies develop elaborate training that includes classroom sessions and PowerPoint presentations that are mind-numbing.

For training to be effective, it's mandatory that the information be easily digestible, memorable and entertaining. When the lesson is not learned, not only is the cost of the training and the time it takes wasted, but more important, the benefit from learning the new information is not put into practice.

There are a number of telltale signs that the message that is being conveyed in group gatherings is falling on deaf ears.

Watch for the frantic "highlighters" in the audience. With marker tightly gripped and their hands moving rhythmically from left to right underlining every word in the speaker's handout. A fluorescent yellow pen is their weapon of choice. If you're sitting next to one of these pen fiends, expect that one of your major takeaways from the training will be the indelible ink stains on your shirtsleeve.

What session would be complete without the obsessed "note taker"? This too common breed writes down every single word the speaker utters, much like a third-grader who is kept after school and made to write 500 times on a blank piece of lined note paper, "I will pay attention in class."

My least favorite in a training session is the "poker." This is the participant sitting next to you who periodically jabs you in the ribs and makes insipid comments, just to prove that he or she is listening even though, of course, he or she is not. This can be not only painful but also annoying, as your own daydreams are interrupted.

All of these types have one thing in common: They'll never again give the topics presented another thought the second they leave the session.

There's a simpler and better way to engage employees and teach them what they need to know. Start by having the speaker use open-ended questions and ask the students to select the correct answer for each question from multiple choices.

One choice might be utterly ridiculous, another downright funny, a third choice is close to correct, and finally, there is the answer that is on target.

I call this "teaspoon" teaching. Small doses of salient information mixed with a bit of sugar (humor) to make the process easier to swallow. In follow-up teaspoon doses, the participants' supervisors later quiz, on a very casual basis, the people being trained as they subsequently go about the day's proceedings or during their daily tasks over the ensuing couple of weeks. Results have shown that retention scores will skyrocket versus those of more traditional and less entertaining methods. There are dozens of iterations of this training method. Just use your imagination and, no matter what, don't be boring.

In many respects learning is about seeing it done, doing it oneself and then teaching it to others. Hospitals have employed this teaching technique very effectively for years.

Being a successful leader requires being a good teacher. When you are not the actual teacher, it is still your job to approve the curriculum.

Manageable doses of knowledge packaged correctly can help guarantee that not only the message is getting through, but it is also being applied outside of the classroom and on the job. Add a little sweetener and the job gets even easier.

What is more important, the icing or the cake?
Are you spending more time and money on form over substance?

This column was originally published in February 2011

E verybody wants to have his or her cake and eat it, too. When a presentation is made to a board of directors or a group of company outsiders, it needs to be right. The presenters always want to appear to have their act together and project an aura of all-knowing. It's part of being human. However, what about important, yet more run-of-the-mill, presentations to smaller groups on nonearthshaking matters? Is the cost of preparation worth the return?

For the last few months, each time I attended a meeting, either within my own company or for other companies and organizations with which I'm involved, I've asked those responsible for the preparation how many hours they invested in producing the final show and tell. Almost without exception, I've been taken aback by the amount of energy expended. This begs the question: What other, more important activities, providing a better return, didn't get done because of this diversion?

Perhaps more startling was the number of hours spent on "dress rehearsal" run-throughs, particularly for internal meetings.

I have no problem with the amount of work it takes for big meetings, particularly with outsiders, who can cause you untold grief if one looks amateurish, indecisive or, worse, a fool. If someone who works for me committed this near-fatal sin of lack of preparation, he or she would receive a quick trip to the proverbial woodshed. On the other hand, I'm a big believer of certain types of less formal presentations that include brainstorming components that are more impromptu, with fewer constraints on form and sharper focus on substance. I'm always pleasantly surprised with the golden nuggets, representing new thinking and ideas, that surface when participants focus on making creative contributions rather than obsessing on what others may think.

So, how do you, as a leader, foster creating acceptable presentation guidelines that will make your people more productive and also communicate to them that not all assemblies are equal? Let's take the work involved for major outsider confabs for investors, bankers, important vendors and customers off the table, while recognizing you're not going to risk taking only half measure just to spare a little work and a few extra dollars. Internal presentations or meetings with external consultants, however, are a different matter. For these types of sessions, the top-of-the-mind methods used by improvisational comedians extraordinaire, such as Robin Williams and Jerry Seinfeld, can be more productive, more fun and produce much better results.

To get your team pointed in the right direction, start asking after each meeting how much time was put into preparation. This simple exercise will reveal if you're getting the appropriate return on the investment. Next, working with your team, create a template that is acceptable for each type of presentation. One size doesn't fit all. A high-powered gathering of movers and shakers requires whistles and bells versus a much more simplified presentation for an intimate get-together of your inner circle. Provide flexible guidelines, including the type of handouts to be utilized and the form of graphics used from very elaborate presentations that would put a Las Vegas chorus line to shame to basic easy-to-prepare flip charts and PowerPoints that more than suffice and make the right impression.

Before any presentation is launched, always ask, 'Who is the audience, and what are the intended results?' By doing this, you will quickly determine if the costs are commensurate with the expected results. There is a difference between an all-hands-on-deck undertaking and a few scribblings on a legal pad for a smaller session's talking points. When you follow this protocol, your people will gain respect for you because it shows that you understand that their time is money and you have an appreciation for what it takes to get the job done.

A long-ago favorite Burger King television commercial portrayed kitchen workers belting out the lyrics, "Hold the pickles, hold the lettuce, special orders don't upset us," with the payoff tagline, "Have it your way." Special orders in the form of elaborate presentations that don't fit the audience should definitely upset you because of their costs. Instead, have it your way by substituting the "burger" with a "cake" topped with a not too rich but still sweet and easily digestible icing.

How best to motivate your team

Use more of the carrot than the stick or just provide lots of thrills and chills?

This column was originally published in July 2011

The simple answer to the age-old conundrum of how to motivate depends on the organization's culture, the leadership style of management and current circumstances, including the economic environment. Since early childhood, we were taught that our actions have consequences. Do something good that exceeds expectations and get something good in return. Run afoul of what's acceptable and be penalized. This positive/negative balancing act sets the tone for our lives from cradle to grave.

Does your company have a "take no prisoners" mentality when it comes to competition and winning? If so, the organization probably focuses more on the stick to motivate, paying albeit meaningful rewards for significant achievements that exceed goals. In this environment, it's expected that winning is the norm and that missteps will receive high visibility. Typically, younger companies drive results this way because of the scarcity of money, the pressures on time, and the realization that mediocrity and too many misses can prove lethal.

In established organizations, a lighter collegial style is more common, as is the frequent use of the carrot. As an example, telephone call centers are noted for celebrating just about everything. A rep receives a relatively unremarkable compliment from a customer and bells go off and high fives fly. Everyone in this type of facility expects to be named Bugs Bunny for a day and to get a carrot on a regular basis. When infractions occur, the supervisor will have a chitchat with the offender, though the talk will likely be punctuated with an abundance of "warm fuzzies."

Many type-A personalities wouldn't be productive nor enjoy a purely "carrot patch" workplace. Go-getters tend to get a high from the pressure always on them to produce. They covet the rush of the thrills and chills of getting the tough job done. Many do their best when they are under the gun, fearing that if they slip and fall they may not get up again. "F of F," or Fear of Failure, is their hot button, as perverse as it may sound. Sure, the carrot does motivate, too, but it's the challenge of the chase, with someone with a stick on their tail, that pushes them into overdrive. Can a company thrive with only type-A employees? Absolutely not, because it's probable that this would create a constant state of anarchy.

Every business needs plenty of the Steady Eddies who can be counted on to consistently do the job day in and day out. This type thrives on predictability and the gratification of periodic attaboys. If the boss were to approach him or her with a stick to make a point, it would scare the bejesus out of him or her.

In between the top and bottom rungs of your corporate ladder, there are dozens of iterations of what it takes to get people to do their best. The skill is in figuring out what size fits each individual category. Creating the appropriate environment for your type of business will set the tone as to how people will respond. A utopia for overachievers could become a living hell for those who prefer a setting in which they can do their jobs where the only excitement is watching paint dry and grass grow. It takes a variety of all types to build an organization and when all are carefully mixed together in the proper proportions the team will jell, and that's what gives a company its unique personality that works.

As people grow and mature, what worked in the past may have to change and the formula reconfigured to fit a company's evolving needs. Also, when economic circumstances outside of your personnel's control deteriorate, smart companies know it's time to lighten up a bit and use more carrots, primarily because the stick can't change the reality of a negative business environment. Much like beating that dead horse, it won't do any good, and it will harm a company in the long run, as employees won't forget how they were treated when the chips were down.

To most effectively craft your company's motivation techniques, you must listen to what your employees are saying and then translate their words into what they really mean.

Learning when and with whom to dangle the carrot, use the stick or add thrills and chills to the work environment will help drive your company's sustained success.

Do your employees sometimes disappoint you?
Maybe it's not them

This column was originally published in August 2011

How many times have you been disappointed because one of your employees or associates didn't produce as promised or as you expected? How many times when this occurred did you merely chalk it up as a black mark against the offender? If this is a recurring theme with those who work for you, then perhaps you should look in the mirror as the problem may be with you — not them.

The fact is that most employees want to do it right. Most actually work diligently at doing what they believe is expected. The best of these employees aggressively make that extra effort to take their performance to the next level.

In order for employees to deliver and excel, it is your job to first thoroughly explain what is expected of them on every major new effort. Failures come in all sizes and shapes, but there is typically one common denominator underlying the miss. It usually starts with a failure to communicate, including defining the key elements necessary to effectively accomplish the goal. Secondly, the necessary check points probably were not established from the get-go to prevent the project from straying off course. Finally, the person doing the work may not have been told the importance of the assignment, and that he or she must ask for help if problems were to arise. Human nature is to "whistle in the dark" and forge ahead even if there is that nagging sense that all is not right.

Let's get down to brass tacks. If you want something done and done correctly you must take the time and make the effort to simply explain the task and provide the pertinent details. If the people undertaking the work understand the purpose and the expected benefits, they'll be more deliberate in producing an appropriate finished product. Understanding the goals dramatically increases the odds of success. If people don't know why they are being told to do something, it's not realistic to expect them to even care.

Too frequently, bosses think that employees will understand what must be done and think this will come about through some magical process or by osmosis. This would be nice, but it just doesn't work that way. Many times you won't get feedback on the task's progress because too many people believe it's a sign of weakness to report in or to ask questions. There is an easy fix to that problem; if you're not getting a sense of the status of what's happening and it's an important effort — you go to them. When you lose touch with the evolution of a significant project, your people could sense this as a sign that it's not important to you.

Too frequently when an effort results in disappointments, everything hits the fan. This causes various degrees of angst on numerous fronts and, most importantly, radically reduces productivity, leads to missed deadlines and, even worse, may result in a costly lost opportunity.

If a project goes south it's mandatory that you find out why. Many times it's too easy and convenient for the boss to say, "handle it," without explaining what "it" means. The combination of those two words, followed by the assignee stating, "I'm on it," without having all the blanks properly filled in, makes it a good bet that the end results will not be pretty.

Clearly, not every undertaking requires a detailed explanation or a well-documented work plan, but even the simplest task needs to be articulated clearly and requires an answer to this question: Is this a "down and dirty" job or do you need near perfection? Also you must provide a deadline. If you don't give one, the employee can't prioritize his or her work.

The much-quoted statement dating back to the War of 1812 proclaimed, "We have met the enemy, and he is us." Business is tough enough as it is; make sure you're not the enemy contributing to a failure because you didn't communicate what needs to be known by all involved so there are no surprises. The first rule of being a leader is to provide explicit directions to those who must follow you. If the employee fails, you're not the only one who will be disappointed — he or she will be, too.

The positives and negatives of jealousy
There's a delicate balance between productive and destructive

This column was originally published in February 2012

At first blush, it might seem a bit perverse that jealousy can be a good thing, a motivator and a catalyst for change. However, like very rich food, ingested in moderation it can be quite good, while overindulgence can bring on a world-class case of heartburn and indigestion.

Like it or not, in life and in business jealousy is always lurking in the shadows. When it rears its ugly head and is not properly controlled in your organization, it can precipitate a problem, do irreparable harm and become a major distraction in the workplace. It also stifles productivity, turning otherwise earnest and collaborative employees into a bunch of rumor mongering, whispering backbiters.

Conversely, a small dose of good or "productive" jealousy can spur others on to new heights. A leader's job is to recognize the point when good turns to bad and to learn how to manage jealousy. This involves encouraging it (read that as creating competition) but also putting one's foot down with a loud thud to get everyone's attention and stopping the bad jealousy in its tracks when it begins leading to potential negative and divisive behaviors.

One of the many challenges of running a business is acknowledging that not everyone is equal, not everyone is motivated by the same factors. Varying attitudes and personalities can challenge the people skills of even the most effective leader. The infamous Rodney King who was at the epicenter of the disastrous 1992 Los

Angeles riots asked the rhetorical question in a nationally televised appeal for peace: "Why can't we just all get along?" The reality was and is, "Rodney, we probably can't, no matter how hard everyone tries." The sobering fact is that anytime there are two or more people together in a room the risk of disagreement and unbridled rivalry emerges and troubles can ignite, many times for inexplicable reasons unknown even to the participants. This is when management has to manage.

Good jealousy is easy to understand and an aware leader knows how to use it effectively. Example: Someone on the team has a unique idea or does something out of the ordinary, which benefits the greater good. The accomplishment is rightly recognized and celebrated by management. There are always people, however, who on the surface join in praising the effort but deep down inside are envious of the other person's accomplishment. You can read the negative expression on their faces like a bad poker player who's bluffing and everyone knows it. Enter the smart boss who helps the seeming ingrate understand that he or she can also receive comparable accolades when warranted. The boss then directs the uninspired employee's envy (jealousy) effectively toward a positive goal, subtly or not so subtly, illuminating a path for the glory seeker to follow to reach a mutually agreed upon outcome.

Bad jealousy, on the flip side, can be like a forest fire that starts quickly and jumps around erratically, destroying anything and everything in its path. The only way to handle this type of negative behavior, which turns cohorts against one other, is with an iron fist and a candid, behind-closed-doors meeting. Typically, this requires identifying the "ring leader" — and there always is one — and then having the boss engage in a very one-sided conversation with that employee to make it clear that this behavior stops when the perpetrator opens the door and exits.

Many times, once unmasked, the naysayers recognize that they'll be under constant scrutiny and become instant cheerleaders for what was accomplished by the other colleague primarily to defuse any future damage in the eyes of the senior management. Good leadership is about steering the ship, managing behaviors, maintaining a constant vigil, watching for warning signs, and then reacting appropriately without hesitation. In the case of bad jealousy, speed counts, as measured in hours, not days or weeks, in stemming the spread of rumors and innuendos.

There is a delicate balance needed to keep a team on track and productive. However, knowing the difference between good jealousy and bad can keep the organization moving forward. We all know not everyone is created equal, and that means different people must be managed differently to accomplish goals and keep the employees and the company off jagged and potentially painful rocks.

Does your management style help or hinder employees?

Filtering too much information clogs up the works

This column was originally published in March 2012

There are hands-on executives who get down and dirty in just about every aspect of a business and then there are leaders who manage from 50,000 feet, rarely calling anything but the big shots. Seldom does a single style or technique always fit every situation. Much depends on the size and maturity of a business and simply how many hands are available on deck to fight a specific fight.

In a startup or younger organization, initially the entrepreneur probably has to do just about everything merely to survive. In a midsize or *Fortune* 500 operation, a good boss, depending on the quality of the team, can pick and choose the level of involvement in a project based upon the complexity, significance and sometimes just the boss's gut feeling or inclination.

Periodically, at one time or another, most leaders miss the forest for the trees, either by not getting involved enough or by delegating too much responsibility. Then, when something goes south, the boss nitpicks his or her way into the company's every twist and turn, driving subordinates nearly to the brink.

Either too much or too little attention is usually well intended, but unfortunately, it can cause more bad than good. Instead, as a boss, one must have a sixth sense of when and, much more importantly, how to get involved and with whom depending how near the undertaking is to getting in big trouble. This is preferable to a blanket mandate that requires an "I must see everything first before going to the next step" policy.

Like it or not, today we're doing business in a 24/7 world and, to accomplish objectives, speed counts. We must be wary of potential bottlenecks that impede process and progress.

One of the biggest obstacles in moving from point A to B is that too many leaders are lousy delegators. Sure, they talk a good game about empowering their people and letting them run with it, but in reality, they hinder progress because they have an insatiable need to function much like an automobile engine air filter. Unfortunately, instead of helping to clean the air, they suck all of the air out of the project.

The "air filter" executive mandates that every preliminary plan, email or even a simple new idea must first be passed by him or her before the undertaking can go to the next step. In a perfect world, this type of filtering might be good. However, at the speed of business today, this type of management style bogs things down or brings them to a screeching halt, as everyone waits for the "air filter" executive to get around to reviewing the latest step. The results include losing productivity, squelching creativity and derailing the initiative of those encumbered by unnecessary oversight.

When this occurs, everybody is negatively affected, including the filterer. Soon the boss who must touch everything gets overwhelmed by what has to be reviewed and, instead of maintaining control, winds up losing it.

There are simple solutions that an effective executive can employ to speed up the work. First, the boss has to be comfortable in his or her own skin about knowing how and when to follow up, intervene or let others keep the ball moving toward the goal line. It's not just about blindly delegating, but instead knowing the skill sets of those to whom the boss delegates and everyone involved having a clear understanding of the parameters of who does what when.

Having explicit ground rules in place, the boss can give subordinates much more rope, not to hang themselves, but instead to throw the lasso much further to snag the bigger prize. This also enables the leader to have many more balls in the air, exponentially increasing the opportunities for success on many fronts and, quite simply, improving the overseer's quality of life by providing more time for the executive to function as an executive. The subordinates win, too, because they have the authority, within prescribed boundaries, to get the job done.

Remember, good intentions aside, it gets down to the fundamentals of how an internal combustion engine functions. If an air-filtering management style clogs the workflow, it can suck the power out of your company's engine, causing it to shut down abruptly.

Managing 'mad'
What is it, and are you doing it without knowing?

This column was originally published in April 2012

In business, too many executives believe that the best path to success is to "manage mad" thinking this will project an image of determination and tenacity, combined with the ability to strike fear in the hearts of any naysayers with opposing views.

Is there a better way, a more balanced method to manage other than by mimicking a fire-breathing dragon? Unfortunately, we have too many bad role models who employ a fearsome persona. There are the pugnacious politicians who make every issue a black-and-white cause célèbre, screaming, "If we don't do it my way, we'll wind up in a shambles on the precipice of extinction." Then there are the professional and college coaches, with seemingly permanent scowls etched on their faces, who shout their mandates to be sure players know that if they don't get the play right, they run the risk of being toast.

Corporate executives from the most admired to the most reviled have adopted this managing mad game face over time, some, perhaps, without even realizing it.

Certainly there is a time and place for a boss to raise his or her voice a few octaves, take on facial expressions of the walking dead and deliver a monologue laced with wakeup calls about either doing it the leader's way or facing possible draconian consequences. This technique is best used very sparingly in situations that warrant an edgy demeanor. However, if a boss constantly plays the managing mad card, it loses its impact and the message becomes diluted as recipients think to themselves, "Same old, same old — just another series of empty threats." Constantly portraying a vitriolic curmudgeon serves only to dampen hope and curb enthusiasm.

A point of clarification: Don't confuse managing mad with being direct and holding people accountable while communicating clearly and explaining the positives, as well as negatives, to a team. This latter method is much preferred by those on the receiving end in order for the team to understand what is being said and, more importantly, what is expected of them.

We have all worked with and known people for whom the use of a smile, a compassionate gesture or a little humor at the right time and place is about as rare as politicians treating each other with respect during a debate. Businesspeople are not elected politicians trying to get votes by speaking the unspeakable with Armageddon undertones.

If you're the boss, ask yourself if you hear what you're saying and how you're delivering the message. Do you need a self-prescribed attitude adjustment and a makeover of your style? If a subordinate projected a managing mad style, you would certainly provide the necessary coaching and counseling. However, if you fear you need this type of tune-up, how can you do it without losing face by asking peers or other trusted associates for a no-holds-barred critique?

There is an easy and effective way to accomplish this self-assessment. Surreptitiously record your next talk to the troops, even a phone conference call or a one-on-one session. Most smartphones have this feature. Before listening to your recording and evaluating your delivery, wait a few hours or until the next day so that you can listen more objectively, being a bit more removed from the heat of the moment. Close your door and use a mirror to watch your own expression as you listen to yourself. You'll immediately know by what you hear and by your expressions in the mirror if you fall into the managing mad trap. Once you're done, take a deep breath and then quickly jot down your own impressions, including the tone, choice of words and substance of the message. The big question becomes, "If you were the audience, would you buy what you're selling?"

If you decide you need improvements, and we all do, use the same voice recorder before you give your next battle cry and rehearse a few times using the device to capture your delivery. Also, do these trial runs in front of a mirror so you can see yourself as others will see you.

When you introspectively examine your technique, you may not like what you discover. However, after the shock of realizing you've been managing mad, you can quickly begin transforming your style, not to morph into a likable wimp but instead to become a thoughtful and effective leader whom others will eagerly listen to and then follow. To get results, it's sometimes not what you say but how you say it.

What took you so long?
Why does it seem like the boss is sometimes the last to know?

This column was originally published in August 2012

We've all seen it before, where co-workers in a company recognize a problem performer, but these same people can't understand why the boss hasn't yet taken action or has taken so long to come to grips with the issue.

Conversely, as the boss, how many times have you made what you considered to be an extremely difficult personnel decision and have done so only after protracted analysis, a fair measure of agony and more than an adequate amount of second guessing yourself?

Case in point: One of your top managers has hit the skids, and in your gut, you know that a change is needed. Fearing the worst, you play over and over in your mind the potential negative consequences that could occur if you were to fire this individual. Finally, after all else fails, you pull the trigger and decide to part ways with the onetime A player. Before you tell associates, you rehearse in your mind how you will explain your decision. Once you gather your lieutenants together and finally utter the previously unthinkable, the reaction is almost a unanimous, "What took you so long?"

After you breathe a sigh of relief, your team members start making not-so-subtle comments suggesting that they weren't surprised, followed by a litany of examples of why your now fallen superstar wasn't hacking it.

This begs a bigger question: Were you really the last one to realize that there was a problem? Furthermore, did it actually take you too long to make that final decision that, as they say in spy novels, this person was "beyond salvage"?

150

This provides a good opportunity for introspective analysis. The end result just might help you understand that you were not the last to know, but in fact, you may have been the first to recognize what was looming on the horizon.

Virtually every leader has to rely on experience, combined with instincts, to decide when to either cut and run or try to rectify a problem. Being an executive requires being a very good teacher. When a pupil is not measuring up, the first question is how can you help and what can you do to improve a person's performance? Most everyone at one point in his or her career hits a rough spot, and with a bit of mentoring, a fair number of wayward employees can turn the corner and again blossom. Also, it's more economical to at least try to turn someone around after investing time and money in developing the individual. After a certain period, the employee has gained valuable empirical knowledge about the ins and outs of the company and, just maybe, a little extra coaching can make the difference.

However, in some situations, your optimism for achieving Mother Teresa status through patient mentoring wanes, and you begin to come to grips with the fact that it's time for a change. You then map out your what-if scenarios. Not only one but several. You ruminate over your game plan until you have the best probable solution locked and loaded in your mind for that moment when you have concluded that you've run out of road.

Most times, trying yet failing is not a bad thing; actually, it is a good thing and the way a responsible leader must approach an important human resource decision. You can never forget that you're dealing with the life and livelihood of a person and his or her family, which can be adversely affected by the decision. Many top employees who veer off course and don't work out were, at one time, effective and loyal contributors to the organization. It's mandatory to make the effort not only to try to stem the negative tide of poor performance, but also to develop an alternative replacement and transition strategy. This takes time and can be a very solitary task depending on the level of the person to be replaced.

In reality, the boss knows in his heart of hearts before most, if not all, others when something ultimately has to give. Being the boss requires making the difficult decisions after meaningful deliberation and then living with them and making them work.

The boss the last to know? Highly unlikely. Instead, he probably is the first to know when the time to act was finally right.

Should you be friends with your employees?

How to have it both ways without crossing that invisible line

This column was originally published in January 2013

What is the best way to motivate employees? Some successful CEOs treat employees as friends, while other equally high-achieving leaders regard employees as merely hired hands, giving them a day's pay for a day's work and nothing more.

What's the best approach to produce the best results for the company, the employee and the employer? Much of the issue lies with one's definition of a friend and the culture of the organization. Many companies boast that their employees are like family. This sounds great, but can it work?

If either party crosses that fine line separating the difficult-to-define business and personal space, both employer and employee can become disenchanted or worse. One way to think of it is friendship is more unconditional. We accept a friend for what he or she is or isn't. On the flipside, reality is most bosses embrace or reject employees for what they do on a consistent basis.

The military has its own way of handling fraternization between officers and the enlisted by making it a possible court martial offense. This stance is predicated on the belief that socializing between these two levels is "prejudicial to good order, discipline and partiality." It is well recognized that business relationships without boundaries can produce too much drama.

Perhaps what we need is a new definition for a nonemotional, congenial, enjoyable and productive day-to-day relationship between leader and follower. This moniker could be employee-friend, or "e-friend" for short. "E-friend" isn't an Apple app, but would describe an employer/employee relationship where there is mutual respect and a genuine appreciation of one another, underscored by an understanding, albeit perhaps unspoken, that when the time for talking is done, the boss has the final word on matters that occur between 9 a.m. and 5 p.m. Using these ground rules, both sides can have it both ways by using good judgment and treating each other as they would want to be treated if their roles were reversed.

The employee should expect from the boss that when the chips are down, either on a business basis or when the employee has a personal problem, he or she knows that the boss will be there for him or her, providing understanding and advice and, when requested, helping the employee maneuver through rough patches. From the employer's perspective, the employee would be someone who, through thick and thin, is there for the company and can temporarily put personal needs aside when there is a business issue that can't be postponed.

The e-friend boss should know as much about the employee as the employee wants the boss to know, which can include sensitive professional problems or even family or medical issues. In a good relationship, the boss could certainly know, as one example, what the subordinate's kids are up to in their lives and be the first to say to the employee that it's more important for him or her to go to an offspring's ballgame or play, rather than putting in extra time on the business project du jour.

Instinctively, employees know if a boss truly cares or is just going through the motions to be politically correct. They know if the head honcho is sincerely concerned about them as a person, not just another set of hands.

Not everything and everyone in the workplace are created equal. There will always be a pecking order; however, there is nothing wrong with truly enjoying the people with whom you work every day and sharing meaningful experiences, all of which lead to a more fulfilling role for both the employer and the employee. The best criterion to avoiding problems is using generous doses of plain common sense.

There is a much-quoted line from the 1987 movie "Wall Street," starring Michael Douglas as the ruthless tycoon Gordon Gekko, who proclaimed "If you want a friend, get a dog." This provoked both laughs and sighs, but in the real world, this attitude makes for a very lonely Ebenezer Scrooge-type life for the boss and a shallow existence for employees who must spend more than half, at the very least, of their Monday through Friday waking hours working.

At times, people can be difficult both to work for and with. However, it's the people who make the company and relationships that combine respect and a form of e-friendship that can make the real difference.

How to create Esprit de Corps in your organization

It's less about creating clever catchphrases and more about seizing unorthodox opportunities

This column was originally published in March 2013

Decent bosses typically try to lead by example. As a leader, you must model appropriate behavior to promote the greater good and to send a constant message with teeth in it.

The French term "esprit de corps" is used to express a sense of unity, common interest and purpose, as developed among associates in a task, cause or enterprise. Sports teams and the military adopt the sometimes-overused cliché, "One for all and all for one." "Semper Fi" is the Marine Corps' motto for "always faithful." We commonly hear, "We're only as strong as our weakest link."

However, the real test of team-building and motivational sayings is that they are good only when they move from an HR/PR catchphrase to a way of doing business — every day.

As soon as you put two or more people in the same room, a whole new set of factors comes into play, including jealousy, illogical pettiness and one-upmanship, all of which can lead to conflicts that obstruct the goals at hand. Certainly, much of this is caused by runaway egos. Perhaps a little bit of it is biological, but most of it is fueled by poor leadership. Everyone has his or her own objective and it's the boss's responsibility to know how to funnel diverse personal goals in order to keep everyone on track. This prevents employees from straying from the target and helps avoid major derailments. Essentially, it all gets down to the boss leading by example with a firm hand, understanding people's motives and a lot of practicing "Do as I say and as I really do myself."

Communicating by one's actions can be very powerful. A good method to set the right tone is stepping in and lending a hand, sometimes in unexpected and dramatic ways. This shows the team that you govern yourself as you expect each team member to govern his or her own behavior. In my enterprises, I constantly tell my colleagues that the title following each person's name boils down to these three critical words: "whatever it takes." Certainly, I bestow prefixes to this one-size-fits-all, three-word title, such as vice president or manager, but I consider these as window dressing only.

After speeches, when I explain this universal job description, I always get questions from the audience about how I communicate this concept. I follow with a real-life experience that played out in the first few months after I started OfficeMax. As a new company, we had precious, little money, never enough time and only so much energy, which we preserved as our most valuable assets in order to be able to continually fight another day.

In those early days, too frequently, I would see what looked like a plumber come into the office, go into the restroom and emerge a few minutes later presenting what I surmised to be a bill to our controller. I knew whatever he was doing was costing us money and probably not building value. The third time he showed up, in as many weeks, I immediately followed him into the restroom (much to his shock and consternation). I asked him what in the world kept bringing him back. He then proceeded to remove the toilet's lid and give me a tutorial on how to bend the float ball for it to function properly. That was the last time anyone ever saw this earnest workman on our premises. Instead, after making known my newly acquired skill, whenever the toilet stopped working, I became the go-to guy.

This became a lesson to my team about how to save money. At that time, 50 bucks a pop was a fortune to us. It got down to people knowing that all of us in this nascent startup were expected to live up to their real, three-word title. This was our version of how to build esprit de corps. Others began boastfully relaying their own unique "whatever it takes" actions, and it became our way of doing business.

The lesson I learned in those early days was that it wasn't always what I said that was important but rather what I did that made an indelible impression. A leader's actions, with emphasis on the occasionally unorthodox to make them memorable, are the ingredients that contribute to molding a company's culture.

The value of being the man or woman behind the curtain

It can provide plausible deniability and build your team at the same time

This column was originally published in August 2013

One of my favorite business books, which also made it as a Broadway play and a big-screen movie, is "The Wonderful Wizard of Oz," written by L. Frank Baum in 1900. My hero in this story is not the young orphaned Dorothy, nor the Cowardly Lion, the desperately in-need-of-some WD-40 Tin Man, nor even the Scarecrow in search of a brain.

Instead it is the Wizard. To understand why the dubious Wizard is my favorite character, one must get past the portrayal of him as scheming, phony and at times nasty.

To appreciate the man behind the curtain, recognize that he is a very effective presenter, though at times this ex-circus performer behaved a bit threatening. OK, he was a jerk, but the point of this column is to take you down the yellow brick road on the way to the enchanted Emerald City and corporate success.

From this tale there is a lesson that one can say all sorts of things, not be visible, and yet still have a meaningful impact.

Another takeaway is that playing this role provides plausible deniability. This absence of visual recognition is particularly beneficial in negotiating when you, as the boss, use a vicar, aka a mouthpiece, to speak on your behalf. This allows you to have things said to others that you as the head honcho could never utter without backing yourself into a corner.

Another plus is you can always throw your mouthpiece under the bus if necessary, of course, with his or her upfront understanding that sometimes there must be a sacrificial lamb. This is not only character-building for your stand-in, but also many times presents an unprecedented opportunity for him or her to learn in real time.

Perhaps the Wizard was the first behind-the-curtain decision-maker, but today this role is used frequently in business and government. In a similar vein, the "voice" of Charlie from the well-known 1970s TV series "Charlie's Angels" was always heard, but he was never seen.

Frequently there is much to be said for using anonymity to float a trial balloon just to get a reaction. Think about a son having his mom test the waters by talking to dad before the son tells him he wants to drop out of junior high school to join the circus. Maybe that's even how our former circus-drifter-turned-Wizard-of-Oz got his start.

In the negotiating process it is important to have a fallback when the talks hit a rough patch by instructing your vicar to backpedal, saying that he or she has just talked to the chief and the benevolent boss said, "I was overreaching with my request."

This also serves to build a persona for the boss-behind-the-curtain as someone who is fair-minded and flexible. All the while, of course, it's the boss who is calling the shots and maneuvering through the process without getting his or her hands dirty.

The value of using this clean-hands technique is that it enables the real decision-maker to come in as the closer who projects the voice of reason, instead of the overeager hard charger who at times seems to have gone rogue.

It actually takes a bigger person to play a secondary role behind the curtain rather than always be in the limelight. It also takes a hands-on coach and counselor to maneuver a protégé through the minefields to achieve the objective.

However, accomplishing the difficult tasks through others is true management and the No. 1 job of a leader who must be a master teacher.

After you have guided a handful of up-and-comers a few times through thorny negotiations, you will gain much more satisfaction than if you had done it yourself, while engendering the respect and gratitude of your pupils. They in turn will have learned by doing, even though they were not really steering the ship alone.

The final step is to let the subordinate take credit for getting the big job done. This will also elevate you to rock star status, at least in his eyes. Soon those who you've taught will emerge as teachers too, and the big benefit is that you will populate your organization with a stellar team of doers, not just watchers.

So, forget about the Wicked Witch of the West and move backstage for the greater good of the organization.

4

Customer Service

Sorry no can do, it's against company policy
A valid excuse or a corporate cop-out?

This column was originally published in March 2006

We have all heard it before and probably even used this age-old lame excuse ourselves at one time or another: "Sorry we can't do that, it's against company policy." Every company, organization and institution has a set of policies guiding its daily life, some of which might even make sense on occasion. On the flip side, however, every organization has selectively enforced or completely ignored policies that are routinely violated without ramifications or repercussions.

Ask yourself this question: How many times do your people say "it's against company's policy" to hide behind doing a little extra work to devise the right custom-made solution for the customer or to fix an internal problem?

Certainly, it is usually easier just to pass the buck and blame everything on an inanimate invisible policy that was created on high and then mysteriously embedded in the underbelly of the organization. Sometimes with this drill whoever asked for the exception upon hearing this robotic rhetoric simply shrugs-off the request and acquiesces. Some policies are stranger than others, where no one really has an earthly clue or there is no obvious rhyme or reason why they were created in the first place. The big problem, however, is that when the perennial policy excuse is used, the promulgator runs the risk of not only losing business, failing to solve an issue or seizing an opportunity, but also diminishes his or her own authority. This can create a negative perception for the entity that is sometimes irreversible.

There is a better way to handle the nonstandard request that when done correctly can lead to a win-win. Every good organization has varying degrees of flexibility when some rule just doesn't fit the circumstances or has evolved into irrelevancy. Management is about taking advantage of opportunities, turning negatives into positives, or affecting change when inertia sets in.

Over the years, I have heard many executives proclaim in meetings, on sales calls and in negotiations, "We have an iron clad policy against this or that."

Talk about throwing down the gauntlet! If nothing else, this attitude can create an adversarial relationship and the perfect storm for the other side to hunker down and fight, or, worse yet, walk away never to return sometimes just because it becomes a matter of principle.

How you deal with so-called immovable obstacles in your company is a measure of your effectiveness. Using common sense and logic to solve an issue without relying on a policy manual as a crutch is a barometer of leadership. Don't get me wrong, some policies are sacrosanct such as: customers do have to pay their bills at some point; employees must show up for work (at least occasionally). There are, however, many times when bending a policy for the greater good makes immense sense. As an example: a customer may want a special concession that has never previously been given, but is willing to give something extra back in another part of the arrangement. Some would say this should not be done because the company does not want to set a precedent. In this case, I say, if the customer is willing to do something special in exchange for the exception, you are not setting a precedent, but instead crafting a customized solution where both sides win. Remember one size does not necessarily always fit all. Market leaders know how to quickly craft "work-arounds."

How is this for a dumb policy? A senior executive wants to bring a non-executive specialist to a high level leadership meeting but is told "Can't do that, our policy is no outsiders — no way, no how." Does it matter that the outsider has the holy grail answer that this august body needs to have more than breath itself? No, this is just another example of "suits" falling back on corporate gobbledygook.

The best way to foster flexibility is to empower your people to make exceptions without having them jump through rings of fire. Make sure that everyone from top to bottom knows that the number one objective is always putting the customer first and then give employees the ability to deliver on that promise.

You can maintain flexibility, without losing control, by appointing one or two people in a work group, division, or business unit to review legitimate and thoughtful exceptions to a policy enabling them to do so as measure in minutes and hours, instead of days and weeks by simplifying the process. Train your people to become problem-solvers, not problem-causers, by instilling in them that when they speak to the customer, they are the company in the eyes of that customer and what they say and how they say it could make the difference between getting the order or sending the customer kicking and screaming to the competition.

And, on those few rare occasions when a change in procedure, process or policy is just not possible, teach your people to "take one for the company" instead of just blaming company policy by providing a rational explanation of their decision. By doing this, it leaves the door open for the next time or for another person within the organization to try again with the same customer.

If your policy is that, it's always business as usual or "this is how we always do it," you have put in place a lumbering bureaucracy that, instead of bending for the right reasons at the right time eventually will break.

A customer/client complaint is an opportunity to turn likely defeat into resounding victory

Worry more about the ones who don't complain about a problem, because they're not coming back

This column was originally published in March 2007

Every time a customer or client is not happy with your goods or services, your business stands at the crossroads. Either that customer will become permanently disenchanted or you can seize a narrow window of opportunity to strengthen the relationship by turning a negative into a positive and solving the issue. The worst is if someone isn't satisfied and doesn't tell you, then the problem can't be fixed. As if that's not bad enough, the disenchanted customer will no doubt recount their unhappy experience at every opportunity. Quickly do the arithmetic and you'll realize that one customer's negative perception can proliferate exponentially to dozens and dozens at a rate that rivals the spread of the E. coli bacteria at a bad fast-food restaurant.

Ensuring an organization has an effective mechanism to discover and solve customer complaints expeditiously and painlessly should keep even the most confident executive up at night.

There is no simple way to guarantee customer satisfaction. A good first step is making sure that embedded in the hearts and minds of every employee is the company's sacrosanct policy that "Customers are always right, even when they're partially wrong." This policy doesn't become a way of doing business simply because it's written somewhere in a manual. Instead, management must educate employees on the domino effect caused by unhappy customers as they repeat the company's transgression every time there's a lull in just about any conversation.

On the positive side, however, make sure your employees also understand the power they possess playing the role of the problem solver by satisfying the customer's problem then and there, with no ifs, ands or buts. My new math of "Customer Reclamation" can translate into huge economic gains for your business. After a negative experience is reversed, the satisfied customer will tell everyone about the positive encounter, and the company's fairness. My experience is that the customer who surfaces an issue does not only want to right a wrong, but also, many times, is subconsciously looking for a reason to continue to do business with the organization. And yes, I guarantee that in the majority of cases, just as the negative bellicose comments from the disenchanted can ruin your business, the new believer can help you prosper.

When I was CEO of my national retail chain, we had hundreds of telephone customer service representatives who were trained to do the right thing for the customer the first time around. The best reps were those who had previously, in another life, been on the losing end of a negative customer experience, finding themselves trivialized and demeaned by a would-be problem solver who only knew how to say "NO."

Periodically, tenacious customers who were outraged by some perceived transgression would make it their mission to find a way to reach me directly. The more creative ones would do some simple homework and get my private telephone number from an accommodating company operator. Actually, they could have gotten through to me directly by simply asking the operator. But that wouldn't be as fulfilling for the disenchanted. Sometimes the chase is better than the catch, as the complainant tried to beat the system to get to the boss by circumventing all intermediaries. Plus, the harder it was to reach the CEO, the madder the customer got and this gave him an added dose of adrenaline and bravado.

I found that when I personally answered my phone after all of the administrative assistants went home, and identified myself by name, the irate caller would immediately launch into histrionics with suggestions that I take the product that was causing their angst and place it where it shouldn't go and definitely wouldn't fit. After the ranting and raving stopped, I almost always solved the problem by immediately saying: "I'm sorry, you're right."

Over time, I became more creative in dealing with less than enthralled customers who called after hours. Instead of answering with my name, I would simply say "hello." I would state that I was the computer tech working on the big boss's computer, but all of us at the company were "trained to stop whatever we were doing and help our customers." The caller would then rationally explain their tale of woe. In just about every instance the issue was more than valid. Playing my role of the customer-centric tech, I would say that I'm writing a note to the CEO to leave on his desk explaining the problem. I also confidently proclaimed I was sure that there would be a more than satisfactory resolution by sundown of the next business day. Many times the now tranquil customer would ask for my name. I would give them a pseudonym so as not to blow my cover and a department number which, if they made contact again, would be directed to my office. Over the years I received many letters of recognition for that "tech" who took the time to listen and bring the dilemma to the CEO's attention.

At the end of the day for all of us as individuals, and for our businesses, we're only as good as our reputations. In my role as the "night-time computer tech" I knew that when I hung up the phone we had again turned a likely defeat into a resounding victory. Using my new "Customer Reclamation" math, I also knew that would translate into increased sales and profits because they were coming b-a-c-k.

When should you fire a customer?

It is not simply a question of dollars and cents

This column was originally published in January 2008

How many of us can say we will do business only with people and companies whom we both like and trust? Probably not too many.

A favorite fantasy of employees is telling the boss to take the job and shove it. For the boss, a recurring dream is to tell that recalcitrant or even more dubious customer to take his or her business and cram it.

Reality is, not many organizations can afford to do business only with like-minded customers whom they really respect and enjoy. It's a big world out there and our customers come in many shapes and sizes with their own idiosyncrasies and personas. Some are more tolerable than others are. If doing business were limited only to customers who were liked, there would be no mega law and giant accounting firms; huge multinational investment banks wouldn't exist; and most companies would have headquarters in offices the size of phone booths instead of skyscrapers. A nice benefit would be all of these service firms would save money on rent, but generating enough volume to keep the doors opened could be an issue. The good news is you're not marrying your customer. Much like holding your breath under water when you were a little kid, you can do it regularly for a certain period and be no worse for wear.

The more salient question is will you do business with people whom you do not trust or who don't meet your ethics standards?

Every organization must have parameters and an internal gauge, which rank the "like" and "trust" factors. When the internal gauge reaches the "red zone," particularly for ethics, then an alarm must sound causing you to ask some tough questions. Over the years, I have written a number of pieces commenting on what I call the "mother rule." Simply put, you shouldn't do something if you wouldn't want your mother to know. Others pose the "front-page" question: would your company do something if it were reported in tomorrow's Wall Street Journal lead story?

Just as individuals should have a moral compass, organizations must employ a similar series of benchmarks or lines in the sand which, when crossed, escalate the status of a customer relationship to a "go, no go" decision.

Maybe most of us do have our price but compromising our ethics can be simply too costly no matter how important a customer's business might be to the bottom line. If a client's methods cause you to wake up with a start at 3 a.m. and ask yourself, "What would mother say?," you must recognize you've entered the danger zone. Whenever that indelible line is crossed, you cannot turn a blind eye to behavior that might be inappropriate.

Periodically any business relationship can enter a gray area. When the alarm bells sound, that does not necessarily mean that summarily, you have to "fire" the customer. Instead, before "pulling the pin" a face-to-face meeting for you to probe for honest answers is mandatory. To prepare for this meeting have all your facts together, avoid allegations of "he said, she said" and glittering generalities. You must be specific as to what transpired that precipitated your angst. After the review of the circumstances is completed, you must be fully prepared to walk away or, depending on what you learn, run from the customer. Sometimes this is more easily said than done, particularly when you have to deal with the mundane, such as meeting payroll and paying your bills. Remember, however, as they say, "You'll either have to pay now or pay later." If you make an exception because the customer in question only occasionally crosses your ethics line, the long-term cost of the infractions might ultimately be much more significant than you ever fathomed, even to the point of being a fatal error.

On the other hand, taking your concerns to a customer might lead to an understanding that allows you to continue the relationship and in some cases not only solidify it, but improve it. You could even be rewarded with a surprising reaction to your assertions of "thank you for having the courage to tell us, we'll fix it."

The best way to do business in today's environment is to have transparency in the relationship, which significantly helps to avoid unpleasant surprises. It also makes for a more satisfying and longer-term partnership with your customers. This criterion will not only set the right example for all of your employees but also will ultimately lead to a much more productive and successful company. As an added plus, you might actually, every once in awhile, even sleep through the night. In terms of doing business only with people you like, it's much akin to the old adage: "you can pick your friends but not your relatives." In the case of business, your customers are sometimes comparable to those "certain relatives." The good news is you don't live under the same roof with your customers; you're just taking their money for services rendered.

Train your team to say 'yes' to customers

In any language, the word 'nyet,' 'nein' or 'no' can translate into lost sales

This column was originally published in April 2010

In order to close a sale, customers must hear the word "yes" before they make a purchase, agree to a service or sign a contract. Few people will do business with a company that makes it a practice of giving a dozen reasons why something cannot be done, instead of figuring out how to say "yes." The word "yes" is the launching pad for every transaction, but too many companies don't seem to get it.

A negative response to a request may at first blush seem appropriate, but a seller must learn how to turn a negative into a positive. There are some easy techniques to accomplish this seemingly elusive feat. As an example, a customer wants a delivery on a Tuesday, when your truck only travels to the customer's area on a Friday. Instead of summarily saying "no" because it does not fit your schedule, empower your people to find a solution. Teach them to be cautious with their choice of words and learn how to use softer and more conciliatory synonyms for "no." For this delivery request example, your representative could say, "Yes, your request is reasonable. We will work on making it happen. However, until we can permanently change our schedule, can we deliver on X day instead of Y day?"

I could never understand why a retail store would put up signs that proclaim what a store won't do for its customers instead of what it can and will do. "No food or drinks allowed." "No checks." "No who-knows-what." Sure, a retailer doesn't want anything spilled on the merchandise and certainly doesn't want to get stiffed with a bad check. However, instead of posting a "no-no" statement, the sign could easily be rewritten to make the negative a positive. A substitute to this same proclamation could be: "We have the lowest prices in town because we don't incur the added costs of processing checks, and we pass this savings on to you. For your convenience, we accept all credit cards." Of course, these illustrations are oversimplifications, but they will point you in the right direction.

Never forget your business needs the customer much more than the other way around. Management's job is to promote creativity and underscore the objective of accommodating your customers' needs with the ultimate goal of exceeding them. You'll never do it if you start with the word "no." The lifeblood of most every company is repeat business. The toughest initial hurdle is to get a customer to try your product or service. This initial trial is also typically the most expensive step in the sales process, but after that, it can lead to a long-term and profitable relationship.

There is nothing worse than telling a customer, "No, it is against company policy," or even worse, "We don't make exceptions, no way, no how."

Recently, I was in a fancy-schmancy restaurant when the waiter began his shtick by rattling off a list of requirements for the privilege of eating at this establishment: "Chef does not allow substitutions, won't prepare the entrée other than broiling and insists on cooking everything medium rare." I interrupted the waiter in midsentence exclaiming my confusion because I thought my guests and I were the customers and the restaurant took the orders instead of giving them. The waiter looked at me as if I were from another planet. He then continued with his spiel. What was the net result of this string of "no's"? First, I had a lingering bad taste in my mouth, and it wasn't from the food. Secondly, I reduced the tip from my usual 20 percent plus. Worse yet for the restaurant, I won't rush back for a return visit and most likely will repeat my tale of woe when this eatery comes up in conversation. You do the math of the cost per letter of the use of the word "no" and what this did to the restaurant's bottom line.

Nyet, nein, no or like words in any language can all have the same effect: lost sales and profits, not to mention a tarnished image. It doesn't get "no" worse than that. Your job as a leader is to find a way for your team to always get to "yes."

Strong caveat to new management
First, do no harm!

This column was originally published in September 2008

Hippocrates, the father of medicine, also knew a thing or two about business. In the fourth century B.C., he crafted the Hippocratic oath. Extracted from this sage pledge came the dictum, "First, do no harm." Even after more than 2,000 years, this oath could be appropriately adopted today by corporate titans. Every day, companies are bought and sold from around the corner to across the world. Organizations of all types undergo management and leadership changes — sometimes as frequently as athletes change their socks.

Many times, changes are necessitated by poor performance or new ownership. The "out with the old, in with the new" actions during transitions are frequently required and appropriate. However, too frequently ill-conceived changes can cause a negative domino effect. Before anyone realizes it, the cure becomes worse than the malady.

New leader, new worries

As the ink is still drying on a new leader's contract, almost instant promulgations are made that the new kahuna has brought in his or her own team, frequently including the head operator, marketing strategist and financial guru. The precipitous action of throwing the baby out with the bathwater can include key people who have the critical "institutional" knowledge of why this or that works or, equally important, why something won't.

Often the first shoe to drop is only the beginning. The usual scenario is that the other executives who come in with the new leader

175

proceed with great dispatch bringing in their own people, further upsetting a fragile apple cart. This exponential process many times causes turmoil and costly business disruptions before anyone realizes the organization is at risk and the troops are not only restless but also operating in a fear mode. Things stop getting done, sales suffer, and customers become unhappy because after these radical changes in personnel nobody knows who's on first and who does what under the new leadership. It's not uncommon for the old team members who stay on to be treated like redheaded stepchildren.

Changes at the top are typically initiated because the former leader simply couldn't get the job done. Most rational business people have no quarrel with this. This doesn't mean the people below the old boss are all bad. In fact, they actually may be very good and understand the intricacies of the business, but because of poor leadership, they couldn't function effectively or their creativity was stymied. However, if the new CEO takes the Hippocratic oath, a great deal of suffering can be avoided.

Wait a minute
Perhaps there is a better way, including enforcing a moratorium on wholesale personnel changes for a specific period of time and certainly at least until the dust settles and a thorough evaluation of existing people and processes is completed. The best of the best buyout companies have a meticulous review and integration process that is launched after an acquisition. This process not only assesses skills but also incorporates sensitivity because new management/owners know they are messing with a lot of people's lives. When changes do begin, they are done professionally, providing dignity to the departed.

Leadership must recognize that during a transition all parties, particularly the employees and the customers, are watching. Indiscriminate changes will long be remembered, and when the employee who does stay receives a new offer a month or a year down the road, he or she will not have forgotten how the company treated its "loyal people" during the change process. Customers, too, have their favorite people in a company, and most times, they are the lower-level support types who are most likely unknown to the CEO. When the time comes, the customer will also vividly recall how the company behaved and treated its customers and employees during the transition.

To avoid the unnecessary rush to judgment of an existing team member, process or strategy, new management must stop, look, listen and learn before acting. Speed certainly counts but not as much as aiming before firing.

When the time comes, as it usually does, for a management transition in your organization gather your top people together and have them raise their right hands and repeat after you: "No matter what changes we make, our primary consideration must be to first, do no harm."

Customers are as mad as hell and aren't going to take it anymore!
This is your wakeup call

This column was originally published in October 2008

In 1976 a satirical movie titled "Network" won four academy awards and quickly gained a cult-like following. The flick centers on an anchor newscaster who's fed up with his job and the world around him. His frustration erupts during a live national TV broadcast that galvanizes the nation with the rant, "I'm mad as hell and I'm not going to take it anymore." This protagonist's action prompts Americans across the country to literally open their windows and shout this defiant pronouncement.

That was then, and this is now. Today, it's not a fictional character, but the public at large that has adopted this mantra. The worm has turned, and now customers have the power — and they know it. No longer do consumers have to accept inferior products and especially dismal service. Most frustrating, according to many surveys, is the "attitude" that accompanies many businesses' lack of follow through and poor service.

In our Internet-driven world, with almost instant communications, blogs and chat rooms, the consumer has come of age. There is a new movement afoot and customers of the 21st century will not be denied!

What does it cost your business when you consistently break promises and disappoint? Most likely, it's not only your potential growth but your very existence.

Each day that your company turns on the lights and opens

the front door, you need to be prepared to keep your promise. Consumers have lost their patience with apathy, incompetence and rudeness. In these difficult times, a number of companies that have been around for years won't make the next cut. This will occur not only as a result of a poor economic environment, but because too many companies just don't deliver.

Disappoint me once, shame on you; disappoint me twice, shame on me

This cliché sums up the new "two strikes and you're out" consumer mentality. There are simply too many alternative companies for customers to put up with an inordinate amount of corporate mumbo jumbo and sleight-of-hand shoddy treatment.

Take for example the experience of calling a company's toll-free number. It's a fair bet that the caller could be disappointed not just because the issue may not be fully resolved but also as a result of the indifference and the negative attitude of the customer service personnel.

On the positive side, there are still standout companies that make customer service their passion. One of the best is the Ritz-Carlton hotel chain. If you have every visited a Ritz and asked an employee the location of a restroom, he or she won't merely tell you; instead they'll accompany you to the facility. This can be a bit disconcerting particularly when an especially enthusiastic Ritz employee initially seems to be prepared to join you in its typically spotless oasis of mirrors, marble and porcelain. Overkill? Perhaps to some. However, to most it's a refreshing example that the Ritz and its employees care about making that extra effort.

Do employees wake up in the morning and want to do a bad job? Absolutely not. The problem doesn't stem from the employee providing the bad service but from the employer that accepts mediocrity and incompetence. In effect, companies become enablers by doing a poor job of training associates and not enforcing customer service standards.

In the land of the blind, the one-eyed man is king

To meet or exceed expectations a company does not have to do anything extraordinary. Most times, just being civil and moderately efficient will win over a customer. For a variety of business reasons, including expense control and the all too prevalent personnel cutbacks, many organizations let customer service go to seed. Make sure you spend your money and devote resources to where you'll get the best return. Customer service should be the very last cut before you're forced to permanently turn off the lights.

This is a wakeup call for every owner and corporate executive to double their efforts to ensure that they are making their customers' life at least tenable, if not easier. Anything less and you run the risk of becoming the target of newly empowered and technology-savvy customers who know how to make themselves heard electronically with a cry that could be heard from every window literally around the world.

Being a big company is not an excuse for being a rude company

How to set expectations using a not-so-subtle nudge

This column was originally published in March 2010

Every business knows that to survive and succeed it needs customers. What is often ignored, however, is that companies also need vendors and suppliers in order to prosper. In too many organizations, this group is not only frequently neglected but also, at times, abused.

A growing number of savvy organizations have come to realize that their vendors are, in effect, their partners. A company's success therefore becomes the vendor's success and is a win-win for everyone.

On the flip side, too many businesses treat their vendors like secondhand citizens who are merely a means to an end. This shabby behavior can manifest itself in many forms, from not returning a supplier's phone call to being down right belligerent.

What I'm writing about here has nothing to do with negotiating the best possible terms with the lowest possible prices from a vendor. It's probably almost biological that buyers and sellers butt heads over price. If we take price and terms out of the buyer-vendor relationship, the question becomes what are the key factors that strengthen the working relationship and what weakens it?

Strengthening the partnership usually gets down to promises made and promises kept. The rub occurs when the little annoying things get in the way of the relationship. A company is judged by its cumulative actions. What may seem to be an insignificant series of slights can be as damaging as a single major lapse in appropriate behavior. The big ones don't happen that frequently.

Here's an analogy. Relatively few people are hit by locomotives, primarily because they're easy to spot, but a huge number are stung by bees because most don't see them coming.

One of my pet peeves is how frequently vendors are kept waiting in lobbies. This sends a signal to the vendor that "our time is more valuable than yours; after all, we're signing your purchase order." The example I'm using in this column is just a proxy for dozens of ways companies send the wrong message and don't even know it.

Years ago, I found an effective solution to reduce vendors waiting time that cost nothing, worked wonders, and kept my employees on the straight and narrow of how to treat visitors.

To get a sense of what was going on in my company, I regularly took walks through all four floors of our headquarters to see and to be seen. There is something about visibility that sends a signal that the boss is paying attention and not just sitting in an ivory tower. During these walks, I would swing through our lobby, where there was always an abundance of hustle and bustle. Often, when I made a second pass through the lobby on the way back to my office I'd see the same people still waiting from my first pass. It was obvious some employees were treating visitors rudely by disrespecting their time.

I thought, "How in the world could we ask a vendor for this or that when we start out by behaving rudely?" It was time for me to take action.

Here's what I did. I had a sign made for the receptionist's desk that bore my signature and read: "If you (the visitor) have an appointment and you're kept waiting longer than 15 minutes, please pick up the red phone next to this sign, which rings directly on my desk. I will personally come down to greet you."

Next, I sent a memo to every employee outlining this policy and the reasons for it. I explained that one of our competitive advantages would be how we treat vendors. I pointed out that this was not to be confused with giving the vendors whatever they asked for just because we didn't want to hurt their feelings. I concluded with the admonishment that if I were called, I would personally rescue the visitor and bring him or her to the policy violators office.

Once the sign went up and my memo went out, things began to change. Visitors were greeted promptly or even ahead of the appointed hour. We dramatically improved our reputation as a company that, although very tough negotiators, respected those doing or trying to do business with us. This created a positive buzz among our vendors.

As a P.S. to this story I never received a call from a single visitor from the date I put in this policy to when I sold the company.

Being big, small or in-between is never an excuse for being rude. And always be on the lookout for bees.

How to repair damaged business relationships
Suck it up for success, because time usually heals all

This column was originally published in July 2014

Most everyone has been a party to a failed relationship, business or otherwise. It's probably mostly about being human and succumbing to hubris, being obstinate or having unrealistic expectations.

When this occurs over time, the gap in the relationship widens, primarily due to intentional or passive neglect. As months turn into years, an invisible long-term breach sets in and the real reasons that caused the rift fade from our consciousness.

Then one day something out of the blue triggers positive thoughts about the supposed offender and you begin to ponder what really went wrong. Maybe an ill-timed comment, an initial misinterpretation or an equally trivial trigger sparked the chasm that took on a life of its own, proliferating seemingly to a point of no return.

If you can't remember the real "story behind the story" of why you stopped doing business with someone, other than possibly because he or she threatened your firstborn or worse, perhaps it's time to reconnect. It could prove to be profitable and, perhaps even more important, personally satisfying.

Get started
In the recesses of your psyche, do a sanity check to ensure you've selected a suitable candidate for reconciliation, not someone who might still be having nightmares about you.

Next, make a list of the gratifying memories you had together before the "black time." Now you're ready to send a note to the target of your reunion. Start by boldly stating, "Out of the blue, Mr. or Ms. X, you came to mind along with how much I previously enjoyed our relationship." Add that you were suddenly overwhelmed with the good of it all and how personally fulfilling doing business with him or her was to you.

From the top of your list cite the most positive memory both of you likely savored. Disarm the recipient by stating, in reflection, you're sorry for what transpired.

Take the blame

Depending how much you have matured since the dark event, how comfortable you are today in your own skin and if you're ready to suck it up, add the comment that you're putting the blame on yourself for what transpired. Even if you weren't the guilty party, this tone will likely crumble any remaining barriers to your efforts to reunite.

The clincher to bridge the existing gap is either to suggest you get reacquainted now or, if you prefer to be a bit more subtle, simply to state, "This communication is long overdue, and I wish you the very best."

Taking the initiative requires the realization that you don't have to win every battle to win the war. Many times this type of unabashed mea culpa can lead to a renewed and sustained relationship that makes the catalysis for the original issue something that both sides can laugh about after the healing process concludes.

Remember, "Time heals all wounds." You just have to be an opportunist to take advantage of this ageless phenomenon.

5

Building Value

Facing your fears
If you're afraid to lose, you'll never win

This column was originally published in February 2005

Almost without exception every success story in business starts with an idea, a concept fueled by a dream. Every day in many ways we hear and read about how these dreams take shape, take hold and come to fruition. We've also all heard the many hackneyed analogies for winning, the most ubiquitous of which are tied to sports in some form or another. Sorry ladies, it must be a guy thing.

There are dozens of these pedestrian lines such as, "if you don't step to the plate, you'll never get on base. If you don't take a shot, you'll never get a basket." Anyway you get the drift. As corny as it sounds these trite phrases apply to much of what we do, particularly in business. Simply put, if you never do anything, nothing will ever happen.

Most, if not all, of us at one point or another have had what we thought was that "big idea." The grand slam concept that will bring us fame, fortune, and for some of us the satisfaction of getting even with that seventh grade teacher who said, "You wouldn't amount to anything."

Unfortunately, many of these great ideas never get traction because we all suffer in one form or another at any given time from the "F of F" or Fear of Failure, which concomitantly almost always surfaces with a slam-bang big idea. We think to ourselves: if I try it and fail I'll embarrass my family, my friends, myself and prove that seventh grade teacher right. Self-doubt and second thoughts come part and parcel with break-through thinking and new ideas. F of F can even be a strong motivator making us delve more deeply, analyze fully, and think through what it will take to make something really work.

On the other hand, we've all experienced or at least observed the effects of analysis/paralysis, where through constant and obsessive study and rehashing, we beat an idea into a dead horse with self-recriminations of woulda, coulda, shoulda. If I do it this way, that will happen. If I do it that way, this will happen. At the end of the process you're exhausted, frustrated and you've taken your rags-to-riches and dream and turned it into a fading fantasy bordering on a nightmare.

As doctors, psychiatrists and psychologists like to say, "When you hear hoof beats, look for horses not zebras lest you cross over the line to the darker side of paranoia."

How do you stop this downward spiral of a good idea and translate it into a reality? There are many effective ways of progressing through the process with different methods working depending on the circumstances. From my experience of coming up with an idea and building businesses from scratch, the best way is to start with the concept and ask yourself a few simple questions. Does my idea fill a niche, provide a solution that no else does? Or, can I take an existing concept, business or methodology and make it better, more efficient, more effective and do it more economically than anybody else.

After I think of an idea I create a mental storyboard much like those used in creating TV shows or commercials. Each frame is a scene and I then fill in the blanks with words and a visual picture of what is to take place at a given sequence or point in time in my plan. I call this process 'sequencing'. As the storyboard progresses, I come up with a quick hit list of additional questions that must be answered. Does the concept have staying power? What will I need in terms of resources, skills, people and how much money will it take to harvest the concept? Once done with my mental storyboard I commit it to writing and then the fun begins. When you follow this scenario, you'll think about the idea or concept intermittently day and night. If it's a particularly good one you'll find yourself staring at the ceiling at 3 a.m. in the morning. You'll ruminate about how to improve it. You'll also begin imagining yourself stepping to the plate, taking the bat off your shoulders and if you're both smart and lucky, you'll hear the crack of the bat and envision that spherical object soaring for the fences as the crowd cheers.

Some of the simplest ideas have become the biggest winners for those persistent enough to stay focused and create their own storyboard of success. This is known as really low hanging fruit. Most people will think of an idea and say, "No, that's too easy. Someone has probably already done it." Because of that always lurking doomsday fear of failure sentiment, or perhaps more aptly put fear of winning, you become afraid to try. The most successful people I have ever met are those who have something to prove to others or more importantly, to themselves. But, you'll never even come close to winning if you're afraid to lose.

You're H-I-R-E-D!

These two words, perhaps not as dramatic as the well-known opposite tv line, but much more important for an organization's success

This column was originally published in May 2005

Unless you've been living under a rock for the past 18 months or so, the CEO boardroom proclamation "You're Fired!," accompanied by a quick flick of the wrist, has become the new corporate mantra for eliminating mediocrity. Recently, life has imitated art with an accelerated steady stream of CEOs' heads rolling as boardroom patience for success has been exhausted.

Certainly to some, the hit TV show "The Apprentice" is not only entertaining, but also suggests that these two simple words, "You're Fired" have become the "holy grail" of solving any and every company's woes.

Firing someone who's not getting it done is at times unavoidable and should never be easy. People change, circumstances change, and sometimes a change for the sake of change can make sense. Banishing a wrong-doer, however, to the unemployment line is not a substitute for fixing a bad strategy.

It may be an oversimplification, but it's a heck of a lot easier to hire the right person for the right job the first time than to create a catharsis by ridding the organization of the person who probably shouldn't have been there in the first place. Consider the impact of making a bad hire. First, it's not only disruptive to the business or organization when a change is made, it's also incredibly expensive. Studies and statistics prove that the cost of firing senior- or middle-management personnel can be as high as 300 percent of that person's annual salary. This includes the disruptive effect, the cost of finding a replacement, training, and ancillary emotional and unsettling peripheral effects. The bottom line is firing is, bad for the bottom line.

How can you stack the deck in your favor when making a new hire? In real estate, it's location, location, location. In hiring people, it's thoroughness, thoroughness, thoroughness. Most of us would never decide to go on a trip, get up in the morning, pack our bags and then start driving without knowing where we were heading. It's shocking to me how many times companies will hire an executive or a manager without really defining the responsibilities, scope of authority and most importantly, the desired results of what the person is expected to do or accomplish. Making a good hire is a methodical process that starts with a need followed by a very tightly structured job description with a lot of definition how the newbie will be measured. Keep drafting and re-drafting until you have a finely tuned outline document that provides the "who, what, why, where and when" of the position. Next, the search begins.

Today, there are a myriad of ways to find great people. Certainly there are the job boards, recruiters, print media; but for top positions, I still prefer doing it the old-fashioned way: find someone who knows somebody who's done it before and done it well. Figure out how to make the contact, then pitch the opportunity. Now the fun really begins with the preliminary telephone interview, followed by the face-to-face meet. Before the appointed hour, know as much as you can about the person, what he or she has done, and equally important what they've not accomplished. This is particularly important for senior level positions.

There are a lot of great search background tools particularly on the Internet, where one can learn almost everything about the person but were afraid to ask. During the interview process, be candid and let the other person speak by asking a lot of open ended questions that require quick thinking and thoughtful answers. Frequently I will ask specific questions already knowing the answers just to see how the candidate responds.

If I had my druthers, instead of interviewing the candidate first, I'd like to talk to the candidate's parents, because I've learned through experience that some of the key basics for success are things that are not learned at school but were taught at home at a very early age. Examples include the fundamentals: integrity, work ethic and commitment. Obviously this is not possible, but there are ways to delve into an individual's background during the conversation that are appropriate and won't get you sued. Much of it is all in how you phrase the question.

After the interview, I always ask the candidate to think about the opportunity; don't tell me then and there if he or she is interested, but instead send me a letter outlining the level of interest, why the candidate thinks he or she can get the job done and what would it take for them to be enticed to join the organization. I do this for a variety of reasons. One, it shows me how the candidate thinks and articulates ideas and concepts; further it reflects the person's sense of urgency and level of interest. I'm always astounded after I interview someone and they write back to me — about three weeks later — telling me they are excited about the opportunity. Obviously they just flunked my urgency test and will receive a perfunctory "have a nice life, but no thanks letter."

My final step when I hone in on the candidate is to have them professionally tested to determine their work style. There are a variety of good and relatively inexpensive work style assessment tests that are very effective in minimizing your downside and that help to ensure you're not trying to put a square peg in a round hole.

Every employee at one time or another would love to tell their boss to take this job and shove it. Equally true, every boss at one time or another would like to use the now infamous two simple words to erase the problem of a bad hire. However, when you proclaim the opposite "You're Hired!" make sure you've done it the right way for the right reason — your organization's success."

It's 3 a.m. and you're still awake

Do you know what your employees are doing right now?

This column was originally published in June 2005

Every owner, manager, CEO or professional periodically has episodes of sleeplessness precipitated by a myriad of demons. These range from utter terror caused by fears of: did you do something that is going to put the business under such as losing a huge customer, or did you forget to think of "this or that" which will drive the big project into a spiraling failure? More mundane causes of corporate and professional insomnia can be: did I unfairly snap at my admin because of my own stupidity and now the admin will pout and punish me with subtle errors of omission for the next five days? Lower on this list is: did someone forget to unplug the coffee pot and the place is burning down as I toss and turn?

I learned a long time ago that there is not much one can do about the less significant humdrum problems that intermittently launch fits of counting sheep. These typically pass quickly and in a few hours one realizes how silly those ghost and goblins really were.

Conversely, I have a possible cure to the three in the morning syndrome that beats taking mega doses of Sominex. The solution lies in the fact that there is strength in numbers. Two heads are better than one when solving problems and the greater the number of people focusing on the same issues, the more likely a successful solution. If you can get your associates, employees, partners, etc. "engaged," you'll have the solace of knowing that when you can't sleep because of issues and opportunities, you are not alone staring at the ceiling in the middle of the night.

My solution is make whomever you are working with participants in the process. One great way is to bring them in to your inner circle and share with them your worst fears and fondest expectations about what must be achieved and when. It always comforts as well as astounds me how people will rise to the occasion when given the opportunity to really become involved.

Equally important to my somniferous solution is giving your key players a piece of the action. This means rewarding those who are joined at the hip with you in reaching key objectives which can produce success or, in some cases, ensure plain old survival.

When I started my company, I used to obsess over the D-word as in D for dilution of my ownership. Fortunately, I realized early on, that to hit a home run or sometimes just to make it through the month, I would have to give up a piece of the ownership or create a slug of money in a bonus pool payable to the folks who could and would make it happen.

There are a dozen ways to bring people into your economic inner sanctum. Take your pick from stock options, profit interest in LLC entities, or sometimes just a well-structured bonus program that is measurable and based on performance. The smartest and cheapest investment a leader can make is sharing the wealth with the team.

Think of it this way: would you rather have a small piece of a very big "profitable" pie, or a huge slice of an extremely tiny much less valuable one? The former is capitalism at its best, the latter is a down right small-minded way to ensure mediocrity or worse. When I was CEO of my *Fortune* 500 company, we had a stock option and bonus program for all management level people from store managers to executive vice presidents. In retrospect, this perhaps was one of the major factors that drove the business from one store to 1,000, with first year sales of $1 million to almost $5 billion 15 years later.

Plus, as an added benefit of having your people as participants, you can take great comfort in knowing that at 3 o'clock in the morning while they are counting sheep, you can be counting your increasing profits, realizing that others are focusing on cracking the code for that important solution.

It's time to start working smarter, not just harder
A ticking clock is your new enemy

This column was originally published in February 2009

The business realities that have followed in the wake of the veritable worldwide economic meltdown during the past six months desperately call for action and dramatic changes in the way we do business. It can no longer be business as usual. The need is immediate for a review and rewrite, if necessary, of every company's playbook and standard operating procedures. The era of unfettered growth fueled by an abundance of available capital has come to a screeching halt.

Lavish perks, such as jets, opulent retreats and extravagant company events, are now not only politically unacceptable but also fiscally imprudent. The same applies to the practice of analysis to the point of paralysis, the expense of redundant layers of management and the luxury of an expansive support staff. Business excesses in any form or fashion have gone the way of yesteryear's three-martini lunches and smoke-filled rooms.

New rules dictated by sobering economic realities require every business to get by with less staff, less cushion and, yes, less money. All managers must take a refresher course in how to "do it once, do it right." Thoroughness and thoughtfulness have become the underpinnings in this new school of business. Superfluous actions must be replaced with an increased emphasis on efficiency, effectiveness, and the elimination of roadblocking and laborious bureaucracy. Time wasters, both functions and people, must be avoided.

Every CEO, owner and senior manager must lead by example. No longer can it be, "Do as I say, not as I do." Success will be measured by results achieved in days, weeks and months, rather than the traditional long-term, five-year plan for every major undertaking.

Wasted motion is management's new enemy. Time not spent on accomplishing specific objectives can lead to a disastrous detour. Leadership must have time to think and act. Distractions must be avoided like a money-borrowing, long-lost, deadbeat relative.

Communications to all constituents must be clear and underscored by facts and reality. Businesses need less talk and more meaningful actions and results. As an example today, the average executive receives more than 100 emails a day and spends more than eight hours a week on electronic communications. New definitions must be established as to what "keeping me in the loop" really means. As a leader, do you really need to know every painful detail of what's happening with all of your direct reports? Descending into minutiae will take you away from strategizing.

Alternative methods of communication need to be reintroduced, such as the unique practice of requiring team members to actually talk to each other rather than texting one another from a next-door office or cubicle.

Today, more so than ever, time means money and must be coveted like one of the most precious assets on your balance sheet. If the clock stops ticking and you run out of time, you most likely will run out of money eventually.

Empower your key people to make decisions to keep moving forward. Teach people to think twice before sending an email or placing a phone call by asking themselves, "What is it I want to report, and is it just nice or is the information really necessary? Will the initial message require another follow-up communication in the next few hours or days?" Before they hit the send button, train your team to ensure that the message is complete and includes the who, what, why, where, when and sometimes how of the subject matter. There is nothing worse than receiving an email that is incomplete, which then requires an email reply asking for clarification. Make it a rule that if your people send you a message, it must be informative and actionable, not just an FYI that has morphed into a CYA.

Discipline your organization to set predetermined follow-up dates on everything of importance. Everyone in the organization must know that if a deadline is going to be missed, he or she must inform the pertinent parties before the clock strikes 12. It's not just a matter of common courtesy; it is about saving extraneous effort. As these new standards are communicated and processes begin to permeate the organization, you'll find everyone becoming more focused and much more goal- and task-oriented. Working smarter, not just harder, must be integral to your organization's strategy.

In these unprecedented times, it's not perspiration, it's performance that counts.

Wise leaders plant trees under which they'll likely never sit

It takes a skillful balancing act to achieve both short- and long-term objectives

This column was originally published in June 2010

Too many businesses are fixated on immediate gratification. All too frequently, a company's worth is now measured almost entirely by the paybacks it achieves in the near term, rather than by its ability to plan effectively and execute a sustainable long-term growth strategy. The use of this barometer to keep score significantly intensified after the economic meltdown of 2008.

Management teams are now on a very short leash. "What have you done for me today?" is the mandate for public companies with their required 13-week earnings report cards, and both public and private companies must typically provide their lenders each month with data that measure results against promised targets. Much of this is appropriate. The negative, however, is that management has less incentive and support to focus on far-off goals to ensure the company is still in business 20 or 30 years from now.

When a company misses the mark, even for a month or a quarter, the team finds itself under the glaring bright lights of intense scrutiny, which can make even the most secure management skittish about undertaking costly programs.

In this current environment, a CEO's tenure is almost measured in dog years. Although definitive figures are not yet available for last year, some estimate that the median average tenure of the top executive at a publicly held company may have dropped to a new low of approximately 5.5 years. This presents a dramatic, more than 40 percent decline from about 9.5 years of service in 1995.

Whatever happened to the nurturing of the CEO by the board of directors or advisers providing him or her time to gain insightful understanding of the intricacies of the business that leads to sustained growth and the ability to implement long-term plans? Isn't the obligation of a management team to ensure that it makes the appropriate decisions to pave the way for the next generation that follows?

Think about it this way: It took more than 100 years to build the great cathedral of Notre Dame in Paris and a span of hundreds of years for Great Wall of China to be built during the Ming Dynasty. Those making the decisions to embark on these massive undertakings surely knew that they would never see the full fruition of their planning. They knew that they were planting trees under which they would never sit.

In modern times, a project that might take a century or more to complete is obviously a bit much. However, for a more realistic example, think about energy companies, which must make decisions today to ensure that we have the energy plants for tomorrow. These expensive, very long-term projects require huge capital, extraordinary amounts of time, and the maturity of management to know that most likely they will not be around to savor the completion of the new facility. Current senior management teams in all companies must understand that what they do on their watch will become their legacy on which history will judge them.

There are dozens of reasons why a company does not plan far enough into the future. Aside from being selfish because current management will not be the beneficiary of the efforts, perhaps a bigger reason is that companies don't have the backing from their constituents to do some of the things necessary for the next generation. In many cases, this would require too big a hit to current profitability. In a more esoteric scenario, some narrow-minded leadership would say, "What's in it for us and our shareholders or investors today?"

There are many excuses, some of which are comparable to a fifth-grader who does not turn in his or her homework and asserts, "The dog ate it."

Companies that make equally absurd statements about focusing solely on the present might be better served by using the dog-ate-it excuse — plus it would probably be more believable and make sense.

Today's leaders must balance short-term, intermediate-term and very long-term objectives in order to satisfy all of their constituents and to improve the odds that there will be a tomorrow.

Being a CEO is akin to being a tightrope walker who must have nerves of steel and very good balance. Unfortunately, we all know what happens to tightrope walkers who lose their balance — they fall, and most times, they don't ever get up again.

There's gold in them there hills
The big question is always: Where?

This column was originally published in August 2010

The opening scene of many Western movies features a scruffy-faced, toothless gold miner who turns to a sidekick and proclaims, as he mystically gazes yonder to majestic mountains, "There is gold in them there hills." This is the sidekick's cue to grunt, thus acknowledging that this utterance is, indeed, fact. In turn, the miner's nonverbal shrug suggests, "But where?" Change the setting and this scene could be two businesspeople staring out of an office window, but standing in for the toothless miner is the eager entrepreneur or CEO, and the man of few words is, no doubt, the accountant.

Reality is it takes money to make money, no matter if a business is just starting out, trying to keep running or growing, the entity needs to find the gold in the hills to move forward. The conundrum is where in the hill is it?

Every month, I receive many comments from both faithful and new readers alike. The No. 1 question I'm asked is, "Show me the money," or, more aptly stated, "Where does one find money?" Anyone running an enterprise can relate to that queasy feeling when the company is bumping up against its credit line, can't get credit at all or is desperately searching for new investors.

After the market meltdown of 2008, we're operating in uncharted waters. Although banks claim they are lending, that's only partially true. For the most part, they are willing to lend money to businesses provided they don't need it, but banks are reluctant to do so for a company whose lifeblood is working capital.

201

This new lender's modus operandi requires borrowers to employ creativity, perseverance and a healthy dose of chutzpah. Make no mistake, there is money to be had, it just may no longer be available from the traditional sources.

For a newer business without a boatload of hard assets to secure a loan, the task is a bit more challenging. What I have advised readers to think about when they are trying to raise money is to ask themselves one important question, which can be expressed as a type of algebraic expression: "My success will = success for ____?" Fill in this blank and the operator will have taken the first step in finding new money. It could be from key suppliers or vendors with which a company creates a new channel of distribution. It might be another business that would be complemented by the establishment of a new business. Rudimentary examples would be a parking lot operator who is located next door to a new restaurant, or a gym that could lease space to a sporting goods store within its walls.

If you're trying to find gold from suppliers, you will have to think of it from their perspective. The win portion of the question could be that the company in search of capital gives warrants or option to the benefactor/lender that entitles it to buy equity into the company either at a prescribed price or under other advantageous terms at a specific point in time.

A midsize or larger company might use similar creativity by refinancing a package of company assets, which have been paid down or owned outright. In addition to paying interest, the borrower might include a "kicker" or something extra that would be provided when the loan matures. In this time of survival of the fittest, there is always the possibility of a merger when going it alone is no longer practical.

Most lenders/investors will need to know: What is the borrower's skin in the game? This means how much of the owner's own money has been contributed to fund the business or has the CEO pledged his or her first-born or other less valuable assets? Also required is a thoughtful plan that demonstrates how one is going to get from point A to point B, travailing any landmines along the way.

To go for the gold takes unique thinking, logic and tenacity.

Another tip: Just because you're told no the first time doesn't necessarily mean you'll be turned down the second time if you provide additional information, a twist to the plan and improved incentives.

Don't just gaze off into those majestic hills, merely fantasizing about finding the mother lode. Instead, gather up your pick and shovel and start prospecting for your future.

Don't confuse doing the right thing with knowing the right thing to do

How to make the right decisions at the right time

This column was originally published in December 2012

Companies typically want to do what's right for those they serve. Key priorities should be customers, investors, employees and the communities in which the company is located — but not necessarily always in this order. The dilemma, however, is that many times short-term decisions can prove to be long-term problems that cause more pain than the initial gain.

It's difficult to make all constituents happy every time. As a result, management must prioritize decisions with a clear understanding that each action has ramifications, which could manifest themselves in the short, intermediate or long term. Seldom does a single decision serve all of the same timelines. There are no easy answers and anyone who has spent even a short amount of time running a business has already learned this fact of life. So what's a leader to do?

It's a sure bet that investors want a better return, employees want more money and benefits, and customers want better quality products, higher levels of service and, oh yes, lower prices. This simply all goes with the territory and is a part of the game. The problem can be that, most times, it's hard to give without taking something away from someone else. Here are a couple of examples.

Take the case of deciding to improve employee compensation packages. Ask the auto companies what happened when they added a multitude of perks over the years, as demanded by the unions? The auto titans thought they didn't have much choice, lest they run the risk of alienating their gigantic workforces. History has shown us the ramifications of their actions as the majority of these manufacturers came close to going belly up, which would have resulted in huge job losses and an economic tsunami.

Basic math caused the problems. The prices charged for cars could not cover all of the legacy costs that accrued over the years, much like barnacles building up on the bottom of a ship to the point where the ship could sink from the weight. Hindsight is 20/20, and, of course, the auto companies should have been more circumspect about creating benefit packages that could not be sustained. Yes, the employees received an increase to their standard of living for a time anyway, but at the end of the day, a company cannot spend more than it takes in and stay in business for long.

Investors in public companies can present a different set of problems because they can have divergent objectives. There are the buy-and-hold investors, albeit a shrinking breed, who understand that for a company to have long-term success, it must invest in the present to build for the future. The term "immediate gratification" is not in their lexicon; they're in it for the long haul. Another type of investor might know or care little about a company's future, other than whether its earnings per share beat Wall Street estimates. These investors buy low and sell high, sometimes flipping the stock in hours or days. And, actually, both types are doing what's right for them. The issue becomes how to serve the needs and goals of both groups. When a company effectively articulates its strategy, it tends to attract the right type of investors who are buying in for the right reason. This will avoid enticing the wrong investors who turn hostile because they want something that the company won't deliver.

When interviewing and before hiring employees, it is imperative that candidates know where the company wants to go and how it plans to get there. Many times, this means telling the prospective newbie that the short-term compensation and benefits may not be as good as the competitors' down the street, but in the longer term, the company anticipates being able to significantly enhance employee packages, with the objective of eventually outmatching the best payers because of the investments in equipment being made today.

The key to satisfying employees (present and prospective), investors, et al, is communicating the types of decisions a company will make over a specific period of time. Communication from the get-go is integral to the rules of engagement and can alleviate huge problems that can otherwise lead to dissatisfaction.

Knowing what is right for your company, based on your stated plan that has been well-communicated, will help ensure that you do the right thing, at the right time, for the right reasons.

The inflection point: when supply meets demand
How to manage the equation for maximum profitability using a mirror

This column was originally published in April 2013

The more there is available of something, the less it costs. Conversely, when there's a limited quantity of that same something, the more it's coveted and the more expensive it is. This is a rudimentary concept, but few companies know how to effectively manage the process to ensure they balance supply with demand in order to maintain or improve the profitability of a product or service. Of course, before you can maximize profitability, you must have something customers want, sometimes even before they know they need it.

Think about precious metals, fine diamonds and even stocks. The beauty and a portion of the intrinsic value of these things are effectively in the eyes of the beholder. In reality, much of their value or price is determined by the ease or difficulty of obtaining them.

As for equities, as soon as everyone who can own a given stock has bought it, then, in many cases, the only direction that stock can take is down because there are simply more sellers than buyers. On the flip side, when few people own a stock but everybody decides they want it, for whatever the reason, that stock may take a precipitous upward trajectory.

A case in point is Apple. At one time, when its per-share price was more than $400, $500 and even $600, everyone thought the sky was the limit and the majority of institutional funds and many home gamers, aka small individual investors, jumped on the bandwagon. The stock reached $705 a share in the fall of 2012, and just when all of the market prognosticators were screaming, "Buy, buy, buy," there were too few buyers left (because everyone already owned it) and the stock fell out of bed. In many respects, Apple was still the same great company with world-class products, but there were simply more sellers than buyers and — poof — the share price evaporated, sending this once high-flying growth stock to the woodshed for a real thrashing.

The question for your business is how can you manage the availability of your goods or services to maximize profit margins? The oversimplified answer is once you have something of value, make sure that you create the appropriate amount of tension, be it requiring a waiting list to obtain the product or service or underproducing the item to create a backlog. However, this is a delicate balancing act, because if it's too hard to get, then customers will quickly find an alternative, and your product will become yesterday's news.

Some very high-end fashion houses, such as Chanel, have it down to a science. It can be very difficult to walk into a marquis retailer today and obtain one of its satchels without being made to jump through waiting-game hoops, just for the privilege of giving the store your money in exchange for the fancy schmancy bag. That stimulates demand and keeps the price up because customers tend to want something they can't seem to get.

As another example, if you have a service business that provides esoteric solutions to thorny issues, the demand increases by having a dearth of experts who can render the unique advice. In turn, the billing rate stays up and clients can be made to "take a number" and wait their turn. The same principle can apply to manufacturing. If you have a market-differentiating product that can't be found elsewhere, you can maintain the price by making it a bit difficult to obtain. Don't confuse this with price gouging, double-dealing or playing outside the lines. Instead, it is just good supply-chain management.

These types of strategies apply to any business. However, to pull it off, you must continue to improve your in-demand product or service, always staying one step ahead of the competition by investing to improve its worth, either real or perceived. You must also effectively position your offering in the market so existing and potential new customers can understand your differentiators. The final step: Don't be bashful about your advantage and create a marketing spin that showcases what you do and how you do it.

Remember beauty is in the eyes of the beholder and you must make sure you're constantly looking in the mirror to discover the hard-to-match differences. Done correctly, you can position your business as a cut above any wannabe interlopers and maintain your profit margins.

Innovator, instigator, administrator or...

What's a leader's single most important skill?

This column was originally published in December 2013

What would it take for a company to succeed if its leader could effectively do only one of the following: innovate, instigate or administrate? We all know that an innovator is the one who sees things that aren't and asks why not? The instigator sees things that are and asks why? The administrator doesn't necessarily ask profound questions but, instead, is dogged about crossing the "t's," dotting the "i's" and making sure that whatever is supposed to happen happens.

Ideally, a top leader combines all three traits while being charismatic, intellectual, pragmatic and able to make decisions faster than a speeding bullet. Although some of us might fantasize that we are Superman or Superwoman, with a sense of exaggerated omnipotence, the bubble usually bursts when we're confronted simultaneously with multiple situations that require the versatility of a Swiss army knife.

Business leaders come in all shapes and sizes with various skill sets and styles that are invaluable, depending on the priorities of a company at any given point in time.

Every business needs an innovator to differentiate the company. Without a unique something or other, there isn't a compelling reason to exist. Once those special products or services that distinguish the business from others are discovered and in place, it takes an instigator to continuously re-examine and challenge every aspect of the business that leads to continued improvements, both functionally and economically. It also takes an administrator — someone who can

210

keep all the balls in the air, ensuring that everyone in the organization is in sync and delivering the finished products as promised to keep customers coming back.

As politicians and pundits of all types have pounded into our heads in recent years, "It takes a village to raise a child." All who practice the art and science of business have learned that, instead of a village, it takes a diverse team working together to make one plus one equal three.

On the ideal team, each member possesses different strengths, contributing to the greater good. The exceptional leader is best when he or she is an effective chef who knows how to mix the different skills together to create a winning recipe.

In many companies, however, leaders tend to surround themselves with clones who share similar abilities, interests and backgrounds. As an example, a manufacturer may have a management team comprised solely of engineers, or a marketing organization could have salespeople who came up through the ranks calling all the shots.

If everyone in an organization comes from the same mold, what tends to happen is, figuratively, one lies and the others swears to it. This builds to a crescendo of complacency and perpetual mediocrity.

There is a better way. Good leaders surround themselves with others who complement their capabilities, and savvy leaders select those with dramatically different backgrounds who will challenge their thinking because they're not carbon copies of the boss. This opens up new horizons, forges breakthroughs and leads to optimal daily performance.

Strange bedfellows can stimulate, nudge and keep each other moving towards the previously unexplored.

To have a sustainable and effective organization, you can't have one type without all of the others. While everyone on the team may not always agree, each player must always be committed to making the whole greater than the sum of the parts.

The single most important skill of the leader who has to pull all of the pieces and parts together is to have the versatility of that Swiss army knife — selecting the precise tool to accomplish the objective at hand.

Is red the new black?
When should the top line overshadow the bottom line?

This column was originally published in April 2014

Most everyone in business has been indoctrinated with an emphasis on the bottom line. Ingrained in the psyche of corporate America is the demand, "Show me the money." If a public company misses analysts' profit estimates, its stock is summarily trashed, and the investment community sometimes even calls for the CEO's head.

In business we're reminded every day that public companies' chieftains are paid the big bucks for bottom line performance, not perspiration. Their brethren in the private sector are instilled with this same mindset.

There are exceptions. Creating value is not always about generating immediate profitability. Recognize either of these names: Tesla Motors and Twitter, just to name a few? These two companies, as an example, simply don't make a dime in profits, yet their stocks have performed better than their most well-endowed, bottom-line counterparts.

Why? Because they're building something for tomorrow. They sacrifice short-term profitability for innovation and market share. They've captured investors' imaginations of what might be, not what is.

The value of the trade-off
How should privately held small-, medium- and even large-sized businesses look at the trade-off between profitability and investing heavily on the "if come?"

The quick answer is that it depends on the industry, the products or services, as well as the depth of the private company's pockets. Forget about traditional banks as a source of funding for the unprofitable business, unless the owners want to personally guarantee a bank loan. The reality is banks take a dim view of companies that lose money. Banks need certainty, which includes a high degree of strong assurance that the borrower will more than likely pay them back at the prescribed time.

There are a number of alternatives for these budding companies that are pushing the boundaries to make it big, but whose founders were not fortunate enough to have been born with that proverbial silver spoon to feed their passion. These include big and small private equity/venture capital firms, which have the money, mindset and stomach to take chances on the unknown. Some are relatively conservative while others are always ready to double down based on instinct and experience.

Many companies are not of the right size, or don't have the sizzle or just may not know how to package their story to attract traditional private equity. There are always wealthy angel-type investors, however, who have already made their big money and want to do it again vicariously on someone else's sweat and tears, or because they just like being in the game.

Take heart; be strong

No matter which type of investor a company chooses to romance, the cornerstone of getting the needed capital is understanding the old cliché that "Money talks and ... Oh well, the other stuff walks." Companies must be weary of wasting their time on the later. So what's an entrepreneur to do?

Colors can paint different pictures. Take the smash hit TV series last year titled "Orange is the New Black," about a gal who finds herself in a women's prison wearing the ubiquitous orange jumpsuit.

Marketing yourself as the company for which "red is the new black" and attracting necessary capital takes a strong stomach and no fear of rejection. Most importantly, you need a decent idea with a practiced ability to deliver a compelling pitch to sell it, backed by thoughtfully researched assumptions.

Never forget, however, that just like the tagline in the oil filter TV commercial, when you take OPM, aka "other people's money," you have to either "pay them now or pay them later" regardless of how you color your story.

A fool and his money soon part

Make sure your kids never go barefoot

This column was originally published in April 2009

This column is a deviation from my usual themes about how to be a strategic leader with an entrepreneurial bent. Instead, this month I explore why executives may be effective at running businesses but frequently fall short in managing their own money. Like many businesses leaders, I thought I was a street-smart steward of my own portfolio of stocks, bonds, hedge funds and private equity. Then came a wake-up call, manifested by what I would characterize as a less than amicable separation between a double-digit percentage of my assets and me.

During recent market gyrations, assets that took most of us years to accumulate and build were significantly reduced in mere months. There were warning signs. One word kept popping up on prognosticators' radar: subprime. This was quickly followed by dire predictions that some of the world's more storied financial institutions could crumble faster, under the weight of toxic loans, than their counterparts did during the infamous 1906 San Francisco earthquake.

Sure, in hindsight, I knew there were troubles brewing. I read The Wall Street Journal daily and Barron's Financial Weekly. In addition, just like President Barack Obama, nothing comes between me and breaking news from my BlackBerry — nothing.

So why did I and the vast majority of other executives experience a precipitous and cataclysmic exodus of assets damaging not only one's net worth but ego, as well?

There are apt comparisons between why the shoemaker's children go barefoot, why the person who represents himself in court has a fool for a client and, yes, why business executives are many times pretty mediocre investment advisers to themselves.

The core issue gets down to priorities, energy and the fact that there are only 24 hours in a day. Business leaders in today's environment must have an unrelenting laser focus on running their organizations. This, however, can result in one-dimensional thinking.

How many times has your spouse or significant other told you that you don't listen? Case in point, at breakfast you review your previous day's business results and your spouse asks you a question, as in, "What would you like to do this weekend?" and you respond by passing the sugar. This is simply an example of time and attention limitations, not lack of interest.

Certainly, you know the mechanics of the markets, you know where you have investments, but at the end of the day, after dealing with myriad business issues and opportunities, you just run out of gas. Because you may be good at making money doesn't mean you have the discipline and expertise not only to preserve it but also to grow it.

What can we do differently to rebuild our assets, while not losing a beat in doing our all-consuming day jobs? Compartmentalize, compartmentalize, compartmentalize!

Just as you set aside specific time to focus on various aspects of your work, you also must compartmentalize your personal investments and then devote time to them on a regular basis.

Start by scheduling some solitary time with yourself to know what direction your portfolio is going and, more importantly, where you want to take it over the next three to five years. It gets down to something as simple as three sessions every two weeks or some sort of quiet time with yourself. During the first session, review whether your portfolio has been either up, down or sideways. In the second time slot, try to understand how and why it got there. Devote the third review to new investment ideas and consider any adjustments.

Managing a portfolio is much akin to playing a hand of poker, during which you must decide to call, raise or fold. Just like in business, if you hesitate too long, you may lose. Treat your investment reviews the same as you would an update with a subordinate. Establish performance parameters, make notes and always assign yourself follow-up action dates.

It's going to take some time to rebuild our portfolios. Remember it took an astonishing 25 years for the Dow Jones Industrial Average to return to its pre-1929 crash levels. However, with some discipline, a plan and perhaps a decent adviser, you can at least ensure that your kids will always have shoes and you won't feel like a fool whose investments deteriorate from passive neglect.

6

Innovation

Stirring the pot for success

This column was originally published in July 2005

As a founder and former CEO of a *Fortune* 500 company, I have given more then a thousand talks and speeches over a 16-year span. Invariably during each presentation's question and answer session that followed, like clockwork I would be asked the obligatory question: What is a CEO's or manager's most important role in an organization? No doubt, the audience expected a pat textbook-type response such as: build a team, accelerate sales and profits, and increase shareholders' value. Sure all of these are "must do" critically important objectives and provide a barometer in one form or another of effectiveness and success.

My answer, however, to this age old question was and still is, "A Boss's Job is to Stir the Pot." I disdain the status quo. The trite phrase "if it ain't broke, don't fix it" sets me off and the comment "same old, same old" about a business's progress is the first sign that the company is heading to eventual obscurity. One of the truly fun aspects of being a boss is that, at times, you get to make up certain rules of exploration and engagement. You establish the goals, create the expectations, and determine the measurements.

One of the biggest ills facing small, medium and, yes, even *Fortune* 500 companies is inertia. If you were at least half-awake in high school physics, you should know that inertia is "the tendency to resist acceleration unless disturbed by an external force." If you are the boss, you need to be that external force for continuous, systematic change and innovation, poised to seize the moment and capitalize on unique opportunities when presented. Good and great companies, institutions, and organizations not only serve their customers' current needs, but also anticipate new needs which customers have yet to even recognize.

Fifteen years ago, did the world know it needed email to communicate? I seriously doubt it. Twenty-five years ago, did anyone guess that cellphones would become virtually ubiquitous around the world carried by tens of millions of consumers from pre-pubescent boys and girls all the way to seasoned executives? I think not. Instead, somewhere, some place there was a leader — a pot stirrer extraordinaire — challenging others to think and to improve a product, process or procedure.

In rare moments of brilliance, companies have devised new products or services for which there was no rational need at the time, but convinced consumers that their revolutionary thingamajig, widget, or service would fulfill their wildest dreams and fondest expectations or something in between. Some were revolutionary such as the computer chip and all of its permutations, others mundane like bottled water that today is sold annually worldwide to the tune of $35 billion with six billion gallons alone in the U.S.

The writer, George Bernard Shaw had the right idea when he authored the line in his play on creative evolution Back to Methuselah: "Some men see things that are and ask why, I dream of things that never were and ask why not." The late brother of President John F. Kennedy, Sen. Robert F. Kennedy, adopted this phase as his passionate rallying cry for change and new solutions to old problems in speeches he gave throughout the early and mid-1960s.

Were George Bernard Shaw and RFK nefarious warlock-type cauldron stirrers with self serving ulterior motives? Depending on one's political persuasion or historic perspective, arguably not. Instead, both were inertia fighters, a title that I think is synonymous with being a great leader. RFK forced people to think and, in short, to challenge conventional wisdom and past practices.

Leaders have to stay one step ahead, at the very least, just to play in the game. When something is working well, they prod and sometimes poke their people to make it work even better and then better again. When there is a possible need, albeit remote, the boss must motivate the team to find an answer. There is a life cycle for everything and the clock is always ticking with the alarm set to ring ushering in the new when someone finds a better way. Just look at the rotary dial phone and buggy whips, washboards and big propeller passenger airplanes. They served a purpose, but their time came and went. Give your people the opportunity to explore, to think, and to dream. You won't be perceived as the Wicked Witch or Warlock of the West, but instead the leader with a recipe for winning — a leader who knows how to stir the pot and let it simmer for success.

Forging unlikely alliances?
How strange bedfellows can make effective strategic partners

This column was originally published in August 2007

William Shakespeare, in addition to being a great playwright, was a very savvy, strategic thinker. His writing reflects insights and valuable business concepts. In his 1611 play "The Tempest" about a shipwreck, Shakespeare's lead character who faces possible death proclaims that "misery acquaints a man with "strange bedfellows." As this literary nugget of wisdom suggests, one can forge an alliance with virtually anyone when the objective is clear and the bottom line results benefit all involved. Who says a partner always has to be on your side? What is necessary is that an alliance be crafted which allows a win/win for each collaborator.

Another theatrical work, arguably of lesser intellect, provides further evidence of this thesis. In the book and movie "The Godfather," Michael Corleone gives an order to his consigliore to arrange a meeting with a rival mob boss moments after he attempted to kill Michael. The young Godfather explained that he was taught by his sage father to "keep your friends close and your enemies closer." For decades we have all heard strategists, diplomats and politicians offer similar pearls of wisdom, including "the enemy of my enemy is my friend."

In the day-to-day business world, you can employ these same concepts to achieve an objective, provided that at the end of the day you are still standing after the unexpected collaboration with your "strange bedfellow." A couple of caveats, however: be sure the bedfellow isn't packing heat and avoid meeting in the back of a dimly lit restaurant near the bathroom where a weapon that could do you harm might be hidden.

Let's examine a situation in which you can create an ad hoc, special-purpose confederacy. Assume for this exercise you are involved in attempting to get a governing body/organization to provide an exception or allow something that has never occurred in the past to take place.

As an example you have big trucks that exceed the weight limit for using a road that could save you 30 minutes each trip to a construction site. Instead, your drivers have to take the long way around to comply with the ordinance. You also have a big competitor who needs to use this same road for a different project but can't because of the like truck weight problem. Working together you could both go to the community and offer to pay for two very expensive, much need traffic lights at either end of the road and to repair the road if the trucks damage it after the projects are completed. Voila! You would have a three-way win for all involved, even though each party might not be too enamored with either of the others. By creating an unlikely alliance, you could gain critical mass and a common voice.

So how do you get the ball rolling? You certainly could go out and hire a bunch of attorneys to write a position paper on why what you want to do is for the greater good. The document could then be sent to the governing body or media to see what happens. With this strategy you can be sure that your fees for getting to this point will be expensive and, probably, there is less than a 50/50 chance that this effort will be successful.

While it may seem counter-intuitive, you need to swallow hard and devise a plan to change the rules of competitive engagement, at least temporarily, by directly or indirectly approaching the heretofore rival head-on. If you aren't comfortable with the idea of just picking up the phone and making your pitch to your foresworn enemy, there are numerous effective methods to broker a conversation and a "meet." Third parties, such as mutual suppliers, your accountant, or even a friend of a friend can do the heavy lifting without you running the risk of personal embarrassment or rejection.

Simply do your homework and carefully outline a script for your vicar representative that succinctly explains what you want to do and, most importantly, why a coalition will work for all parties. You just might be very surprised at the positive back-channel response you receive to your offer.

This type of scenario is played out daily in government, diplomacy, and even in junior high school with a seventh grade boy having another classmate (not even a friend, but someone who has something else to gain) ask the cute freckled-face girl for a date on his behalf. Don't get hung up on this self-serving collaboration as it does not mean that you will have to stop preaching to your employees and associates, in sometimes graphic and candid terms, why your competitor or competitors don't deserve this or that. A temporary "détente" does not signify the end of a war.

If you still can't suck it in and be comfortable with "sleeping with the enemy," just tell yourself: "It's nothing personal, it's just business." A line we've all heard dozens of times for the past six years on HBO on Sunday nights at 9 p.m. and in hundreds of grade B movies. The truth is, if you're an innovative thinker, it really is just business … smart business.

Follow the leader
Why it's not always the best game to play

This column was originally published in August 2008

How many times have you stood at a busy crosswalk with other pedestrians waiting for the "Don't Walk" signal to flash to "Walk"? How many times have you along with other unsuspecting pedestrians entered the crosswalk before the sign changed because one "leader" prematurely elected to proceed across the street? The lesson in this example is that blindly following the leader is not always to your best advantage and can sometimes be downright dangerous.

Think about where most leaders get their ideas and inspirations. Certainly, they do some analysis, read the papers, watch TV and check the Internet. No doubt, they also talk to associates, consult the usual suspect experts, such as barbers/hairdressers, taxi drivers and probably even have periodic pillow talks with whomever, just like all of us. After digesting and distilling all of this critical data, the experts have an "aha" moment and promulgate their epiphany of the next trend, be it where the stock market and economy are heading, what the consumer will need tomorrow or how companies must change. Just as sure as the sun sets in the west, the majority of business executives aren't much different from the people at crosswalks. Without any qualms or questions, they fall into lockstep and follow the leader before really thinking about where they're going and if it's even safe.

In business, wisdom is the ability to discover alternatives. Let's examine other methods of creating a new strategy, playing the stock market, buying real estate or pursuing whatever else is your vice or pleasure. No matter what you're trying to accomplish in order for your company to cope with change, fundamental bottom-up analysis is the best starting point. You must also think as a contrarian and create alternative scenarios that are applicable to your specific circumstance. Be creative in your thinking but not outrageous. You're not looking for a one-in-a- million chance to win the lottery. Instead, figure out how to adapt your business to meet your customers' altered needs and counter their resistance points.

Dreaming of "what could be and should be" has a place in your analysis process. However, your dreams must be grounded and fact-based. Look at your current business environment and then ask, "How can we do it differently from others, and how can we turn a negative into a positive?" Don't be intimidated by what the leaders are saying and doing, but instead, study what your customers want and then figure out creative methods to deliver it in a manner that will knock their socks off.

Here is a hypothetical solution using contrarian thinking. Assume you own a health spa 50 miles from the center of town. Gas prices are reaching new highs every day while environmentalists are turning up the volume about the negative effects of gasoline on the planet. Prominent "thought leaders" aggressively tell the populous to stay close to home to save money on fuel and, at the same time, help reduce air pollution by driving less. If you simply played "follow the leader," you'd be calling a real estate agent to move your spa from its pastoral setting to the urban center. Instead, you turn lemons into lemonade by adding free luxurious limo pickup and return service for your clients so they don't have to pay for the gas. To deal with the environmental piece, you promote the fact that your limo is a hybrid or runs on big electric batteries and/or has a very long extension cord.

In 1929 when the stock market crashed, many investors were doing half gainers off tall buildings while others on Wall Street wisely chose not to follow and instead became buyers. After the devastating trauma of Sept. 11, New York City real estate prices plummeted over predications of pending economic doom. However, the "smart money" started buying previously coveted properties at bargain prices and eventually reaped huge profits.

Use difficult times to your advantage by challenging common

wisdom and searching for innovative opportunities and solutions. Following the leader can sometimes be OK, but very seldom are the results great. Buying straw hats in the winter and not becoming an automaton follower can be very profitable for your organization and you.

An exaggerated sense of your own importance can stifle new ideas

Simple techniques to discover fresh concepts and solutions

This column was originally published in April 2011

As an executive, do you walk down the hall of your office, store or factory with your head down, lips sealed and eyes riveted to the floor? If you do, you're creating a barrier that is sending signals that say, "Don't speak to me, I am not approachable, and I don't care about your opinion or ideas. I'm the head honcho; I already know it all." Conversely, if you traverse the halls and byways of your facility with your head up, a smile on your face and making eye contact with those you encounter, you're telling employees, "Talk to me, tell me what you think, suggest how can we do it better."

Nonverbal communications speak volumes about your style of management and how receptive you are to new ideas without worrying about who comes up with them. The best CEOs are the ones who know their people's first names, a little bit about their personal life and their jobs. They also regularly communicate with their associates by asking questions and seeking suggestions. If you don't want to speak to anyone, just don't look at them, and they'll get the message, but you'll run the risk of ignoring that low-hanging fruit that is always there if you just look for it.

Many good ideas come from people who spend their time in the trenches, building the product, dealing with your customers, or listening to their concerns and complaints. The best ways of turning negatives into positives are first understanding the problems and then discovering alternatives to prevent them in the future. No one knows these issues better than the people in your organization who have to deal with them every day.

To get your people to open up, first you have to get out of your own office and become visible. When you're visible on a continuous basis, you become accessible. Accessibility leads to innovation as well as creating solutions to issues from the mundane to the complex. Once you start walking about on a regular basis, you also have to learn how to ask questions when the opportunity arises. Certainly, it's fine to ask someone, "How are you doing today?" Not only is it polite, but it also reflects that you care about the individual. However, combining that inquiry with one of more substance that deals with known problems can lead to effective solutions or put you on the right path to solving the problem by getting input on the circumstances that may have caused it in the first place. Most everyone has an opinion, and all of us want to have a sounding board. If that sounding board is a top executive or the CEO, that's even better. Asking relevant questions engages employees and encourages give-and-take communications.

Try this technique the next time you walk through your facility. Before you get up from behind your desk, ask yourself what the problems du jour are and what do you need to know so that you can solve them. As a simple example, if there is a known bottleneck in the shipping and receiving area, instead of just reading a memo about the problem from the supervisor, take a stroll over to the loading dock with a couple of questions in mind. There is no law that only good ideas have to come from you and your management team. By asking those involved with the process why there are problems, you might just get an answer or two that spawns the fix you need. Listening is a skill that all of us have to develop and nurture. But, before you can listen, you have to be sure that your people are willing to talk to you and with you.

It's almost guaranteed that if you have an exaggerated sense of your own importance, you'll not only stifle new ideas but you might never find answers to nagging problems. One little gem, one golden nugget of information can translate into bottom-line improvement. An ongoing string of these gems can help make your company an industry leader while enhancing your employees' sense of importance and ownership in the process. These methods also show you value employees' opinions and you expect them to have opinions on how to do their job better. Tomorrow, leave your ego at home and start your discovery process, then watch your business grow.

If it ain't broke, break it now

Every business must change or become a victim of change

This column was originally published in January 2012

One of the worst hackneyed clichés is "If it ain't broke, don't fix it." If this is your way of doing business, then it is a good bet that it's just a matter of time until you hit that big bump in the road and the wheels fall off your wagon. It may start as a small crack in the underlying pavement of your strategy, manifesting itself as a minor issue with an inquiring customer asking when are you going to do this or that, but you can be sure that this slight whisper will build to that proverbial shout. Face it, whether you like it or not, you're doing business and competing in an age where existing and prospective customers have access to instant information. This includes quickly discovering the first inkling of the "new best thing" that the "next Steve Jobs" has cooking in his or her garage — something that just might be a breakthrough or meaningful, innovation in your industry.

Customer loyalty today is based on a "What have you done for me lately?" mentality. It's mandatory that your employees be on a constant vigil for how to improve. For customers to be loyal to you, they have to know that you're always improving and on the prowl for how to do it better or how to find new solutions to new problems sometimes before your customers even know they might have a problem.

To be a player, you have to devote time, effort and, yes, money to perpetual research and development. R&D is not just for tech companies or manufacturers but also for companies that plan to be around tomorrow. Even small businesses, as basic as a cleaning service, have to be on the lookout for anything that can do it better: from the latest vacuum to a new cleaning chemical that proves to be a better solution (pun intended). Retailers, too, are constantly changing store presentations as well as merchandise. In most businesses, the real villain is inertia, which leads to complacency from within and customer boredom from the same old product even if it's working. When each side of an ongoing relationship starts taking one another for granted, it's just a matter of time before problems begin to percolate.

Certainly money is tight for small and big companies alike, and the bean counters are quick to give R&D expenses an evil eye. Unfortunately, and even understandably, it's usually the first thing cut when sales slow and when banks start tightening leading covenants. The justification is typically that innovation needs to be put on hold because there is no immediate return on the investment.

The bigger question for the CEO is, "Are these types of expenses nice or necessary?" I vehemently would argue it's the latter. Why do car companies perpetually come out with new models with new gadgets every year? Why do technology companies introduce version 1.0, and then, six months later, come out with version 1.1? The answer to both is, "to keep a product fresh and compelling." It's about creating a degree of planned obsolescence to ensure that a product doesn't become commoditized, which can spell the beginning of the end. As soon as that happens, a company's trophy product will be knocked off and made more cheaply by someone who doesn't have overhead expenses as high as the originator and who will surely cut the price and the incumbent's heart at the same time.

Make sure you're stirring the pot, asking questions of your team members, making it their charge to dig for even the most elusive answers. This leads to innovation, which is followed by creating elasticity for your products because you'll have found a way to make your widget better and more economical. In turn, this can increase demand and produce planned obsolescence for the older version. To do otherwise, companies run the big risk of being victims of their own initial success.

It all gets down to changing or being a casualty of change. When you improve your business, you can continue to dazzle your customers and hopefully keep them, which will make your business grow, allow sales and profits to increase and create more jobs. This is the heart of capitalism. So, if it ain't broke, make sure you break it.

Reliable but not predictable

Keeping employees guessing can be effective in driving creativity

This column was originally published in May 2013

When you flip a light switch, turn on the water or start your car, you expect reliability every time. For employees, it's just as mandatory that they be reliable, by showing up on time, completing the tasks at hand and basically doing their jobs time and time again.

By the same token, your employees expect you, as their leader, to be reliable. This means when you say you'll do something, you do it, when they need direction, you provide it, and when the chips are down, you'll be there for them.

Being reliable is good, but being too predictable — not always. In fact, being too conventional can make your company a "me, too" organization that only reacts to what the competition does, rather than taking the lead. It can be a bit more daring to set the trend, but if managed and controlled correctly, the rewards dramatically outweigh the risks.

Warning signs that your leadership has become too predictable occur when your subordinates begin finishing your sentences and know what you will think and say before you utter that first word on just about every topic. Compounding the problem is when your employees begin to perpetuate the negative effect of you being so darn predicable by believing it themselves and telling others, "Don't even think about that; there's no point bringing up your idea about X, Y or Z because the boss will shoot you down before you take your next breath." This bridles creativity and stifles people's thinking and

234

stretching for new ideas.

It's human nature for subordinates to want to please the chief. Under the right circumstances, that can be good, particularly if you are the chief. But it can be a very bad thing if you are looking for fresh concepts that have never before been run up the flagpole.

Uniqueness is the foundation of innovation and the catalyst for breaking new ground. George Bernard Shaw, the noted Irish playwright and co-founder of the London School of Economics, characterized innovation best when he wrote: "Some look at things that are and ask why. I dream of things that never were and ask why not?"

The "why not" portion of this quote is the lifeblood of every organization. A status quo attitude can ultimately do a company in, as it will just be a matter of time until somebody finds a better way.

As a leader, the first step in motivating people to reach higher is to dispel the image that you're exclusively a predictable, same-old, same-old type of executive who wants things a certain way every time. There are dozens of signals that a boss can give to alter a long-standing image and dispel entrenched mindsets. You can always have a midlife crisis and show up at work in a Porsche or Ferrari instead of your unremarkable Buick. This flash of flamboyance will certainly get people questioning what they thought was sacrosanct about you. The cool car might also be a lot of fun; however, the theatrics might be a bit over the top for some, not to mention a costly stage prop just to send a message.

A better solution is to begin modifying how you interface with your team, how you answer inquiries from them and, most importantly, how to ask open-ended questions that are not your typical, "How do we do this or that?"

Another technique is when somebody begins to answer your question, before you've finished asking, particularly in a meeting, abruptly interrupt the person. Next, throw him off guard by stating, "don't tell us what we already know." Instead, assert that you're looking for ideas about how to reinvent whatever it is you want reinvented or improved in giant steps as opposed to evolutionary baby steps. If you're feeling particularly bold, for emphasis, try abruptly just getting up and walking out of the meeting. In short order, your associates will start thinking differently. They'll cease providing you with the answers they think you want. Some players will hate the new you, but the good ones will rise to the occasion and sharpen their games.

If you want reliability, flip the light switch. To jump-start innovation, you could begin driving that head-turning sports car. Better yet, get your team thinking by how you ask and answer questions and by not always being 100 percent predictable but always reliable.

How not to paint yourself into a corner
Use a bucket and never say never

This column was originally published in June 2013

This column is not a how-to painting guide for business executives — I'll leave that to the experts at Sherwin-Williams. Instead, I offer a few suggestions on preserving ideas for future exploration and innovation. Let me explain further.

Hindering creativity typically rears its inhibiting, ugly head when you make definitive statements, either verbally to others or in the confines of your own mind, and too quickly dismiss new ideas as being too farfetched. We've all been there. How many times have you said, "Not on my watch," or, "I'm drawing a line in the sand on that matter," and sometimes adding for emphasis, "That will happen only over my dead body"?

Eating your words, even years later, can likely cause severe indigestion and can sometimes result in choking that could bring on a premature demise of that next big thing. Littering the bottom of the corporate sea are concepts with promising potential that executives, with the flick of the wrist, pooh-poohed. Most times, that was simply because there wasn't enough time to deal with the unknown or because of myopia and the lack of an inclination to push the envelope. It doesn't take much talent to say no, but it takes leadership and creativity to take a germ of an idea to the next level. And it takes true vision to shepherd a new anything through the difficult trial-and-error gauntlet.

Close-minded responses to the unproven are not just limited to management. Politicians particularly have a unique knack of painting themselves into a corner with unlikely promulgations that frequently

237

come back to haunt them in November after the opposite occurs. Backpedaling is probably the method most politicians use to get their exercise.

In a 1966 *Time* magazine print edition feature story, this then-prestigious publication asserted, "Remote shopping, while feasible, will flop because women like to handle the merchandise and, with so much time on their hands, want to get out of the house." Someone might want to email Time and ask the publisher how to spell Amazon.

There are alternatives to summarily stymieing thoughts, dreams or unproven methods. Certainly, there is a time and place for everything, and frequently, you or your team may not have adequate resources, at a particular moment, to pursue every idea that comes down the pike. Instead of saying no, a more fitting response is to say or think, "Let's put that idea on a back burner so that we can for the moment focus on more conventional solutions, at least, for the shorter term." This leaves the door open for continued research and refinement of an idea that could ultimately evolve into something meaningful.

Here is where the bucket from my headline comes in to preserve an incomparable yet promising notion that, at the moment, might be superfluous to the task at hand but, at the right time and place, proves to be a killer idea. I use the word bucket as a euphemism for a holding place or repository for things that I may want to explore when the time is right. Certainly, one cannot investigate every idea ever pondered, but at least by retaining all such ideas in one place, they are always there for future consideration when either more is learned about the subject matter or when comments begin surfacing in the media or elsewhere touching on that similar idea you've kept tucked away.

Your very own bucket can also become a temporary refuge merely to take your mind off other, more thorny problems or a simple respite from the day-to-day grind when you're looking for a new inspiration. Alternatively, at the end of the year, remove the mothballs from your bucket and review what you've deposited. A fresh look just might ignite a former idea, which then takes on a new life of its own.

Anyone who has ever painted a room already knows not to wind up in a corner, lest they may never get out. Worse yet, more open-minded competitors could use that bucket to throw cold water on an idea that you had earlier but never capitalized on it while they did.

Why every company needs an additional type of COO

They march to a different drummer; are hard-to-find; and some companies don't admit they have or covet one

This column was originally published in March 2014

We all know what traditional chief operating officers do and what characteristics typically make them tick. There is another type of COO that every company needs — whether they admit it or not — who shares the same initials as the former, but who has diametric responsibilities.

This person is a chief opportunity officer, although the title sometimes varies because the word opportunity conveys the wrong message to the less pragmatic.

The characteristics of this rare bird were probably honed when he or she was a small child. Most parents didn't talk much about this offspring's special traits outside the home.

High-energy personalities

We have all seen these kids in action. They have too much energy, are in perpetual motion and feel compelled to touch everything in sight.

They also ask questions and make statements that can shock or antagonize even the most understanding adult.

When they go off to school, they're the ones who neglect to raise their hands when answering questions, but instead blurt out their responses. And most of the time they're right, which tends to further aggravate teachers.

At their first job, they continue to be in constant motion,

questioning everyone, everything and sometimes ignoring the chain of command. At the same time, however, they seem to discover previously unthought-of alternatives to thorny issues.

If they're lucky, a more senior manager spots the hidden talents of this potential COO and begins instilling a little, much needed, discipline and tutoring on the realities of being politically correct to get things done.

In short order, this heretofore rogue player begins to climb the organizational ladder, scoring a series of meaningful and unique accomplishments. This garners heightened recognition and a reputation as someone who can think outside the box and isn't afraid to take well-calculated risks.

Making waves comes easy
Many of these iconoclasts' ideas seem at first blush to be prosaic — the idea so obvious and simple it leaves everyone in the organization scratching their heads asking, "Why didn't I think of that?" Other times, what initially seems to be an off-the-wall concept suddenly takes shape and emerges as a breakthrough.

We all know the names of innovators who have excelled and possessed the characteristics described. Some are famous business rock stars, such as the legendary Steve Jobs of Apple or Facebook's Mark Zuckerberg. Others are unknown hidden gems within the ranks of America's most admired, successful companies.

Many times companies don't parade them in public, due to the commotion they invariably cause — the same reasons their parents exposed them sparingly to outsiders.

This type of innovator devotes his or her energy to looking for low-hanging fruit, or that special something that can transform a business from the ordinary to the extraordinary.

Their techniques are non-conventional and they frequently ruffle feathers. Usually for them to succeed, they must work in an organization that recognizes the fact that not everyone has to be cut from the same cloth.

Every once in a while, these one-time outcasts emerge as the leader of the enterprise with the letter "E" replacing the middle "O" in their earlier title. After that occurs, the newly minted CEO will deny to the death that he was ever the kid whose parents were reluctant to take anywhere.

7

Overcoming Challenges

Who is in charge?

For business as usual consensus management works, but when crisis strikes it's time for a benevolent dictator to take charge

This column was originally published in December 2005

The tragic events of this fall's Hurricane Katrina that devastated the Gulf States and flooded much of New Orleans are now indelibly etched in our collective memories. During a two-week period from the onset of this storm until the crisis ebbed, Americans were transfixed on the television coverage which not only brought us graphic examples of the fury of Mother Nature and human suffering, but also provided a classic business lesson on the effects of poor preparation, mismanagement, and accountability. The initial mishandled response begged the question: "Who was in charge?"

A lesson learned from the handling of this disaster should also be permanently ingrained in the minds of all organizational and corporate leaders. Fact is bad stuff happens. Unfortunately, it usually happens when it is least expected and the only way to deal effectively with bad things is to be prepared and determine beforehand who will be the boss — who is in charge.

Virtually every business and organization, no matter the size or scope, needs a plan of action to deal with contingencies. These contingencies can be anything from an employee strike, a natural disaster, all the way to a bank or credit agency calling a loan or cutting a rating with a myriad of other possibilities in between such as a restaurant patron finding a foreign object or worse in its soup de jour. The Boy Scouts motto says it best: "be prepared" all the while hoping your response guide will never have to be taken from the shelf, dusted off and implemented.

Obviously it is difficult to anticipate every possibility, but with a good general road map of what to do, you will have a working model to guide you when the unthinkable surfaces. This plan is prepared in the same manner, with the same meticulous thought process that goes into a business or financial plan, a marketing strategy, or dealing with a worse case scenario.

Start by creating the following:

1. Predetermine when an event arises, how it will be communicated and whom within the organization must be alerted. In crisis mode, there is no time for "cover your backside" type emails. Instead the word needs to be spread the old fashioned way, by walking over and telling whomever needs to know. If the people who must be brought into the loop are not all in the same building, use the phone, and the best practice is, try and gather everyone together within a room and/or by telephonic conference call and do it as measured in seconds and minutes not hours.

2. Have a pre-established method and protocol for gathering as much information as fast as possible on the situation preferably from someone at ground zero. Designate the people who will manage the problem and be sure they each have a proven track record of dealing in facts, rather than succumbing to emotion. This is no time to have anyone involved who has a propensity for hyperbole or hysteria on your management response team.

3. If there is a physical or safety problem, take care of the people first and foremost, and the organization's assets last. This isn't just good PR and associate relations; it is the right thing to do.

4. Rehearse scenarios on how to handle the most likely events. We all did it starting in elementary school with fire drills, and flight attendants do it every time before a plane's wheels leave the runway.

5. The person put in charge, must take charge. He or she must provide leadership, make decisions and be prepared with plan

A and B. When plan A is not working, much like what occurred in the first few days of the Katrina response, have stand by plan B ready to pull from the hip pocket. Most importantly, don't be afraid to make changes quickly. In crises, people need and want to follow. There is only room for one boss. During Katrina, the government finally came to its senses and put a cigar-chomping, three-star Army Lieutenant General, Russel Honoré, in charge. Aptly he was known as the "Ragin' Cajun" and a throwback to another era replicating the flamboyant general from a scene out of the movie Patton. This leader in New Orleans knew how to take charge, make things happen, and didn't mince words or stand on ceremony. He also quickly manifested a sense of hope.

During business as usual, there can be an important need for consensus building management; but in a crisis, it is time for a benevolent dictator to take over quickly.

When establishing your crisis plan, let everyone in the organization know in advance who's running the show by putting it in writing. An example of the wrong way to do it was when former Secretary of State Alexander Haig proclaimed in March 1981 after President Ronald Reagan was shot, "I'm in control here." The lesson to learn in this case is that one cannot be a self-appointed leader in a crisis situation. Secretary Haig neglected a minor detail of the Constitution which provided for an order of succession which was different from his promulgation.

We all hope in our personal lives and business that a crisis never occurs. However, when it does, be prepared to triage the situation and have your team ready to take control. There is no genius involved in this process, as it is probably closer to 1 percent inspiration and 99 percent perspiration, but it has worked in the past and it will work in the future when those involved know who is in charge and the leader takes charge, although cigar chomping is certainly optional.

Solving problems before they rise to biblical proportions

How to run a small business like a *Fortune* 500 company, and a big business like a startup

This column was originally published in October 2006

From time to time we all want to be something we're not. Running a *Fortune* 500 company, as I did for many years, I would bemoan the trials and tribulations of dealing with layers of management, outside and inside auditors, various and sundry attorneys and ubiquitous regulators. On the flipside, when I first started the company, I frequently fantasized about what it would be like to be a CEO of a huge organization with a bevy of executives doing the day-to-day heavy lifting, with legions of lawyers, and all kinds of accountants to calculate and analyze anything and everything.

So where is the happy medium, when you can have your cake and eat it, too? In my case after transitioning from a startup to a medium-size and then multibillion-dollar company, I realized you can have it both ways. The best of both worlds is to run a company the same no matter the size, number of employees, or geographic breadth. Sweat the little stuff while focusing on the big picture. Recognize your customers' needs, preferably before they do. and execute your plan efficiently and effectively with a sense of urgency. One of the few big differences is that when the company is big there are many more "zeros" at the end of the dollar sign. However, when starting out the smaller number of "zeros" after the dollar sign is just as important, if not more so, in terms of succeeding or just staying in business.

In a small company you keep your ear to the ground, usually knowing the answers before others even ask the questions, and watching the cash every single day. Equally critical understand the trends, your employees' biggest concerns and your competitors' strengths and weaknesses. In a *Fortune* 500 company it's not much different except that your reports and P&Ls are delivered to you in fancier binders. Typically you'll review the figures weekly instead of daily, and if you're smart you will still think and worry about them every day anyway.

Big, small or in-between, you must frequently hold both formal and informal updates with your key people. My style was to do it weekly or bi-weekly unless the project could be a deal-breaker or ship-sinker, in which case I'd be briefed as needed, even once or twice daily. Size should never be a factor governing the flow of critical information. Opportunity many times comes disguised as a negative and your job, no matter the size of your company, is to develop that "sixth sense" to recognize the issue and then take action.

You must structure lines of reporting and methods of operation, no matter the organization's size, to always allow you and your key people to keep your pulse on the business in real-time. History has proven that it doesn't take long, sometimes measured in mere weeks, to have a business "turn south" with a vengeance.

Some may say if you're staying on top of the business you're a "micromanager." I say, bunk! If you're in charge, then take charge. When things go wrong because someone let something important fall through the cracks, nobody is going to remember that you were "The Great Delegator." During the first 18 months of my then new company, I required every store to call my home seven nights a week to give me the sales for the day, which I would then record in a simple ledger bound book. This was an easy task when we had the first two or three stores, but it became more of a time commitment when we got to 25 outlets, mitigated by geographic locations in different time zones. However, this ritual enabled us to rapidly grow the company by managing cash flow with an emphasis on accounts payable down to the last few dollars.

Every night, albeit way past midnight, I would know what vendors I could pay the next day. Micromanagement? You bet and proud of it! This protocol not only accelerated our growth but set a management style for executives to operate their own areas in a similar "know what's happening" fashion. After our next surge of growth I reluctantly took my wife's strong suggestion, stopped the incessant nocturnal phone calls and graduated to a headquarters' answering machine for stores to call. This was finally followed by the inevitable computerization. As we broke through the ranks from small to large, the procedures weren't much different other than the daily cash management was delegated, and my senior executives and I reviewed the numbers at the beginning of every week.

As they say "the devil is in the details." That doesn't mean that the CEO has to manage the details but, if not, the CEO must be sure that the person delegated to do so is inflicted with at least a mild dose of paranoia and a smidgeon of fear of failure, which tends to keep the best managers on top of their game.

At the end of the day, to prevent small, garden variety problems from accelerating to Biblical proportions, you must manage the process and be tuned in to the flow of factual information on a real-time basis. The delicate balance comes into play knowing how and when to run the place like a *Fortune* 500 company, or a Ma and Pa Candy Store, depending on the circumstances. Remember, one size never fits all and events and circumstances dictate your tactics. This means that you as the boss, must instinctively understand when to be an observer and when you must get your hands very dirty, very quickly, to survive, to succeed or to excel.

What to do when the wolf is at your door

Make sure that all the huffing and puffing doesn't blow your business in

This column was originally published in November 2006

One thing that everyone who runs a business or organization knows is that typically, when you least expect it, "stuff" happens. Sometimes that "stuff" can potentially be very, very damaging. So what happens when you find the wolf huffing and puffing at your front door?

How should the CEO, owner or leader react and respond to a negative situation? One thing that never works, and can sometimes dig one into a deeper hole, is to claim immediately and summarily there is no problem. The worst tactic is to deny, deny, deny, before knowing all of the facts, only to find out thereafter that there are issues that need addressing.

Like it or not, perception many times becomes reality. If someone is claiming there is an issue, then in some form or fashion it must become your immediate issue. The urgency with which you respond to the situation depends on who's doing the huffing and puffing. In the back of your mind never forget that usually where there is smoke there is fire, and becoming instantly defensive because you've been challenged or your ego is bruised can set you and your organization up for even more ancillary problems. Reacting with righteous indignation is a no-no.

Every day there are new reports about this company or that organization which finds itself in the spotlight, and it's not because they're about to receive an Academy Award. Just read the paper any day and you'll learn about claims being made against a myriad of companies. It can be anything from the current, infamous transgression of backdating stock options by a public corporation in order to give the option recipients a lower strike price, to facing an environmental claim, an accounting problem or the ubiquitous employee harassment charges. Union threats and problems are also guaranteed to send chills down the back of even the most stoic CEO.

Once the gauntlet has been thrown down by an accuser — be it a government agency, shareholder, employee or whomever — it is time to move to the military's most serious readiness level, Defcon One, more commonly known as "Red Alert." This translates into a process of ready, aim, fire — not ready, fire, aim. Don't deny anything just yet, but instead respond by stating that the matter will receive immediate and thorough attention at the highest level of the organization. If appropriate, outside specialists must be called upon to provide a disinterested review.

Never, and I mean never, try to sweep any problem of magnitude under the carpet. After making your initial stop-gap announcement immediately bring your team together and provide leadership by meticulously vetting the initial allegations. Secondly, appoint a spokesperson who will be responsible for responding to all of your constituents, the media and public in general as, in a time of crisis, an organization/company must speak with one voice. Under certain circumstances and depending on the issue, it may be necessary to remove either a senior person who may have a vested interest in the outcome or even yourself from the review process. Impartiality and objectivity are central to resolving the issue quickly and removing any clouds of suspicion.

As soon as practical, after you have determined there is merit to the claim, move for swift resolution. Draconian albatrosses in the form of besmirching a company's reputation can linger like the scent of cheap perfume.

If you find that the negative assertions are true, or even partially true, determine an appropriate course of action commensurate with the problem and then take your medicine, no matter how bad it may taste going down. If that means terminating someone from their position for the transgression, so be it. If it means publicly stating your organization did something wrong, get on with it and just do it.

In taking action it is mandatory that you package your response so that it is comprehensive and forthright, addressing the cause of the issue. Be diligent about not insulting the public's intelligence by offering up a mere placebo or band-aid fix. The public today is cynical about business so make sure you do the right thing. It will be easier in the long run.

On the flipside, if your due diligence finds there is no merit to the claim, then weigh the cost consideration of the struggle ahead for vindication from an economic as well as time, effort and diversion standpoint. As much as I hate to say it, sometimes it's just not worth fighting the fight. However, if there will be meaningful and measurable damage in any form to your organization then prepare your defense, have your facts in hand and charge into battle, not in an emotional frenzy, but instead employing a methodical and strategic approach. As in the story of the Big Bad Wolf, just because the wolf said "Let me in, let me in" doesn't mean all the huffing and puffing will blow your business in. To refresh your memory, at the end of the fable, "The Three Little Pigs," the Wolf got just what he deserved when he was boiled in a kettle of water. Sometimes, there is justice in this world.

When to tidy up your dirty little messes

Bad economic conditions provide unique opportunities

This column was originally published in April 2008

We all have them. Some are hidden in obscure corners of a business; others are slung around the neck like the proverbial albatross. Much like barnacles that build up on the bottom of a boat, at first, they don't cause many problems, but as they accumulate, they start to slow things down and damage the veneer. Every business has its inevitable little messes — some self-inflicted, others created through being at the wrong place at the wrong time. It can be a bad hire who just doesn't get better, a less than stellar contract, or a costly piece of equipment that just never performed as promised. Like those annoying barnacles, they hang on and don't go away by themselves.

It's just a matter of when and how before you must stop ignoring these issues. The question becomes, is it better to clean up all of these transgressions in one fell swoop or endure the perpetual agony by successively fixing each problem as it becomes unbearable?

How to handle mistakes and missteps depends on a number of factors, starting with, do you own the business and report to no one, or do you have investors, banks or others to whom you are accountable? Out of the necessity of using OPM (other people's money), most businesses aren't completely independent. It's the old story about investors and lenders: You can't live with them, but most of the time you can't live without them or at least their money.

Public companies can take a page from the playbook of their publicly held cousins to learn how they deal with their big bloopers

253

and blunders. History shows us that most public companies tend to take their lumps all at once, employing a kitchen-sink strategy, ridding the organization of anything that doesn't measure up.

Dealing with these issues is much like having a terrible cold. When you're knee-deep in cough drops, decongestants and Kleenex and with aches and pains, you think that the big one is coming, and you'll soon be on your way that special boardroom in the sky. A week later, when the symptoms have subsided the good news is that brush with the Grim Reaper is all but forgotten.

Sure, public companies know that when they launch the clean-up process, their stocks will go down, the media might trash them, and investor activists and class-action attorneys will likely rattle their sabers. However, just like that bad cold, if handled properly, this too shall pass. Nonetheless, by moving with great dispatch and with a little luck, the cathartic company will be in a better position after the housecleaning and when the bumpy ride ends.

There is strength in numbers. Frequently, stocks of companies in the same business sectors move down in sympathy with each other. That's why public companies take advantage of periodic economic dips because they know they'll have the necessary cover to make their fixes. Actually, if a company is one of the standout performers in its group during tough times, naysayers will assert that it's just a matter of time until the other shoe drops and the last man standing (the company performing well) is pulled down with its peers.

For the unseasoned, all of this may sound very cynical and disingenuous. However, the ebbs and flows in the business cycle are much like biology — it's just nature's way of cleaning things up.

When business is great, almost no one thinks the trend is ever going to turn bad, and when it's bad nobody ever thinks it will get better.

To be rid of your nasty little problems, it gets down to making hard decisions. If you know something will never work, seize the opportunity at hand, and jettison the excessive baggage. Few mere business mortals are miracle workers and can fix everything without divine intervention. Learn to leave those type situations to a much higher authority.

One caveat — this cleansing cannot be undertaken in a Machiavellian, take-no-prisoners manner. Instead, have a methodical, well-reasoned plan that you share with your team as you move through the process of discarding the bad and strengthening the good.

When possible, do it at a time and place of your choosing for the greater good of all of your constituencies. The first step is to stock up on an ample supply of those cough drops and tissues to treat your woe-is-me sniffling and then begin building for a better tomorrow.

OMG — panic in the streets!
Survival lessons that must not be forgotten

This column was originally published in December 2008

OMG, texting generation's abbreviation for "Oh, my God," aptly describes the near cataclysmic financial market gyrations during the infamous last weeks of September 2008. Businesses must never forget the survival lessons that these events teach.

During those tumultuous days, Lehman Brothers, the venerable white-shoed investment banking firm, folded after 158 years. Lehman's fall followed on the heels of the Bear Stearns demise that rocked the investment world several months earlier. Little did we know that we had not seen anything yet. Next came the collapse of Fannie Mae and Freddie Mac, along with the rescue of AIG, the world's largest insurance company. Just when we thought the worst was over, Washington Mutual was seized almost in the dead of night and sold, making this the largest bank failure in history. Next came the Fed's shotgun arranged marriage, with Citigroup agreeing to buy the failing Wachovia Bank only to be usurped by Wells Fargo that triggered a shootout between the two rival bidders, which was ultimately won by Wells Fargo.

If most people hadn't been so scared or lost so much money, this wild ride would have been intellectually fascinating.

OK, what is, is. However, have we finally learned our lesson? Only time will tell. For common variety executives or owners with no hope of a government bailout if they mess up, they'd better take note if they want to continue to play in this risky game of business.

There are numerous lessons to learn from the last eight to 10 years of excess and reckless behavior that almost shattered the foundation of our system. So what were the biggies to remember and etch into the minds and hearts of your teams?

If it is too good to be true, don't believe it; it will never last.
Unprecedented growth, with little or no regard for common sense, combined with loaning money to someone who might be light on the old-fashioned requirements, such as a job and at least a credit history that provides a 50-50 chance for repayment, is a recipe for disaster. Call me a dreamer, but collateralizing a loan with something that has some value near the amount being borrowed makes good sense, too. The harsh truth here is a sobering case of financial reality — as in how many zeros are in a near trillion-dollar rescue? Here's another novel thought: Don't give customers credit when you have no clue if they can pay you back. Moreover, once you do extend credit, be all over them like a cheap suit if they start paying late.

Your first loss is your best loss.
Just ask the dead men walking — former CEOs of Lehman or Bear Stearns — who kept saying, "It isn't as bad as it looks. We'll save ourselves. We've done it before, and we can do it again." Hello bankruptcy, goodbye billions! If these Pollyannas had acted a few weeks earlier, they would have at least salvaged something for their investors. The lesson for all businesses is, always have plan A and plan B covering worst-case scenarios. Then, if everything hits the fan at once, don't be afraid to pull the trigger. Survival takes a plan combined with guts.

Forget Gordon Gekko from the movie "Wall Street" who said, "Greed is good."

It's not, and he was a jerk. There is nothing wrong with making it big, but not at the expense of others. Good business is not a zero-sum game. Always take care of your customers, investors and employees. You'll be amazed at how much good comes to you even if you're not first in line. There are many equalizers in the business world that work in mysterious ways.

This September, we saw what many pundits think was the closest thing to panic in the streets and a near meltdown that may have rivaled the big crash of 1929. What transpired in the last 15 days of this month from hell paralyzed some executives from taking action. Others had their heads on straight, such as the CEO of Merrill Lynch who saved what there was to save by merging before the lights were involuntarily turned off. Your job as an executive is to know your business and anticipate a crisis before it occurs. However, when your worst fears materialize, don't behave like a deer in the headlights.

The Boy Scouts still have the best idea: "Always be prepared."

Jumping through hoops and dodging bullets...

The new CEO two-step dance for survival

This column was originally published in January 2009

There is a new world order for CEOs and business leaders, fueled by the dramatic global economic upheaval that has sent the stock and credit markets into turmoil, not to mention the depressing effects on consumer and business spending. Today's executives must start dancing to a different tune by doing a new iteration of the traditional two-step of jumping through hoops and dodging bullets just to survive.

Warning: Previously tried and-true methods may not apply to the future and could definitely be hazardous to your very existence.

Are these words scaring you? They better. The time to act is now. You must marshal your forces to start thinking and behaving differently. There are dangers ahead as well as new positive opportunities for those who are fleet of foot.

Wisdom is the ability to discover alternatives. Challenging existing practices must become SOP, or standard operating procedure. No longer can any executive enjoy the luxury or indulge in the hubris of waiting for things to improve. Instead successful leaders will be the ones who challenge, rechallenge and, in some cases, force change by taking their people kicking and screaming over the finish line, whether they like it or not.

No area of a business can be exempt from this review. Everything is subject to scrutiny, and everybody must search for better ways.

Organizations must simultaneously start at the bottom and at the top and meet in the middle to ensure every aspect of their go-to-market process and strategy is examined. The goal is to find ways to increase revenue while reducing expenses. This sounds almost ridiculously simple, but it's surprising how many companies don't think this way.

In this new era, businesses must cut out fat and at the same time not be afraid to add initiatives that can produce a satisfactory return on a new investment of money and effort. Inertia is the enemy. Leaders must also ensure that everyone in the organization knows the promise to the customer. In retailing, it's called a "never out list." This means that if you operate a grocery store, as an example, you can never be out of milk or bread. If the store starts to run low and can't be replenished through normal sources, you must go buy these items from a competitor rather than disappoint one customer — which could lead to losing that customer forever.

Begin your challenge process by asking your team to examine everything and ask themselves the question, "Is there a better way?" The better way can be eliminating the redundant and the nonproductive or simplifying the too complicated, while finding new hot buttons that will better serve your customers.

Don't be bashful about promoting the new "whatevers" that will help your customers survive in this new world order. Don't worry about being a fear monger promoting concerns and the booby traps that lie ahead. However, when you show the negatives, also serve up solutions. Your customers are desperately searching for new ideas in these frantic times.

When you ask your team to look at the old and find the new, it's guaranteed that some will say, "We do it this way because we've always done it this way." That will be your cue to go ballistic and remind the person that it is no longer business as usual.

Ask your direct reports to make two lists. One should include existing things they currently do as possible candidates to change. The second should be a list of new initiatives that can serve the objective of boosting revenue and producing a return. In some cases, this type of request has been known to cause severe pain between the ears of some, but refusing to do a deep dive to engage in intense thinking is not an option in this environment.

Also, make sure all of your direct reports push this same exercise down to their people. Most importantly, you can't just promulgate the need for change without creating a formal process to vet each worthy recommendation.

Within short order, you will have a series of initiatives to take to the next step. If only a few pan out, you'll be ahead of the game.

Taking all of these steps will help ensure that if the music ever stops playing, you won't be the last man dancing with no chair on which to sit.

Penny-wise or pound-stupid?

Don't make knee-jerk decisions that could come back to haunt you

This column was originally published in May 2009

The hits just keep on coming. It started last fall with the banking industry crisis and stock market meltdown that left most everybody shocked, awed and a whole lot poorer. These events triggered reactions, some knee-jerk, causing businesses to rethink and adjust their modus operandi to ensure that they could live to fight another day.

The government came to the rescue with the TARP bailout, followed by "Son of TARP," aka the stimulus package. These elixirs included everything from stemming mortgage foreclosures all the way to fostering pork-laden catalysts to spur new jobs.

Culminating a now infamous all-night February congressional drafting session, Congress passed this imperfect panacea, more than 1,000 pages of legislation, and our new commander in chief signed the plan, making it the law of the land. This marked yet another well-intentioned but questionable "Hail Mary" government set of solutions. From the get-go of this economic debacle, few organizations escaped unscathed. Sales and profits withered and liquidity evaporated as consumers worldwide went on a protracted spending hiatus.

In response, companies around the globe started paring costs and programs. Virtually everyday businesses proclaimed that because of the bold steps they were taking, they would ultimately emerge stronger while crossing their fingers and thinking, "From our lips to

God's ears."

The question now emerging is: Were these newly minted methodologies and cuts penny-wise or just pound-stupid?

With the probability of little immediate relief from the sagging results on the horizon, management must again examine the newly made promulgations to ensure the decisions actually accomplished a goal.

In good times, smart businesses and organizations share the gains. Now, it is appropriate for companies to have their employees, suppliers and even tangential partners share the pain. The trick is that whatever is done must serve a purpose that can sustain the test of time. The worst scenario is eliminating something only to reinstate it, often at a much higher cost, because it was quickly recognized that the medicine was worse than the cure.

Most companies' short list focuses on hunkering down and pruning excesses, be it people, processes or even unprofitable customers. Certainly, saving money in most cases makes sense, provided savings for the sake of savings don't cause even further damage. As an example, is it smart to stop face-to-face meetings with your best customers just to save the price of a no frills, coach-fare plane ticket? Remember, if you're not staying in front of customers, it's a good bet your competition will be your more-than-willing substitute.

Not spending money to improve or maintain mission-critical undertakings can translate into huge blunders that companies will live to regret in the months and years ahead.

Here are a few penny-wise steps that could produce tangible benefits. Instead of arbitrarily implementing an across-the-board RIF (reduction in force), consider creative alternatives that will better serve the greater good of your employees, customers and business. Rather than the traditional spare-no-department layoffs of X percent of people, ask employees to take a temporary pay reduction. Turning this negative into a quasi-positive, tells employees that they will need to endure this pay hit for, say, only six months. Then add the twist that normal pay rates will resume in November and December to make the holiday season just a little more tenable.

Do the math and determine if this savings tactic gets to the same bottom line number as more disruptive firings, while allowing you to maintain your full existing work force for the better days ahead.

Also, be creative with your suppliers. One example is if you have equipment coming off a lease, instead of replacing it with the latest and greatest updated version, make a deal to keep the older devise for a longer period of time and negotiate a meaningfully lower monthly fee. This is a real win-win, as your vendor continues receiving revenue on something that is possibly already written off of its books while you can reduce your cost.

Focus on the end objectives and consider made-to-fit alternatives, rather than using off-the-shelf traditional methods. Don't be afraid to spend money to make money, and be weary of actions that risk saving yourself out of business.

Executives are paid to make the tough decisions and then sell them to key constituents, whether they are popular or not. Abdicating a thoughtful risk-reward assessment of significant economic counter-measures is not penny-wise and can prove to be painfully pound-stupid.

You'd better start
sweating the small stuff
Little problems can lead to huge failures

This column was originally published in August 2009

How many times have you heard about CEOs who espouse the theory that, in the larger scheme of things, seemingly smaller issues are not worthy of a Big Kahuna's attention? Put another way, these top dogs keep telling themselves they don't want to lose sight of the forest for the trees.

This concept of managing from 50,000 feet seems logical when times are good and sales cover a multitude of sins. However, history has proven that this type of detachment from the deceivingly mundane does not always work in practice when companies are travailing through difficult economic patches.

The streets are littered with the figurative carcasses of leaders who subscribed to this hands-off style, only to be dragged down by something that started as a whisper and built to a deafening shout. A small faux pas or error of omission or commission can grow exponentially. Unfortunately, in many organizations, it is just not CEO-ish to sweat the small stuff.

Here are a few infamous stumbles that probably started small but ultimately led to painful "flat-on-the-face" falls.

A bank executive in 2007 somewhere in a palatial office is talking to his or her loan officers stating, "There is nothing wrong with granting equity home loans to the creditworthy-challenged. So what if these poor schleps don't have jobs or may never pay back a single debt? Give them the loans because it will help our bottom line, and if the borrowers default, who cares? By that time, we'll have sold the loser loans to someone else or the property value will have gone up and we'll be better off anyway."

Famous last words.

How about the now infamous auto executives who flew to Washington on their majestic corporate jets in search of government handouts? No doubt they thought, "No one will notice the planes, and if they do, who cares anyway because we need to secure billions to survive, so what's a few hundred large to fly a measly 395 miles each way." The Big Three CEOs would have been smarter taking the Grey Dog (Greyhound Bus) to D.C.

Pretend you are a bug on the wall in the Oval Office around August 24, 2005, when the red phone rings and it's Al Roker, America's favorite weatherman, alerting the president to the pending precipitation that is expected to hit New Orleans in the form of Hurricane Katrina. The leader of the free world responds, "What's a little rain? It can't make a difference; no need to jump through hoops to prepare. Plus, isn't a little water good for the grass?" Ask the people still living in FEMA trailers if they agree.

Who knows if there may have been a client of Bernie Madoff, the grand shyster of all shysters, who looked at his or her monthly statement and thought, "Gee, it's strange that this statement is printed on paper more indigenous to a lavatory than a top-tier money management firm." So what if the money market fund Madoff used and listed on the report didn't inspire confidence because alongside the name was the fund's slogan: "Find someone we paid and will pay you." It's a good bet the client dismissed these little details, fondly pondering the extraordinary month after month returns that America's now most despicable con man claimed to achieve.

Each of these issues started small but ended big, hairy and very ugly. In business, every day, executives see things and too many neglect to anticipate the larger ramifications. Common thinking is, "Let my person call the other guy's person and have them work it out."

Successes are built on a series of small, seemingly inconsequential steps. However, not minding the details, thinking someone else a few levels below will catch it or relying on the good fairy to solve the issue just doesn't cut it anymore. Apathy and turning a blind eye provide the makings for a perfect storm.

In today's precarious and volatile business environment, leadership must set the tone and the standards. This includes paying attention, watching for warning signs, constantly looking for chinks in the armor and always asking the tough questions when something does not pass the smell test.

Many executives want to distance themselves from the nitty-gritty and deal from on high. The best CEOs, however, when necessary, act like hands-on managers to prevent a broken branch from becoming a falling tree that hits them in the head.

A straight line is not always the best route
Short detours can sometimes save you time, money and angst

This column was originally published in September 2010

As smart as most seasoned executives think they are, many have prematurely pulled the trigger because of the need for speed. The pressure is always there: Do it now, get it done, make it happen — today. Most of the time, experienced managers can pull this off with minimal damage. But every once in a while when the stars and moon don't align as planned, a serious misstep can occur and be darn near lethal. In the rush to solve problems or take advantage of opportunities, executives take shortcuts — as well they should provided they pause periodically for a sanity check to ensure they're not sacrificing quality for speed.

The reason we accelerate at breakneck speeds is probably because from day one we have been taught that the shortest distance between point A and point B is a straight line. Much of the blame emanates from ninth grade geometry class. With a protractor and compass in hand, it probably makes sense to use this mathematical discipline to solve problems or accomplish objectives. However, this is not necessarily the smartest trajectory to employ in business.

Whether it's creating a new business methodology, developing a unique marketing strategy or building a business, many times a deliberate detour or zigzag, can save time, money and angst. Anyone that's been in the game of business for even a short time learns quickly that there is seldom a cut-and-dried solution where one starts at the beginning and proceeds directly to the finish line. Most times creating something new is an iterative process that requires flexibility and occasionally a jagged line to produce what is promised.

Let's say that your plan is to create a new product by following a traditional process and timeline. You devise all of the steps necessary to assign the tasks, priorities, critical steps and a comprehensive action plan. When done, the good times are supposed to roll. Instead, the reality of the creation process usually has a variety of twists and turns with which you must deal. Following your script in order to get the new product to market, you follow time-proven prescribed steps. However, at midpoint someone discovers that the color, the size or the smell of the widget just won't fly.

Instead of panicking or pulling the pin on the project and its development, the leader decides to call a timeout, take a deep breath and launch a series of additional consumer focus group sessions to do a deep dive to determine what's wrong and what are the real hot buttons with the targeted consumers. Sure, this will cause a temporary delay and cost a few extra dollars, but at the end of the process, it will likely accelerate the positive results because the product will go to market hitting the bull's eye of what the customer really wants and needs. Alternatively, if the team simply forged ahead in order to bring the product to market on schedule, it might have been completed, but simply put, the product would have flopped like a bad Broadway play.

At that point, the new product might be killed not because it's the wrong product, but because it's the wrong color or size or it smells funny. This results in numerous confessions of mea culpa, heads rolling and money wasted.

Certainly speed counts and getting it right the first time without delay is a very good thing, but in the real world, unfortunately, it just doesn't happen that way most times. Running full out with the gas pedal to the floor might make it seem like you're leaving the competition in the dust, but in actuality, you could be making flawed decisions that come back to haunt you.

Everyone knows somebody who perpetually leaves the stadium before the big game ends, jumps in the car drives home like a maniac only to get in the house plop down on the couch and proclaim, "I'm home." Now what? Getting the job half done because you draw a straight line between two points is like going hell-bent for election, but forgetting to stop to take voter polls along the way. This usually results in defeat.

How to keep Humpty Dumpty on the top of your wall

Stopping the fall is easier than trying to pick up the pieces

This column was originally published in May 2011

We've all read or heard the perennial favorite old English nursery rhyme about Humpty Dumpty who fell from that darned wall, was irreversibly damaged and could not be put back together again. In business, we spend a lot of effort fixing what has been broken, rather than preventing the breakage in the first place. Think of your own organization and recall how much effort went into trying to fix that last big problem that could have been critical to your business and, ultimately, sales and earnings. No doubt that once the issue reared its ugly head, you went into fire drill mode, barking out orders to get to the bottom of the problem and fix it immediately, as measured in hours and days, not weeks and months.

Stop and think about the cost, the interruption factor and diversion of effort this "pick up the pieces" exercise inflicted on the organization. Key people had to drop everything and scramble, not to make a penny but to stop the loss. Of course, every business periodically hits a slick spot and has to maneuver quickly to regain control; it comes with the territory.

Wouldn't it have been easier, however, to prevent the crisis before it became one? Just ask BP about its oil spill last year and what it cost in hard dollars (or pounds), not to mention the almost irreparable harm to its reputation and perhaps long-term future. This is a dramatic case of failing to take the necessary steps to avoid the oil damage itself, as well as the near cataclysmic peripheral stumbles made in handling communications. The amateurish PR efforts are what really pushed BP's Humpty Dumpty, aka the Gulf of Mexico Deep Water Horizon spill, off that proverbial wall. What actions can your company take to ensure you don't encounter your own Humpty Dumpty?

Sure most companies have risk management programs, which involve assessing potential dangers, working to prevent them and determining the costs if the unimaginable does occur. Unfortunately, too many companies apply the risk management thought process only to issues that are most associated with accidents. The Humpty Dumpy theory has to be extended to all areas of a business, from customer service to employee productivity and everything in between.

It starts with paying attention and sweating the small stuff and taking action when the first whiff of a problem occurs. It's almost a gut feeling that surfaces when good executives encounter something that just doesn't seem right. Call it a sixth sense, but it can happen at any time and in some of the most unusual places.

As an example, you're reviewing an internal report on an important new project, and as you study the material, something just doesn't seem right. The numbers add up, but nonetheless you know that all the dots aren't connecting as they should — you're just not sure what's wrong. You pause and put the report down for a few minutes, and then it hits you. Kaboom, a subtle yet critical step was omitted from the plan. Now that you've found the missing piece, you make a few calls and a potential problem that could have easily morphed into a big issue is squelched.

These same gut feelings apply to "reading" people, not necessarily by what they say or do but many times by what they don't say or do. Here's another scenario, your biggest vendor normally touches base with you like clockwork, sometimes if only to say hello. One day you realize you've not heard from this supplier recently. You wonder what's up with this? However, you're busy and the thought quickly passes. Big mistake. You should have picked up the phone, found out what the story was, and if there was an issue brewing, fixed it then and there.

It all gets down to trusting your instincts and recognizing when your Humpty Dumpty might be leaning too close to the wall's edge. That's the same wall from which anything can topple and shatter beyond repair. Preventing that from occurring requires paying attention, looking for telltale signs of change and then being perceptive enough to know that there is something that needs scrutiny — even if you can't pinpoint exactly why or what.

The risk in your own little kingdom is that when your Humpty Dumpty falls you may not have enough of the King's horses and men to put the pieces back together again.

What to do when everything hits the fan at once

Be prepared to compartmentalize big problems

This column was originally published in May 2012

Unfortunately, when everything hits the fan, it won't be at a time and place of your choosing, and most likely, it won't be just one issue.

When you least expect it and when everything seems to be going OK for the first time in awhile, a severe lightning strike may occur, seemingly out of nowhere, even when the sun is shining brightly. Worse yet is that first bolt may be followed by multiple booms, bangs and claps in rapid succession.

It may start with a phone call informing you that the unspeakable has occurred. One of your top people encountered a personal problem that will shed a bad light on your company, or you get a FedEx letter from one of your biggest customers stating: "It's been fun while it lasted; have a nice life. Sayonara." As a wave of nausea sweeps over you, your chief accounting lieutenant barges into your office, holding your auditors' notice and stammering, "earnings restatement."

Trouble comes in many sizes and shapes, and as the boss, you must always be prepared to provide direction. While any one problem could be monumental, two or more are almost debilitating. What can you do; what must you do?

First, figuratively and literally, take three deep breaths and count

274

to 10. Pick up a legal pad and write out the key issues, crystallizing options and setting priorities of who on your team does what. Also write out some ideas of how to get started. Step two, clear your calendar and focus.

The trick in attacking multiple major problems simultaneously is to compartmentalize each of them, quickly determining the downside risks and coming up with temporary fixes to stop any bleeding, followed by long-term solutions. Let's say another crisis hits when you receive a notice that your largest plant has become the target of a unionization drive. You quickly recognize that if this effort is successful, then your other facilities run the risk of a similar fate. The economic consequences could be enormous, and as equally disturbing is the fact that fighting this will be incredibly time-consuming, costly and will surely divert the attention of management away from sales and earnings goals.

Rather than bemoan your current state of affairs, gather your team together, contact your attorneys and find out what precipitated this situation. Was there an underlying morale problem in the plant, or did the union simply choose your company because it was an attractive target? Don't always expect the worse, but plan for it. Maybe you'll get lucky and find out that it was a simple misstep by a lower-level supervisor that antagonized a very small group of otherwise well-meaning employees, which can be more easily fixed.

If the earnings restatement is the biggest threat, then most likely you will take charge of the accounting issues and have your vice president of human resources tackle the union problem. Time can be your biggest enemy or your greatest ally. If you procrastinate and don't swing into action, the situations will simply proliferate. If, however, you jump in with both feet immediately, you may be able to stem the tide in your favor much more quickly. One thing is for sure: The good fairy won't solve these problems and your only choice is to take charge.

Of course, you'll have more than a few restless nights; your calendar will become an instant nightmare as you deal with these problems du jour. Nevertheless, at least you'll have started the compartmentalizing issue process.

A few words of caution: Certainly delegate aspects of the problems to your best and brightest but also make sure you're constantly kept in the loop. An effective leader is much akin to being a juggler and having the skills to keep all of the balls in the air simultaneously.

One consolation is that if being the boss was so easy, then everyone would do it. In fact, being a good leader takes a keen mind, often an incredible sense of urgency and a strong stomach.

Troubles come with the territory. However, there is one major consolation: When you're at the top, the height can be a bit frightening at times, but the view is certainly spectacular.

Welcome to the new 'normal'

What produced success in the past may not work in the future

This column was originally published in October 2012

The number of seismic changes in the way business is done during the past 10 to 15 years is unprecedented. Just ponder the magnitude of all that has occurred as you read this list: Cellphones became ubiquitous, and computers with 24/7 Internet access moved from the strident screechy tones and beeps of telephone dial up to today's broadband connections that transmit huge amounts of data in seconds, resulting in virtually everyone being constantly connected.

Instead of getting the latest news at 11 p.m. and sleeping on it, we now receive a constant stream of information in real time. Reaction time has moved from digesting the myriad of hard copy reports that awaited you at the office each morning to now making decisions simultaneously with that first sip of morning coffee while reading data on a smart device.

In addition, the era of easy money is also long gone, along with what seemed to be extraordinary and unlimited growth where the average company would do just fine, propelled by a rising tide of good times.

The tragedy of Sept. 11 jolted the world permanently, altering the way people live and think about the future. There are no more givens that one will grow up, go to school, get a job, have a family and live happily ever after. Two major wars have lingered beyond anyone's worst expectations. Then came the economic meltdown of 2008 when the wheels came off the wagon and the music stopped playing while everyone frantically searched for too few remaining chairs. With

277

the stock market crash and the banking/lending meltdown, even the most sanguine turned jaundiced toward their views of government, business and what the future holds.

Even those businesses naively ensconced in their fairytale cocoons realized it was no longer business as usual. What worked for years would no longer move the needle. Customers' attitudes and loyalties could no longer be taken for granted as businesses acknowledged that future success and prosperity could well be the exception, rather than the rule.

Does this mean that everything that we've learned in the past has gone swirling down the drain, including basic business principles and practices that were sacrosanct?

There are no pat answers to deal with almost revolutionary metamorphoses, if you don't change, you most certainly will become a victim of change.

Welcome to the new 'normal.' If you're leading an organization today, you must devote the majority of your time and efforts to looking ahead and trying to find the answers before your competitors even know the questions. Change has become how we must do business. What worked for your company previously is, at best, a fleeting memory overshadowed by the customers' mindset of "What have you done for me today?" In short, there are no guarantees other than you'll have to continuously get better or be gone.

A scary thought? It all depends how you approach this new reality. With changes come new opportunities, new ground rules and the ability to find a better way and deliver that better way more efficiently and effectively.

So how do you go about preparing for the future? Certainly use all of the new tools that are at your fingertips. Instant information on the Web is available to all of us with a few keystrokes directed at a growing number of sophisticated search engine. Data that took weeks and months to gather can now be gleaned in minutes or hours. While Americans are graying as the over-50 crowd mushrooms, don't ignore the young who know only this new way of life. Does this mean you should add a few 14-year-olds to your board? Maybe not a practical idea, but be sure you're at least talking to a couple of them on an ongoing basis. Ideas come in many forms, many times from the most unlikely.

You must retrain your team to challenge virtually everything and find a better way, envision products, goods and services that no one knows they even need yet, and create a strategy to deliver them compellingly and creatively.

Will there continue to be business casualties? You bet. Much more importantly, however, there will be many business successes for those companies led by visionaries who answer that morning wake-up call each day with an open mind to the new normal.

Do you believe in magic?
Click your heels twice
and see what happens

This column was originally published in February 2013

Should hard-nosed, thick-skinned, ice-water-running-through-their-veins executives who live and die by facts and profit and loss statements believe in things they can't totally understand and certainly can't explain?

We have all been there. At various times, for virtually inexplicable reasons, an undertaking that has been struggling suddenly takes a 180-degree turn and begins an upward trajectory. There was no indication from the numbers, substantively nothing extraordinary was changed, but all of a sudden, it's as if the sun, moon and stars all aligned and you are heading toward Fat City.

Of course, we've all experienced the converse, when everything seems to be jelling and all of a sudden out of the blue your project takes a nosedive, plummeting to earth faster than the fastest falling star — or the stock market crash of 2008.

Even though you fancy yourself as tough as nails, you must hope against hope, experiment with unusual fixes, devise out-of-the-box solutions — do just about anything, including making promises to a higher power, along the lines of, "Let me get through this, and I'll never _____ again." (You fill in the blank as it is best kept between you and the great power in which you believe.)

Don't get me wrong I don't really believe in the good fairy or the ability to make everything better with the wave of wand, but I do very much believe what the famous New York Yankees manager Yogi Berra once said, "It ain't over till it's over."

There is "magic" when some inexplicable ingredient kicks in that enables the best leaders to continuously generate "what if I try this" scenarios and then, out of nowhere, one of those ideas turns sure defeat into a salvageable success. Is this skill and intelligence at play? To a certain extent, yes, but there is more to it than that. The only thing I believe about unadulterated pure luck is the explanation from that overused phrase, "The harder one works, the luckier he or she gets." The real answer more likely is a combination of knowing how to run a business: using your head, your heart and your gut to tackle a dilemma, recognizing that on any given day one of these faculties will get you through a difficult issue. On a great day when all three kick in, it's almost as if it were magic, and you start hearing sounds that become music to your ears as the needed solution suddenly emerges.

In reality, the "magic" is having faith in the people with whom you work, maintaining a strong belief that for most of the seemingly insurmountable questions there are answers, trusting that good things do happen to good people, and knowing that every once in a while the good guys do win. This doesn't mean becoming a naive Pollyanna. Instead, it all gets down to not throwing in the towel until you have exhausted all possibilities and logically and systematically explored all the alternatives, some of which may be very nontraditional.

This approach is also a direct reflection of positive thinking and mindfulness, which is the practice of purposely focusing your attention on the present moment and ignoring all other distractions. In essence, some psychological studies have shown that when one is committed to success and has the discipline not to let the mind travel down a negative path, the brain can focus on producing unique solutions. Using positive psychology techniques can result in intense absorption that can lead to coming up with unlikely fixes. Some shrinks call this increasing mental flow. I call it a little bit of magic.

My simpler explanation for this phenomenon, which I've written about many times, is that success is achieved when you combine preparation, persistence with a bit of perspiration, along with a few ingredients that can't always be explained, including having a little faith.

My advice is don't always worry about your image of being a buttoned-up, corporate type. Instead, when the going gets particularly tough, it's OK to become a Dorothy, as in "The Wizard of Oz," click your heels twice and quickly repeat to yourself, "I believe, I believe."

8

Evaluating Opportunities

A primer on spotting and dealing with time wasters, users and hangers-on

This column was originally published in November 2005

We all know them, they are fairly easy to spot and just like day-old fish, you can almost smell them as they hone in on you. Somehow you can even pick up their scent via email and telephone. Who are these annoying and costly parasitic-types? They are time wasters, users and various and sundry other types of hangers-on. They have a central commonality: they sap you of your valuable time and energy and almost never provide a return. Don't get me wrong, everything doesn't have to have a pay-back. Sometimes we should do something just because it is the right thing to do or because it makes us feel good and that in itself is more than adequate payback.

These wasters, et al come in all sizes and shapes. You find them at every turn, and they always stand out in the crowd. As an example: if you are selling products, goods or services to a customer and all of a sudden at the first meeting the potential buyer starts talking about huge orders, putting you on the map, making you rich and famous, you have just encountered your first warning signals. There is always a catch with these waste-type customers, before they give you the biggest order on the planet, they always have a few minor requests. Typically, not only do they want you to jump through hoops, but also make you do this or that, which takes your valuable time. It could be a free study, in-depth analysis, meeting after meeting, but the net result is always the same: nada, nothing, zilch.

There are also wasters and users who have infiltrated companies and organizations impersonating productive employees. They are the ones who have the great idea that never seems to pan out. They are also the people who, to get to the next step, want to have numerous meetings with you and ten of your closest associates, only to have you sit down and find out that these users haven't a clue how to get started. Worse yet, they are poorly prepared for the meeting they have called to kick-off their project. They rehash old ideas and play woulda, coulda, shoulda games squandering your time and energy. Avoid these associates like the plague.

The best way to deal with them is suggest having the meeting that they called standing up, walking about, or better yet, alone in a phone booth where they can waste their own time talking to themselves.

Some of the worst offenders are people you don't really know. Perhaps you meet them at a conference, on an airplane, and all of a sudden, they are your best friend. On the plane, before its reaching cruising altitude, you have heard about their dramatic successes, their third wife, and how they are on the verge of hitting it even bigger. By the time you touch down, the cabin door opens and the flight attendant utters the obligatory "bye bye" you think, "I hope I never see this guy again in this lifetime." No such luck, whether it is a few days later, a month later, or even longer, you get the call from your former seatmate saying, "Just checking in." You think to yourself, "self, what does this knucklehead think I am, a Continental Airlines ticket agent," only to learn that your new found friend wants to "network with you" and be introduced to anybody and everybody you know so he can "help them get to the next level." Translation: your former co-passenger has probably lost his job, has no contacts left who will speak to him, and wants to use you any way and every way he can. Of course, he suggests breakfast, lunch, dinner or drinks and if you are foolish enough to do it, no doubt you will get stuck with the check, too.

The best way to handle this type is when he or she suggests lunch on, let's say, a Thursday and asks if that works for you, your response should be: "No, Thursday's out, how about neve — is never good for you?" This sardonic retort is from a cartoon in *The New Yorker's* May 1993 issue, a reproduction of which hangs in my office as a reminder that we all have choices. So what is the best way to handle these situations and at the same time not come off as a jerk? No easy task, but a straightforward approach works best. Listen and learn, and quickly size-up those with whom you do business, recognizing if what they are saying makes sense, and you can reach their expectations or theirs yours, and do so in an effective and economical manner. If the answer is no, walk away.

For the co-workers who spend more time calling meetings than producing results, make them put in a memo what the purpose is of the meeting they are proposing, how long will it take, provide an agenda, and an objective. For the airplane hangers-on, a briefcase full of work or a good book with your nose buried in it from takeoff to touchdown is the best antidote. Alternatively, stare at your laptop with these words typed on the screen "if you can read this, you are too damn close." It's a real conversation stopper.

On the flip side, learn to spot people who might be dreamers, but are also doers. People who may need a favor or a contact, but people who don't over-use their welcome and who might return the favor someday. Remember what goes around, comes around. Finally, make sure every encounter passes the smell test because as they say "no good deed ever goes unpunished."

How to overcome analysis paralysis
Manage your business with your head, heart and gut

This column was originally published in February 2008

There is a delicate balance between using facts and employing intuition to make important decisions. Combining the use of both the right-brain for creativity with the left-brain for analytics has been the formula for many a great success.

Managers typically use a myriad of proven methods to launch the decision-making process. Rarely, however, is there a single protocol or technique that always works the best. How one approaches an undertaking depends on circumstances including time and resources. Sometimes genius results from painstaking, laser-like focus on a specific goal and other times it's that fleeting thought that germinates into a newborn winning concept.

Under certain circumstances, it makes sense to drill down on what needs to be done and then as Nike asserts in its advertising: "Just do it." This cavalier method using the right cranial hemisphere is recommended when you are well versed on the subject and have successfully done something similar in either your current role or another life.

More often than not, you need to build a very tightly crafted road map, which takes you through each step whether it is launching a new product or service, starting a business, or reformulating a troublesome strategy. In cases such as this, it is not only understanding the variables and paybacks but also a matter of down and dirty scrounging for the available information and then testing and analyzing assumptions and hypotheses before proceeding.

Analysis is a prerequisite to establishing parameters and arriving at a go/no go decision. The process must often include a healthy dose of "time outs" when applicable to re-think pieces and parts of a project for either a sanity check or just a double check.

Before passing the Rubicon, or point of no return, knowing how to proceed with an undertaking must include digesting and interpreting data based on facts as well as history. It is pure bravado to pioneer without first learning from what others, including competitors, have done previously to determine what worked and, equally important, what didn't. I am not a big fan of pioneers because as history taught us in the seventh grade, they were the ones who were frequently found face down in the mud with arrows in their backs.

Analysis traditionally is an integral piece of any puzzle. However, just like everything else, analysis can be and often is overdone. In many cases, analysis can lead to paralysis, which in business can be fatal. The government should require a "Black Box" warning on every business book and corporate business plan, similar to what is mandated for cigarettes and certain pharmaceuticals, which might read, "Caution: excess and repeated use of facts and figures can lead to permanent paralysis."

In a perfect world, one uses both hardcore analysis and creativity as the tools to reach a conclusion. The best executives use their head (for analysis), their hearts (for supplying the passion and inspiration), and their gut (for intuitively and inexplicitly propelling them in the right direction). On a bad day, any one of these faculties will get you through the decision-making gauntlet. On a good day, all three kick in and suddenly, you can see through those nebulous clouds that have plagued your project, with spot-on acuity leading to the granddaddy of all solutions.

However, there can be a big downside to too much analysis. It occurs when one wants zero risk through even more study and research before pulling the trigger. Analysis then becomes an excuse for delaying or never making a final decision. I have seen it in meetings a thousand times when someone will assert after months of fact finding, digesting and dissecting that the team still has to look one more time in one more place to validate, double or triple check the data and the conclusion. This can become an exercise in futility and it is when the team leader has to assert, "Enough is enough."

Today we do business where "mind to market" is measured in days and weeks, not months and years. As they say "he who hesitates is not only lost, but can be toast, too." Many times, it is better to launch and then fix rather than continually postpone. Software companies have been doing this since zeroes and ones were first strung together to create computer programs.

Typically, there are two types of people. The first include those who are almost exclusively fact-driven and the second are those who seem to shoot more from the hip at times and are considered by some as just lucky when their ideas succeed. Given the choice I would rather be lucky than good. Many executives are very smart but not particularly lucky. They're the ones who, no matter how hard they work, never seem to catch that brass ring. They're always talking themselves out of taking the next step until updated facts are available. Conversely, I know a number of extremely successful people who always seem to arrive at the right decision at the right time.

Are these leaders lucky or good? It's probably a combination thereof. I believe that to be lucky one also must be smart enough to know that he or she is being lucky and then simply seize the opportunity. The best executives use their left-brain to interpret and analyze data but give equal weight to all three finely honed biological tools we have: our head, heart, and gut. Sometimes no decision (aka analysis paralysis) is worse than the wrong decision.

Is victory at any cost a real victory?

Should leaders change their mantra?

This column was originally published in July 2008

There are many CEO types, some successful, some not, who have taken a page from the playbook of the legendary Green Bay Packers' football coach Vince Lombardi. He was known for proclaiming his hard-nosed theories about winning, some say, at any cost.

Then there's the hugely successful, yet equally infamous, Indiana college basketball coach who believed more in action than words. Unfortunately, his actions sometimes included hurling objects onto the court when he lost.

Similarly, too many business leaders focus almost exclusively on winning for the sake of winning without fully understanding the economic and human energy commitment needed to reach the goal.

It's well established at self-help meetings that each attendee must stand before the group, introduce himself or herself by first name and state that he or she has a problem. For those in business who are addicted to the need to win without regard to ramifications, imagine this assertion, "Hello, my name is (you fill in the first name here) and I'm an irrational, compulsive winner."

Every organization has associates who must always be first, be right and never lose. The problem is, many times, the cost of being numero uno is simply not worth the price. Remember, your team doesn't have to win every game to win the championship.

As leaders and managers, we must recognize when an all-out effort is warranted and, just as important, when it's not. In addition, we must train our associates, particularly the younger ones, to know how

290

to assess the cost of a victory and how and when to pick their spots.

"Business is a marathon, not a sprint." This is an overused saying but, nonetheless, it's dead-on right. Leaders must operate their organizations to achieve continuous progress and growth, not to win one every single battle just for the sake of the fight.

The concept of zero defects, the same as in always needing to win, is not only unsustainable, but it is also simply too costly and painful.

Sure, if you're the maker of airplane jet engines, then I'm all for zero defects, particularly if I'm flying on the plane. However, if you're the producer of a widget that is not essential to maintaining safety, it's cheaper and more practical for the end user to replace the widget as needed rather than to pay the higher price for zero defects.

There are some simple practices to follow to ensure you invest your organization's resources wisely to achieve a win.

First, before you start any project, determine what the payback is. Certainly, all victories contribute something, but they're not always of equal value.

It's critical to know when enough is enough and it's time to just pull back and settle for second, third or drop out completely. This is easier said than done because there are many factors at work, including the mysterious chemicals that drive the alpha male and alpha female.

One problem is that for type A personalities, winning sometimes just feels so darn good.

A second consideration is burnout. You can't let your employees put in 100 percent or more on every undertaking. Associates who constantly do so serve you well for a short time, but, in the end, they unceremoniously fizzle out like a cheap firecracker. Unfortunately, most times, they also don't rebound, even after you have made them take a forced time-out.

Third, when launching every meaningful effort, create a one to 10 scoring scale, with the lower numbers representing the less important goals/projects. You must communicate with your people when the effort is worthy of a nine or 10 so they know to turn on the adrenaline for success.

When dealing with something rated a one or a two, they must certainly try but also know how much it's worth investing to achieve the goal's desired outcome.

As a sanity check, tomorrow morning when you awake, look in the bathroom mirror and then audibly introduce yourself to yourself. If, in your heart of hearts, you hear a little voice saying, "Hello, my name is (fill in your name here) and I am an irrational, compulsive winner," you'll know it's time to reprioritize because it does matter how you play the game if you want to win consistently year after year.

Trust, but verify

If it walks like a duck and quacks like a duck, then it probably ain't a zebra

This column was originally published in March 2009

The playwright Oscar Wilde wrote, "A cynic knows the cost of everything and the value of nothing." By nature, most successful business executives tend to be more optimists than cynical naysayers.

The leaders who are the best of the best, however, have an internal mechanism that allows them to dream, dare and do while simultaneously knowing to challenge and question. The good leaders probably possess a yet undiscovered gene that automatically flashes a yellow warning sign in the back of their heads reading "trust, but verify," when they're introduced to the unproven or unknown. Experience, judgment and wisdom are the tools needed to distinguish between dismissing an idea as flaky and accepting it at face value.

Case in point is the now infamous Bernard Madoff, the Ponzi-practitioner extraordinaire, who also had a bit of Houdini in him because he could touch a dollar and make it instantly disappear. His signature pièce de résistance was the vanishing act of putting other people's dollars in his own pocket by using a sleight-of-hand maneuver, most likely in the form of a glib smile and nifty software program. The software produced a faux monthly statement that recapped the bogus previous 30 days' perennial successful results. This led trusting investors to believe they could sleep soundly thinking that their money was not only safe but also growing exponentially.

This garden-variety swindler, who makes the Wild West bandit Jesse James look like a saint in comparison, certainly did not discriminate. Reportedly, he purloined more than $50 billion from supposedly savvy fund managers to unsuspecting charities with no doubt a few widows and orphans sprinkled in for good measure.

How could this have happened? First, people wanted to believe. Secondly, most of us have an innate desire to be associated with winners. However, eventually, we all learn the cold reality that if it is too good to be true, then more than likely, it is too good to be true. Worst of all, some professional "money managers" turned over unimaginably huge sums to this Ponzi-artist without apparently doing their own due diligence, which is not only an ethical prerequisite but also an exercise demanded by common sense if not common law. Had the unsuspected subscribed to the principle of "trust, but verify," this scheme would have failed. Instead, decades passed before the genie was out of the bottle, and it took the biggest stock market disaster since the Great Depression to defrock this con man.

How can executives learn from this debacle and translate the concept of "trust, but verify" into a safety net to protect the enterprise without dampening creativity and enthusiasm that could lead to the next great business success?

Every stockbroker must learn the Securities and Exchange Commission's Rule 405, which is 'know your customer." This same requirement must apply to businesses. At a very minimum, have a sense of whom you are dealing with. Is it coming from a trusted peer or subordinate or the nephew of your brother-in-law's barber? The best bets are made on those who have done it before and have done it successfully. Some call these habitual achievers "serial entrepreneurs," but they also can be innovators who toil down the hall from you and constantly deliver on promises and concepts. Good leadership requires the discipline to hear out a proposal yet employ finely tuned instincts and cunning, sometimes indelicately referred to as the "smell test."

Sniffing out the nuances of the real story to discover hyperbole or worse takes discipline and patience. Once the answers sort of make sense, move to phase two by doing some quick back-of-the-envelope calculations and research to determine if there is at least a snowball's chance that whatever is being proposed won't melt away as soon as your check clears the bank.

Finally, talk to others who may have tried something even remotely similar to what has been proposed. You'll be amazed at what complete strangers and even tangential competitors will tell you when you simply pick up the phone and ask.

To build, grow and succeed, every organization needs a constant inflow of new ideas, be it products, services or a better way to skin that proverbial cat. Somewhere between an optimist and a cynic is a realist who always knows the difference between a quacking duck and a striped zebra.

If you bat 1.000 in business, you'll eventually strike out
Risk-taking and defeats are a big part of the game

This column was originally published in May 2010

Every business executive wants to make the right decisions that lead to a win, be it completing a transaction, launching a new product or orchestrating a mega deal. However, reality is that there are few, if any, players who are always right and who always win.

Think about it this way. A great major league baseball player such as the Yankees' Alex Rodriguez has a lifetime batting average going into the 2010 season of .305, with more than 2,500 hits, including 583 homers. For this, he has a current contract worth about $275 million, which is nice work if you can get it. A-Rod's average means, however, that for every time he is at the plate, he gets a hit less than one-third of the time.

Using baseball batting averages as a benchmark puts into perspective that being great or batting a thousand in most anything is virtually impossible. In business, it can mean a leader is afraid to take a swing when he or she steps up to the plate. It's hard to get on base and ultimately score if an executive is unwilling to take appropriate and measured risks. Baseball is a game where failing seven out of 10 times is a success, not to mention very lucrative. In business, a good leader who makes the right decisions between 60 and 70 percent of the time is a darn effective mover and shaker who will consistently delivery top and bottom growth.

Now ask yourself: What is your batting average? Equally important, what's the average for the top members of your management team?

Do you reward your players for taking chances even if they don't always pan out, or do you subtly punish an associate for daring to try something different? Sometimes it is difficult to swallow a loss; however, a mistake or a series of controlled misses can lead to uncovering that next big success.

The true game-changer in business is to be sure that you and your team are taking enough chances, new routes if you will, and breaking fresh ground. This is not a loosey-goosey process or just a thoughtless periodic roll of the dice. Risk-taking requires discipline and confidence. The discipline portion is setting a course for which you've never previously traveled and then progressing deliberately yet cautiously. This includes having safeguards in place to recognize when the undertaking isn't quite right, at which time you must take a timeout and make a few tweaks or even change direction. As a company explores new avenues, there must be safeguards in place to avoid painful missteps. These include setting parameters for the dollars you're willing to risk and the time and the resources you can devote to the effort.

The confidence portion of the equation is not being afraid to be wrong, admit it and to try again another day. It all gets down to the risk versus the possible rewards. Certainly if you do nothing and it's the same old, same old every day, you might keep going for some time. During this period, you could bat a thousand, but it's just a matter of time until you strike out. As the old adage states, there's nothing more certain than change. Those who don't change will ultimately be the victims of change.

As a leader, you have to set the standard for change and communicate the virtues of discovery and new alternatives to your team. Growth is all about making sure you always have enough lines in the water that provide the possibility of finding that better way or new widget.

The best hitters in baseball have a career that can span many years. The flash-in-the-pan players who are great one season and forgotten the next are equivalent to executives who only had one good idea. When they stepped up to the plate the next time, they were afraid to take a swing. Three out of 10 is terrific in baseball and six or seven out 10 in business might just get you into the hall of fame.

Second thoughts can be a good thing
But the timing of when they occur is everything

This column was originally published in March 2011

It's happened to all of us. One night you go to sleep without a thought in your head, and inexplicably, you awaken at 3 a.m. and find yourself sitting ramrod straight up in bed with an idea in your head that you think could change the world, which will make you a legend in your own time. You may have no clue where the idea came from, but at that moment, you are energized with the possibility of fame and fortune. In a panic, you scribble your thoughts on a bedside pad of paper in fear of losing them. You then pause for a few minutes before your somniferous state overcomes you, and you fall back into la-la land.

Fast-forward about three hours and you get up feeling a little restless, not totally recalling the epiphany you experienced earlier. Then it comes back to you as you find your notes. You begin to sort out the elements of your holy grail discovery and begin to apply logic to your revolutionary concept. Then it hits you. Perhaps, what you thought was an earth-changing breakthrough might just be more of a jumble of fragmented elements that no longer pass the smell test. You just experienced the inevitable second thoughts.

This reconsideration is completely normal, very necessary and a part of the discovery process. Second thoughts are critical and invariably occur with just about everything we do in business, but it all comes down to the sequence and timing. Second thoughts are good most times, except in situations where you've already made a commitment, made your idea public or, worse, promised

299

to do something. They are particularly bad after the wedding vows conclude with the obligatory "I do's" or after you decide that you can beat that train at the crossing and then change your mind as you hear the "thump, thump" of your tires rolling over the railroad ties as the freight train's bright light shines in your eyes.

In business, second thoughts should be your standard modus operandi when you or one of your charges comes up with that possible big idea. It's important to use that time between an idea's inception and the launch of implementation using a simple discipline that can help ensure you're not off on a wild goose chase.

When you have your next revelation, begin the process of evaluation knowing full well that you may have second thoughts, and either bag your little gem completely or fine-tune it further after it has been time and stress tested.

First, flesh out your original notes and prepare a basic outline of what it is you may attempt, what it will do, and how and why it could pay off. Don't waste time on form; just drill down to substance. Secondly, sleep on it, either literally or figuratively. Think about the idea for a night or two before you drift off to dreamland. Alternatively, put your narrative in your top drawer for a day or so. After this mandatory timeout, pull out your notes, read them thoroughly, thinking of the ramifications and nuances, and then, if it all still makes sense, take your thoughts to the next step, which can include discussing the idea with a colleague, friend or significant other.

This simple respite in your race for success can give you the opportunity to bag the idea and move on, concluding your concept was nothing more than the result of a little too much indulgence of food or drink before you hit the pillow on that fateful night. However, if you make the decision to continue to proceed, the rest will come naturally as you more fully flesh out the concept during the ongoing discovery, fine-tuning and testing stages. New ideas are almost always an iterative process often with the finished product emerging dramatically different from the initial idea when lightning first struck. Creation is one of the most exciting, yet challenging, aspects of building a business, but without following the vetting process, it's almost guaranteed that inertia will set in and your concept will drift into oblivion.

Second thoughts are an integral safety valve for success. Taking an idea from mind to market is all a matter of sequence and timing, and when done right it can be satisfying and very lucrative.

Prepare or perish
God gave us Google;
teach your team to use it

This column was originally published in September 2011

It is a given in the academic world that for a professor to succeed, he or she must publish or perish. In the business world, the admonishment must be prepare or perish. This should be a given, but we all periodically need a mandatory refresher. Consider this it.

We've all been there, seen it and, as much as we hate to admit it, done it. The "done it" in this case is when we've tried to wing it with little or no preparation and found ourselves in that proverbial prone position, face down with our noses buried in the carpet realizing that the jig is up.

As a leader, you must require your team to take the time and effort to prepare for anything of value — be it a sales call or a major presentation. This doesn't mean dredging up worthless minutia about what is to be discussed. Instead, preparing means getting the basics down cold, so that whatever is pitched can be done so effectively and convincingly because the presenter had sufficient background on the prospect. There is nothing more annoying than a presenter turning glassy-eyed, with perspiration running down his or her forehead, while he or she grapples to answer a simple question, such as, "Tell me what you think your company can do for mine and what you think of our products." Without preparation, there are usually three utterances from the presenter in rapid succession: "Uh, uh," and a final "duh." The translation is that the presenter didn't do enough homework and now looks like a fool and, worse yet, made your company look just as bad.

Here is a tale of two cities that I recently experienced. Tale No.

1: A very close business acquaintance and good friend called and asked if his long-lost college roommate could have a 15-minute conversation about how his business might help me. I told my friend, it's all a matter of who does the asking, and of course, I would speak to his former roommate. At the appointed hour, the call came in, and right off of the bat, once we got past two sentences on the weather, it was obvious the caller had no clue about what my company does. But, because the caller was a friend of my friend, I politely — well, maybe not so politely — told him if he expected to take the conversation past the climate, he would have to do some homework, all the while I was thinking, "This guy is a big time-waster."

The homework could have been accomplished in no more than 10 minutes by simply going to Google and typing in the name of my company and seeing a complete description of the business. This wannabe super salesman would have then had enough information to get at least to first base with me. Instead he struck out and embarrassed his friend to boot.

Tale No. 2: I received a telephone call from another friend who asked if I would spend a few minutes talking to a recent graduate about job opportunities with my organization. Normally, this is something I avoid like the plague. However, I realize friends are hard to come by, so I consented to the call. A few days later, a young lady reached me and immediately proceeded to tell me about the attributes of my company, how she saw us positioned and what she thought she could do for us. Best yet, she even skipped the two-sentence preliminaries on the weather and current barometric pressure, which saved us both time.

How did this 20-something person not only get my attention but also motivate me to pave the way for her with our HR director? She was well prepared and ready to talk business, unlike the other friend's bozo college roommate who, though 25-plus years older than the newbie, had no clue of what to say once we got past the temperature.

The tools to prepare are at everyone's disposal today and are simply phenomenal. With a few clicks of the computer mouse, one can become informed on almost any subject matter in a matter of minutes. God gave us Google and its competitors, and it's your job to be sure your team uses these types of tools. Make it mandatory that your people be prepared, and make it known that if they aren't, their career with you may also perish.

Things you should stop worrying about, but can't
Second-guessing wastes time and leads to nowhere

This column was originally published in November 2011

In business and in life, we all spend time conjuring up negative thoughts that are not only unproductive but also make us crazy.

Do you sometimes second-guess yourself after a meeting with that important client? Maybe it was something that just jumped out of your mouth before you considered the consequences when you were talking to someone important or something as simple as wondering why did he or she look at you "that way." It's even worse sometimes when you're the CEO or leader and you browbeat yourself over and over, pondering if you got the intended message out with the right balance of firmness, yet warmth and caring.

It is unrealistic to believe we should think only good thoughts, particularly in business when things move at a lightning pace and the path to achieving objectives is littered with potholes just waiting to cause a serious blowout. We must always be playing what-if games in our heads to determine a course of action if something isn't working the way we expected. This means having plan B at the ready or even C and D if you're losing ground and your worst-case scenario suddenly becomes your living nightmare.

All of this can lead to analysis paralysis and sometimes overwhelmingly questioning your own judgment. The difference, however, between an effective leader and one who is constantly gripped by second thoughts of uncertainty is the ability to compartmentalize negative thinking. Sometimes that's easier said than done. However, with a little practice, you can turn your focus away from thoughts that are an exercise in futility, either because what is done is done and there's nothing you can do about it or the odds of that doomsday scenario actually occurring are minuscule.

There are numerous techniques to employ to minimize incessant rehashing of our actions or decisions. Too many times, excessive indulgence in drink, food or other dubious activities is used as an antidote to ward off our demons. But at best, these diversions are temporary, extremely unhealthy and, many times, lead to even more serious problems.

Exercise, on the other hand, has been proven to have numerous psychological benefits. In my case, the best way to take my mind off business problems or my errors of omission or commission is to take a vigorous run or do an aggressive workout, and soon, the pain from my aching joints almost magically erases those irrational concerns that crept into my head just a few minutes earlier. It's sort of like having a stomachache and then someone punches you in the nose, and all of sudden the only thing you can think about is the new pain in your nose.

A more disciplined and less painful approach is to chronicle all of your concerns, putting them in writing on a legal pad or tapping them out on your computer or iPad.

If you have multiple negative thoughts, list them starting with those that you perceive as the most serious. Under each concern, try to define the problem in as few words as possible. If you think you spoke out of school and said something you shouldn't have, jot it down. Finally, go ahead and really beat yourself up by spelling out on your list the worse possible consequences. Once you see them in writing, much of your concern will suddenly dissipate as you realize your problems or missteps don't seem all that daunting anymore.

For those remaining concerns that don't make the "it ain't worth thinking about" cut, the next step is to focus on what you need to do to mitigate any damage. You might just find that after you crystallize the issues in writing, you will stumble onto heretofore unthought-of remedies to your problems or your narrative takes on a life of its own and leads you in a new direction to find new answers for which you didn't even have questions.

This method of mitigating concerns by reducing them to their lowest common denominator won't cure all your problems, but it just may enable you to put your priorities in order and eliminate time-wasting worrying that leads to nowhere. As the often-recited Serenity Prayer states, "Grant me the serenity to accept the things I cannot change, the courage to change the things I can, and the wisdom to know the difference."

What do good CEOs have in common with a fisherman?

Knowing when to fish or cut bait in business

This column was originally published in July 2013

This is no fish story. Instead, this column is about one of the most important roles an owner or CEO must fulfill on an ongoing basis.

Leaders spend an inordinate amount of time dealing with the issues du jour. These range from managing people, wooing and cajoling customers, creating strategies, searching for elusive answers and just about everything in between. These are all good and necessary tasks and undertakings. Too frequently, however, these same leaders delegate this effort to others or ignore it altogether. To be "in the game," you have to know when to fish or cut bait.

Successful fishermen know that to catch a fish they have to sometimes cast their lines dozens of times just to get a nibble or bite. The first bite might not result in reeling in that big fish. Frequently, a nibble is just a tipoff as to where the fish are swimming.

The same applies to reaching out — casting a line, if you will, to explore new, many times unorthodox, opportunities for your organization. These opportunities can be finding a competitor to buy, discovering an unlikely yet complementary business to partner with or snagging a new customer from an industry that had heretofore gone undiscovered.

All of this takes setting a portion of your time to investigate unique situations, as well as a healthy dose of creativity and the ability to think well beyond the most obvious.

Too many times even the most accomplished executives lack the motivation to look for ideas in unlikely places. Some would believe that it's unproductive to spend a significant amount of time on untested "what ifs." Just like sage fishermen, executives can also cultivate their own places to troll.

Of course, networking is a good starting point, particularly with people unrelated to your business, where sometimes one may fortuitously stumble onto a new idea that leads to a payoff.

Other times, a hot lead might come from simply reading trade papers, general media reports and just surfing the Internet. The creative twist is reading material that doesn't necessarily apply to your own industry or to anything even close to what you do. New ideas come disguised in many forms and are frequently hidden in a variety of nooks and crannies. This means training yourself to read between the lines.

Once something piques your imagination, the next step is to follow through and call the other company or send an inquiry by email to state that it might be worth a short conversation to explore potential mutually beneficial arrangements. This can at times be a bit frustrating and futile. That's when you cut bait and start anew.

However, reaching out to someone today could materialize into something of substance tomorrow. The often skipped but critical next step, even after hitting a seemingly dead end, is to always close the loop with whomever you made contact. Even if there is no apparent fit or interest at the moment, it's easy and polite to send a short note of thanks and attach your one-paragraph "elevator" pitch.

That same person just might be casting him or herself, be it in a month or even a year later, and make contact with a different organization that's not a fit for him or her, but recall you because you followed through and created awareness about your story.

This just might lead the person with whom you first spoke to call you because you had had the courtesy to send that note. Bingo — you just got a bite all because of continuing to cast your line.

Good CEOs and honest fishermen also have one other important characteristic in common: humility. They know that when a line is cast it won't result in a catch every time. But if nothing is ventured, it's guaranteed there will be nothing gained. Don't let that big one get away. Just keep casting.

Keep your eyes open and your mouth shut

How to find new ideas in the most unlikely places

This column was originally published in October 2013

Most weeks I get on a plane and attempt to have an out-of-body experience to deal with all the hassles of flying as I travel from point A to point B. When flying, I have a few simple rules. One, I almost never eat the food. Two, I attempt to talk to no one other than obligatory hellos. Three, I never argue with or say a cross word to flight attendants.

One other very important practice I follow on land, sea and especially in the air is that I constantly scan my surroundings for potential troubles and new ideas.

On a recent flight, upon boarding, I quietly and obediently proceeded to my designated seat.

As I began to sit down, a gentleman asked if I would mind trading seats with him so that he could sit next to his wife. Like most seasoned travelers I try to accommodate reasonable requests. In this case it seemed a no-brainer to agree to move.

Notice the details

As I started to settle in and fasten my seatbelt I noted that my new seatmate was very hot. No, it's not what you're thinking. I mean she seemed to be flushed and radiating heat, ostensibly from a high fever. I'm thinking, this is not good, plus it proves the age-old adage that no good deed goes unpunished.

In the next minute I had an epiphany, which happens frequently as

I believe that many problems come disguised as opportunities.

I rang the call button and, when approached, asked the cabin attendant to please bring me two cloth napkins. I stated that the purpose was to construct a makeshift facemask by tying the two pieces together to prevent possibly contracting some dreaded disease.

I feared that my intentions could be misinterpreted if I were to don a mask without an explanation; this could cause a well-meaning passenger to drag me to the floor thinking I had nefarious motives.

The stewardess smiled, nodding approvingly of my plan. She then summoned all her co-attendants to my seat and proceeded to whisper what I was attempting. Otherwise, she explained, they, too, could misunderstand my appearance and cause me bodily harm.

As founder and CEO of Max-Wellness, a health and wellness retail and marketing chain, I'm always looking for that next special something to share with my team. Therefore, while burying my now masked face in a newspaper so as not to frighten or offend the sick seatmate, I began dictating a memo to my merchandise product group proudly asserting that I just had another "aha!" moment, for which I am well-known, among my colleagues. For full disclosure, however, I am sometimes known for being a bit "out there" on occasion — but no one bats a thousand.

Turn an idea into a product

This particular predicament gave me the idea to develop a product kit that we could sell to weary travelers in our stores and in airports. I suggested a handful of complementary products, including a mask, a disinfectant spray and, if all else fails, relief remedies. I also noted that it probably would be prudent to include a cigarette pack-type "Black Box" warning stating that the mask is not what some suspicious flyers might think, but instead it's for prevention of disease only. I even proposed we market these kits directly to the airlines to dispense as an emergency prophylactic for passengers exposed to airborne (pun intended) pathogens.

Fleeting thoughts have value

A key role for business leaders is teaching a management team to use fleeting thoughts as a springboard, to pair common problems with sometimes-simple solutions.

Just because it is a simple fix, though, doesn't mean the idea couldn't be a lucrative breakthrough.

When something sparks an idea it needs be taken to the next level before being pooh-poohed. Most likely the vast majority of these inspirations won't see the light of day, but that's OK. Just think — what if one transient idea translates into the next Post-it Notes, Kleenex or bottled water?

The next time you sit by a masked man on a plane, it most likely won't be the Lone Ranger. Instead, you might be witnessing the incubation of the next best thing since sliced bread.

The melting ice cube syndrome
The clock can be your friend or enemy

This column was originally published in September 2014

No, I have not made a new discovery in chemistry/physics. Nor is the syndrome in this headline a medical finding that will lead to yet another worldwide woe. Instead, the melting ice cube syndrome affects every business at some point.

Organizations have a limited amount of time to solve problems or take advantage of opportunities, and the second hand on every clock is always moving. Almost every major sport, except baseball, also must deal with the melting ice cube in the form of a ticking clock.

When a team is winning, it works to turn up the heat to exhaust the time and quickly melt the ice cube so that the opponent can't score. If a team is losing, it must take advantage of every second in order to score again or create a freezing effect to slow the process.

Decide not to decide

Sometimes with a particularly serious problem, time can be a powerful tool because rather than taking action, it is better to move into a watch-and-wait mode. Often, the best decision is no decision and coming to that conclusion takes evaluation, highly educated guesses and even a bit of luck.

Too many times, we spring into action and wind up doing more harm than good. Conversely, other times we wait and hope, and the problem escalates into a disaster because of its exponential effects.

Frequently it seems we can't win for losing and no matter which way we turn, we have issues. So what's the best solution?

Effectively using a risk/reward inventory can point us in the right direction to improve the odds of choosing the best course of action. Many also call this an upside/downside assessment. In its simplest form, it's really taking the time to make the effort to stop, think, research and then formulate a plan before pulling the trigger. Haste makes waste, but a "do nothing" strategy can also work against you.

A leader must train his or her team to use a disciplined evaluation process on just about anything out of the norm, any matter in which making the wrong decision could prove costly or painful.

Make a work sheet
This can be facilitated by creating your own simple work sheet whereby on the left side you list the course of actions that you might take and on the right side you make your assessment using a one to 10 numeric gauge, with the lowest numbers indicating unlikely to help and a 10 indicating the best shot at working.

When you're done, you eliminate those low numbered actions, as an example, any with a rating of four or less. You then focus on the remaining actions scored five or higher, which are most likely to be effective, and don't exceed your threshold of pain. This thoughtful and disciplined process simply improves the odds in your favor both when solving problems or jump-starting opportunities.

The clock can be your friend or your enemy; you just need to learn how to estimate what can be accomplished in the amount of time remaining before the ice cube melts and evaporates forever.

9

Negotiating

If you don't ask,
you'll never get

This column was originally published in November 2004

Pretend for a minute that you're a door-to-door salesperson. You drive to a nice neighborhood. After parking, you take out your sample case of goods and proudly and confidently march up the two steps leading to the house with the quaint white picket fence. You proceed to the door, knock twice and hear the squeak of the hinges as the door opens. Without really looking, as you take a deep breath, that audible signal tells you it's show time. You immediately descend into your sales pitch with a generous dose of boast and brag assertions about your bag of must have, can't live without products.

When you're done you resume breathing.
Instantly, you note that you are looking through to the kitchen, but you don't see anyone until you move your head down 20 degrees and suddenly realize that the person in front of you is a bit short, about 3 feet 1 inch tall and around 5 years old.

Not to worry, you are on a roll and in seconds a 5-foot-4-inch replacement appears, and you simply start over. When you're done this time, you close your bag and turn away, exclaiming as you walk out of sight "have a nice day."

What's wrong with this picture? You forgot to ask for the order! Sound strange? Maybe for a professional door-to-door salesperson who can put food on the table only if he or she makes the sale. However, in my experience, many executives forget this last important ingredient and worse yet, many don't realize it.

As CEO of a *Fortune* 500 company for 16 years, I can recall dozens of times when people came to see me, about million or multimillion dollar programs, but left without making the ask. It is sort of like a bad love story. There is a beginning, middle, but no ending.

I was always astounded by how easily people gave up. If I looked crosswise at them, or seemed bored, or if I inadvertently even yawned, some would simply pack up before actually asking what they came for, apologize for taking my time, sometimes the more down trodden mumbled "excuse me for breathing," as they walked out the door.

Unfortunately, little did these uninspired closers know, many times, they were so close, yet so far away because they couldn't suck it in and ask me to sign on the dotted line.

In my early years of running a startup, I quickly learned that one either had to lead, follow, or get out of the way, but never, never forget to ask for whatever it is that was needed to survive.

In those first years, I asked for hundreds of things from various constituents, including vendors, investors, and customers. Sometimes, I was initially told "no," but I always went back and rephrased, reoffered or did whatever it took to get what we needed.

One of my favorite real-life experiences occurred in the first year of my company's operation. We were doing business with a huge Japanese electronics manufacturer that was about as personal as dealing with the post office by phone asking for a zip code, or worse, the IRS. Actually, in those days, most of our dealings with this Japanese company were through a U.S. intermediary who had the title of Credit Manager and who, no doubt, was also a part-time bouncer. Our dilemma was we only had a $25,000.

merchandise line of credit, and every time we asked the Credit Manager for more credit, he would dig into his lexicon and respond with his usual one syllable answer — "no." If he was feeling particularly verbose, sometimes he would say "no can do this because of my Japanese bosses' policy."

I needed a plan to bypass this Mr. No credit manager. Finally, it came to me; I would write directly to the Japanese company's CEO and plead my case, asking for an increased credit line and explaining what's in it for his company. I knew I'd have to be very creative to get the CEO's attention. First, I needed to do some homework. I went to the library and skimmed some business books on Japanese business culture.

I confirmed that the Japanese were fiercely proud, very formal, and keeping their word was paramount. The light again went off in my head, and I had a strategy.

First, I drafted a letter in English emphasizing what I needed, why I needed it. Next, I found a local Japanese student studying here and paid her to translate my letter, long hand, into Japanese. Then, I sent it Federal Express, with the label written both in English and in Japanese, addressed directly to the CEO.

About two weeks later, I received a person-to-person telephone call through the international operator who stated that the CEO of the Japanese company was on the line with an English-speaking translator.

The CEO asked me many questions in his native language about my business and me, and then the translator interpreted. It seemed like the conversation was going on for hours. I was just thankful as a startup; I wasn't paying the long distance charges.

The gist of the comments from the CEO was that this was one of the very few times a U.S. company of any size had ever made the effort to write him a letter in Japanese. At the conclusion of the conversation, the CEO asked me one final question. "If I give you the increased credit, how do I know you will pay us?" I paused and quickly remembered my research, and then blurted out with confidence "because I'm giving you my word." The CEO then said something very quickly in Japanese, and the interpreter translated his words saying "you now have a million dollar line of credit."

The next morning, the now humbled U.S. credit manager who had received word from the land of the rising sun, called congratulating me on my creativity while, no doubt, thinking he'd been had.

The bottom line is if you don't ask, you'll never get. Do your homework, create a plan and ask. Oh yes, it's also a good idea, just in case, to never forget to look down too.

In negotiations, it is sometimes what you don't say that really makes the difference

This column was originally published in September 2005

During my career I have been the primary negotiator on literally thousands of transactions. Everything from store leases to basic vendor contracts, labor agreements, all the way to major acquisitions amounting to somewhere north of $3 billion, including the sale of my company. A deal is much like a love story. You have the beginning when both parties have great expectations, the middle when everybody reaches the frustration point, and the end when boy gets girl — or, in the case of a business deal, where handshakes, high-fives and guffaws abound. The best deals are when both sides feel they won, and for icing on the cake outsmarted, outmaneuvered, or gotten the best of the other guy.

Similar to a major league baseball player who steps to the plate and takes an indeterminable amount of time pulling and tugging on various parts of his anatomy and uniform before he is finally ready to accept the pitch, the negotiator, too, has his or her own quirky obsessions before sitting down at the table. Although I don't tug on body parts, for me it is wearing that lucky suit, donning that special "power tie" and using other accouterments, such as a "magic pen" that I carry just to sign deals.

Once I am past the superstition phase, I actually go through a thorough cerebral process and "deal inventory." I ask myself: "Do I really want to do this thing?" "Am I sure I want to make it happen because it adds value and it is not just about winning?" and "At what point I'm prepared to say 'thanks, but no thanks' and walk away?"

Make no mistake about it, there are a lot of theatrics in the negotiating process. Some people like to play the tough guy, others the country bumpkin, and a few love to portray an aura of total and utter indifference. Just like a good thespian, you pull out the best costume from your wardrobe for the circumstances to create the character you want to play, and then it is almost show time. But first, one of the most crucial exercises is do your homework. Find out all there is to know about the opponent. What is his or her track record in previous deals? Talk to people who know the person's style of doing business. Just like Wild West gunslingers, negotiators have a reputation.

Next decide where to meet. Do you want to try for home court advantage and control the environment by meeting in your office? Or, perhaps you will give the other side the sense that they are in control by meeting at their place. For most of my bigger deals the first session typically takes place in neutral territory, be it a banker's or attorney's office, or a quiet restaurant. In an eatery always sit with your back to the wall (which is a lesson learned from Godfather type movies). From a more practical standpoint, if your opponent has that power seat, you'll lose concentration as you watch his eyes darting hither and fro, observing who is coming and going. Another hard learned lesson is to try to meet one on one to avoid having the opponent waste time trying to impress the others whom he brought along. A key component of the process is to be sure the person with whom you're talking has the juice to do the deal, not just someone taking messages back and forth.

Once the preliminaries are behind you, it is time to get down to business. Whenever possible, force the other side to make the opening offer. Sometimes it is what you don't say that matters most. I have been in talks where the other guy was negotiating with himself — asking the questions and then answering them before I could open my mouth. We have all experienced or heard of a seller offering a price range, for example, between $2,000 and $3,000. Oh sure, you are going to say "I'll pay the higher price." I don't think so. Instead, let the other guy show his cards first.

Attention to body language plays an important role in understanding the dynamics of the negotiations. There are always plenty of little signs that point the way providing clues as to what the other person is really thinking. Watching closely, you can pick-up on these subtle signals: the glisten of moisture at the hairline or on a moustache (anxiety), the thumping of fingers (impatience), the Adam's apple bobbing up and down (panic). One of my favorite experiences was during the negotiations for a $400 million chain of stores where I picked up on my counterpart's habit of slouching in his chair when he was being less than truthful. Each time he stretched the facts, he would slide down even further. I knew I had him when I could only see his eyebrows above the table.

Be patient. Transactions take time. You have to be prepared to let them play out. When you are overly eager it shows. You pay more as the buyer and you get less as the seller. I have used other techniques, albeit slightly rude, such as being late for a specific session or even not showing at all. Of course, I would always call to apologize with a good excuse such as my dog ate my deal work papers. In a few past transactions the other side walked away, sometimes for a few weeks, one time for a year. Always be prepared to leave the door open when the talking stops, but also know when you're at the end of the road. It is the old story "be careful what you wish for." To make a deal just to make the deal can be costly and painful in the long-run.

Another tool is the use of throwaways. A throwaway is something you ask for, but you don't really care if you get. Using this approach, you can show a spirit of compromise and allow the other side to negotiate away what you consider to be meaningless items.

Finally, never make a promise you can't keep. Never offer something you are not prepared to give. Most importantly, it is the things you don't say that can be the difference between a long-term profitable transaction or a money loser.

Don't negotiate
with yourself

Woulda, coulda, shoulda mind games
will drive you over the edge

This column was originally published in March 2008

Everyone who is anyone has a top 10 list of this or that. So why should I be any different? At the top of my list of the biggest time waster is, "negotiating with yourself." It's superfluous and an exercise in futility. The only good news is if you're an investor in the makers of Maalox or Valium, it is a proven revenue enhancer.

Asking yourself repetitive and numerous rhetorical questions will thrust you into a vicious cycle on a road to nowhere. It's much like playing pingpong with yourself: There is never a winner.

From time to time, we all engage in this exasperating process. However, when negotiating with yourself becomes a habitual routine for you, you're well on your way to diluting your effectiveness and driving the people around you to distraction or worse.

Do not confuse this negative mental gymnastic with the more productive process of playing "what if" games. The difference is with "what if" scenarios you should deal with a series of facts to which you can add various suppositions to predict the most likely outcomes. This is simply good business and prepares you for whatever battle you're about to embark upon, such as buying a competitor or making almost any type of deal. A thoughtful and reasoned negotiating strategy is loosely similar to the lessons of physics, which teaches us that, "For every cause, there is an effect; for action, there is a (predictable) reaction." On the flip side, it's of no value to negotiate with yourself, without concrete facts, trying to guess what someone is going to say or do.

Negotiating with oneself can migrate from the subconscious to the conscious and then erupt into a full-fledged traumatic episode. After submitting your proposal and before you receive any feedback, you conjure up a myriad responses that you think you might receive, engaging in a second guessing game of woulda, coulda, shoulda. In the cross-examination of a witness, attorneys call this "asked and answered." This may play well on the TV show "Boston Legal" but in real life business, it's a waste of energy.

In essence, under the majority of circumstances you can predict with a relatively high degree of certainty how the other side will respond. As a way of an example, let's examine the key factors in a typical acquisition by one company of another. First, company A decides to buy company B because there are management, market and/or economic synergies. Company A makes its offer and the decision usually gets down to three fundamental considerations.

First, what is the price, as in "show me the money?" Is it fair or a low-ball offer? Moreover, who gets how much and when? Secondly, at the end of the day, which side will get to call the shots in the newly configured venture? Combining management teams and calling it a merger of equals and keeping everybody happy is about as likely as finding peace in the Middle East in the next 30 days. It sounds great, but, unfortunately, the desired results are usually nothing more than a PR spin based on fairy tales. Thirdly, which side will be perceived as the winner in the public's eye? This is particularly significant in public company transactions. Keeping these types of predicable formulas in mind because, based on empirical results, they are good antidotes for negotiating with yourself.

Here is a simple preventative method to avoid endless self-doubt during the downtime between when you make your offer and when you get that first response. After you fire your opening salvo in the form of whatever you're offering, then stand down and wait until there is something to respond to other than your own self-doubts and negative thoughts. Although it will take a herculean effort and willpower, refrain from questioning your proposal and always give the other side first opportunity to respond. This will eliminate or, at least, dramatically reduce your own internalized histrionics. You'll not only be more productive, but you'll be a better leader and possibly a happier executive.

Remember, there are a lot better ways to get your exercise other than playing a game of pingpong with yourself.

Something has to give

How to go over, under or around to accomplish your objectives

This column was originally published in September 2009

There is a great oldie but goodie song, "Something's Gotta Give," that hit the top of the charts many years ago but still provides a valuable lesson for today. The basic thesis of this catchy ditty, applicable to any business, is that when an overwhelming force meets an immovable object to progress, there has to be movement.

Any time two groups with differing views get together, either they have to compromise or one side has to cave in order to move forward. The latter is not likely; therefore, the trick is to get off the dime as quickly as possible by removing that figurative blockade to get to the next step.

There are always two sides to every story and then the truth. Usually, in negotiations, both sides are convinced they're righteous, fighting the fight for truth, justice and capitalism. This may result in an immovable object, with one side of the negotiations butting heads with an irrepressible force, as in the other side. After the early rounds of mental gymnastics and histrionics, typically inertia sets in and a wall emerges between the parties built on a foundation of emotions.

There is nothing wrong at the beginning of a discussion in seeing how much you can get in your favor. A hundred percent is great, but typically unattainable. We see it every day in offices, in the boardroom and, yes, the nursery school where two toddlers fight over the same toys. We all get the toy tug-of-war thing, but grown-ups behaving like nursery-school students becomes an exercise in futility, fueled by frustration. After the obligatory pushback, which is part of the deal-making process, it is time to stop, think and determine how to accomplish the goal of getting past the wall.

Essentially, it gets down to physics. If it is impossible to move the wall, those involved have to figure out how to go over, under or around whatever obstacle is blocking the path. One does not need to be a rocket scientist to do this. Just put yourself in the other side's shoes and play out in your mind how you would react if you were the opponent being asked to do what has been proposed.

For example, if the problem is economics, think of what besides money you can use to sweeten the deal and get to a yes. It could be something as simple as agreeing to throw in a nonmonetary concession that makes the other side feel like they "won," such as moving an office, changing a meeting venue or the like so that the guys whom you now view as wearing the black hats feel that they won something. It could be improved payment terms, free this or that, you fill in the blanks. Most business executives don't know when to say when and will continue to fight for something that, at the end of the day, does not make enough of a difference or even matter in the bigger scheme of things. Fine-tuning your skills to discern when it is time to take a new tact is where real talent is required. It's exhausting to the opposition and yourself when both sides start fighting for the sake of fighting and forget what the goal was when it all began. This happens frequently and aggravates everyone, wastes time and money and runs the risk of ruining a relationship or deal that would have been productive.

Watch for telltale signals in the negotiations and you will know when it is time to try a different strategy. Sure signs are when the other side starts muttering under their breath or rolling their eyes when you speak. Another good bet that all is not well is the sound of slamming doors and those across the table talking to one another in front of you but referring to you in the third-person as if you were not even in the room.

You can be the savior and the big winner by throwing out a "gimme" that provides creative alternatives so that the opponent feels better about the arrangements.

As the lyrics in the song reveal, "Fight, fight, fight it with all of (your) might. Chances are on some heavenly star-spangled night, you will find out, as sure as (you) live, something's really got to give." Most times, it is just a matter of reading the tea leaves to find a way to go over, under or around that immovable object by putting yourself in the other person's place.

The dumbest farmers grow the biggest potatoes
How to outwit the guys who think they're the smartest ones in the room

This column was originally published in June 2011

Early in my career, I worked for a CEO who was fond of pontificating about how one doesn't need to always project an image of being the most brilliant, sophisticated businessperson and that this power image could actually be a detriment in certain circumstances. He would conclude his mini-sermon by flashing a smirk and reciting his favorite old German saying: "The dumbest farmers grow the biggest potatoes." I was in my mid-20s in those days, and in hindsight, I most likely didn't fully appreciate my boss's words of wisdom because I had assumed the best tactic was never let them see you sweat, although under your outer layer you were consumed by fear and soaking wet.

Today, that farmer's adage now rings true with me. I have seen executives over the years who, with an exaggerated sense of their own importance, have invariably put their foot in their mouths. These pundits, most always, come across as very slick, certainly articulate know-it-alls who are so impressed with themselves they frequently miss the forest from the trees. Another trait of these self-anointed moguls is that they are usually afraid to ask the questions for which they need answers because they don't want to diminish their image and have those with whom they're working or negotiating think they might not be perfect.

Not seeking the truth or failing to discover the underlying facts can, and often does, play into the hands of the "farmer type" my former mentor idolized. Instead of systematically working to flush out a concept that passes the important "smell tests" or probing to actually determine what works either economically or functionally, the high and mighty will simply wing it because they really think they are smarter than everyone else.

I love negotiating with these types because they never bother with the details, thinking, "who cares," that will be handled by the "little people." This fixation on image and sacrificing substance for form typically results in a lot of money being left on the table primarily because of blinding hubris.

Meanwhile, the mild-mannered farmer with that "aw shucks" persona, who is by no means average, gains the upper hand by asking many different questions and sometimes the same questions, using different words, and doing it more than once. Each inquiry produces a better understanding of the issues and opportunities and how to turn them to his or her favor. While this grunt work is going on, our boy- or girl-wonder is too busy hypothesizing and contemplating about this or that and is only available to hear him or herself speak.

At the end of the meeting, the too-slick-for-their-own-good, buttoned-up types with every hair in place, go off, normally without a clue that they've been had and that the enemy was really themselves.

The old TV cop show "Colombo" and its more modern-day version "Monk" are indicative of how to underwhelm the other side. These detectives on the surface seemingly unaware, a bit disheveled, somewhat babbling and incessantly asked the same question a zillion times in different ways until they get the needed answers to solve the mystery.

How can you use this low-key approach to outwit the competition? First, always do your homework. Give the opposition the benefit of the doubt by assuming they are very good at what they do, and don't underestimate them. It's better to be over prepared and overestimate an opponent's abilities than find yourself on the short end of the discussion because you've failed to fully prepare. And, never ever be afraid to ask any questions. My view is the only dumb question is the one you never ask. So what if the other smart guys snicker at what they perceive as your sophomoric questions? Many times, shrewd businesspeople ask questions even though they know the answer just to learn if the other people in the room know their stuff. Finally, don't be too quick to volunteer information. It's much better to be a good listener and learn as you go, than to be a fast talker.

When you harvest your next crop, be sure you produce the biggest potatoes by knowing what you don't know and being smart enough to understand how and when to ask the right questions. Doing this will produce an abundant yield more times than not.

What's the most important question to answer before the negotiations begin?

Sometimes it's best to start at the end

This column was originally published in September 2012

In developing a strategy, creating a new business or launching a product line, intensive preplanning is what can make the difference between success and failure. This same principle applies to negotiating just about anything. No matter what you want to achieve, be it selling a new customer, buying a competitor or hiring a superstar, you must determine what is the end result you want before you put pen to paper or make that first introductory call.

We've all heard hundreds of times about the importance of "putting yourself in the other guy's shoes" or showing some empathy. Good basic advice, but do you really follow these suggestions?

In many business relationships, if it becomes a win/lose transaction, at the end of the day, one side is going to be very unhappy and the other side, albeit temporarily satisfied, could ultimately lose, too. In most instances, both sides have alternatives. Unless you have found the holy grail that no one can live without, the other side always has choices. One of which can be to do nothing and take a hike.

Most negotiations begin with the thought, "What's in it for me?" Instead, the first question should always be, "How can we enable the other side to win (or feel as though they have won)?" It's all about looking at the objective through the other person's eyes. This simply translates into giving the "opposition" something that they must have, even if they've yet to realize it, while meeting your own needs. Rather than start with figuring out how much can you make on the deal or the positive result that will accrue to you if you hire a particular superstar, ask yourself, "What can I do to make the other side feel like the winner?"

For your next initiative, start at the end and work toward the beginning. You might just be pleasantly surprised with the road map you construct using this technique. Here are a few examples.

You want to buy a competitor because it has a product that will enhance your offering, but you don't need all of the other widgets that this target manufactures. The traditional strategy would be to make an offer knowing that, if you succeed, you'll scuttle all of the company's other operations, cherry-picking what you want from the carcass. This could work and might be the easiest way to achieve your goal, but this Machiavellian method of taking no prisoners likely won't play well with the target company owner, who has spent years building it and is emotionally invested in the business and the organization's employees. When you look at the situation through the lens of the founder, you determine that a different approach, such as paying a good price for the entire business, plucking the item you want from the company, and then selling the rest of the company back to the employees could be the ticket to getting discussions started. This way the owner gets his money, he is a hero with his employees, and you acquire the product you need to grow.

Let's say you want to hire the best salesperson in your industry who, unfortunately, works for your competitor. Instead of just going in and offering a big salary and bonus, which he or she most likely has already been offered by someone else, try to determine, after doing your homework, what this superstar's hot buttons are. Maybe he has made it known that he would like to work remotely from a desert island while continuing to build his book of business. Looking at it from his perspective, you figure out that you can buy him his piece of sand somewhere with a beautiful view, obtain high-speed Internet connectivity to his paradise and allow him to work six months per year in his dream location. Rather than just making a cash-rich offer, start the negotiations by providing a solution to your target's fondest expectations.

Putting yourself in the other guy's shoes is far from a new idea. However, too many executives forget that creating a win-win is preferable to having it only your way. Remember, many times, instead of just knowing the answers, you first have to figure out what questions to ask to ensure success.

Beware of red herrings

... why an executive must learn to be both a detective and an interpreter

This column was originally published in January 2014

First, a quick refresher. The term red herring is derived from the practice of training hounds to follow a scent, or distracting them with a different smell, during a fox hunt. In a story it can be a clue that leads the reader towards a false impression or conclusion. Not to muddy the waters, but this term also refers to a preliminary prospectus sometimes used for an initial public offering (IPO) that intentionally provides only a portion of a company's vital data.

A red herring can also be a diversionary tactic used in business to make an argument, or raise a concern, that is not relevant to the central issue, but appears initially to be plausible.

Has the tide turned?
Here's an example: You have been working on an acquisition and finally the other side has agreed to a face-to-face powwow on your turf to seal the deal. After months of sweet-talking, playing nice and being on your best behavior, you think you can make this transaction finally happen.

Then out of the blue, a few days before the visit, you start to get not so warm and fuzzy emails from the other side referencing the offer price. Your touch-base calls suddenly go unreturned and you get that sinking feeling that the tide has changed.

What gives? First you must take a step back and retrace everything that has transpired since the tone began changing. Once you're sure it's not you, rather than improving the deal, you move to a watch and wait mode.

On the appointed day your guests arrive, you rush into the room, hand extended with a big smile on your face, but they signal indifferent expressions and reciprocate with wimpy handshakes.

To avoid making a huge tactical misjudgment, you must immediately move to detective and interpreter mode. The detective portion of this persona requires you to look beyond the obvious, not accepting circumstantial evidence as gospel, learning to think like Sherlock Holmes — assessing information and searching for real meaning from scraps of random comments and innuendos.

Part and parcel of this is also the need to function the same as a United Nations-type, interpreting words and body language to translate what is said into what is really meant. Effective managers instinctively can read between the lines to drill down to the lowest common denominator to get beyond red herring statements that merely become diversions to solving the real problem.

Playing a bargaining chip

Fast forward to the end of this dramatization and we learn that the visiting team was simply trying to put you on the defensive by employing a "big chill" technique to cause you to second guess your economic offer.

Their real objective was to gain a bargaining chip to get you to agree to allow them to keep their existing titles so they could save face in the community. This is right out of Red Herring 101.

Red herrings might provide some direction but, more frequently than not, they can send you down the wrong path.

With a little practice, a degree of healthy skepticism and a resistance to jumping to conclusions, red herrings can be readily spotted once it's understood how people use them, either intentionally or inadvertently. A good starting point is to remember that red herrings, just like their real life namesakes, don't pass the smell test.

'No' is one of the most dreaded words in our vocabulary

But sometimes, 'no' is simply the word 'maybe' in disguise

This column was originally published in May 2014

"No" is the one word we all hear too often. It can invoke everything from a mere sigh with a shrug of the shoulders to the sense that a dagger has been driven into our hearts.

The word "no," according to child development experts, is learned around the age of 8 months and is easily understood, particularly when delivered rapidly in a high-pitched voice. From there it goes downhill.

Throughout childhood and our adult lives, "no" is that feared one-syllable word in response to a hopeful kid's request, "Can I have an ice cream cone?" and to the nervous, hormones-raging teen's question, "Will you go to the dance with me?" and as adults we've all at one time breathlessly asked, "May I have a raise?"

Do your own research. Pick a day and keep track of the number of times you're told "no" by those you encounter, or how often you say "no" to others. This little exercise will serve as a report card as to how effective you are in convincing others to do it your way or, conversely, how frequently you shut others off with a premature negative response because of the way you were asked.

Not the final answer
Does this unwelcome pejorative really mean all is lost? Perhaps not.

To avoid the feared "no," guard against asking questions that can be summarily dismissed with this two-letter declarative. To get to the opposite response, try employing the lessons from the marketing acronym "AIDA," which stands for Attention, Interest, Desire and Action.

Here's an oversimplified example: Rather than ask, "May I have the order?" which could invoke the path of least resistance ending in a "no," paint a verbal picture by grabbing the listener's attention and asserting, "I can double your business in three months."

Next, for the interest piece, state, "I can make this happen for a mere $100." For the third component of this formula, top off your request with a sprinkling of desire by uttering, "Everyone who has done this has been promoted."

For the pièce de résistance, create action by proclaiming, "You must let me know in three minutes."

When you follow this road map you just might get lucky and the recipient of your words of wisdom will call for action and grab the order sheet from you and immediately sign.

Avoid setting up for failure

To get to "yes," don't set yourself up to fail by neglecting to soundly and factually explain what's in it for the other guy. Too many people make a request without romancing the "ask."

Sometimes "no" just means you didn't do an effective job of presenting your request to motivate a positive response. Many times a "no" is merely a "maybe" in disguise and is your cue to forge ahead to explain the features and benefits.

Accepting a "no" can be an excuse to stop trying. Usually a "no" means "no" only after the 10th time or when the other person walks out or hangs up.

10

Competition

Stop the "woe is me" and turn your David into a Goliath

This column was originally published in October 2005

Every company, every institution, every anything always believes the competitor is smarter, better, or stronger. It must be something that is mysteriously embedded in every organization's DNA. I don't care if it is Microsoft or Wal-Mart, Intel or Chrysler, I guarantee you they all are borderline paranoid thinking that even the most miniscule competitor is gaining on them in some form or fashion. In many respects, a small to moderate dose of paranoia is a good thing. It forces organizations to change, improve, grow, innovate, and execute.

Don't you think that the Board of GM is convinced that "Ford has a better idea" or the Trustees of Harvard might fear that even little Podunk U. in nowhere U.S.A. might overtake them in some obscure rankings?

While watching every move of the competitor is good, and a little fear of failure isn't bad, I think too many organizations of all types spend too much time looking over their shoulder. Way too much energy is wasted playing "what if" mind games. If we did what they do, we would be where they are at; if only we would have thought of that before they did, we would be number one. These thoughts underscore the old adage: "if you had wheels, you would be a wagon."

Instead of devoting your time and effort in this woulda, coulda, shoulda exercise in futility, pick your priorities and decide how you want to be positioned before your competitors do it for you. Every organization has its strengths and weaknesses. The best and the worst of organizations have their hidden warts. The way to beat the competition is to pick your battles and fight them at the time and place of your choosing — not theirs. We all grew up hearing our parents, teachers, whomever, constantly telling us "always pick on someone your own size." Bad idea! This concept implies a 50/50 chance of winning and of course, losing as well. I am not big on fair fights. Therefore, find your strength by taking advantage of the other guy's weakness.

The smarter approach is to figure out how a David can take on a Goliath and prevail. There is a process that can get you there. First, identify your competitor or competitors and learn everything there is to know about them. Read every word ever published about your foes, read their press releases, and study their ads word for word, comma-for-comma. Talk to their customers, employees, their supporters and detractors. When you are all done, do it again, but this time read and listen between the lines. Think about how your organization is different and what works and what doesn't. I promise you that the competition has many of the same issues you have. They may have instead cracked the code for an effective work-around, making a negative a positive. Also, when reading, don't believe every word that is written. A company's public relations and projected persona can be mighty weapons in diverting attention to one subject so competitors don't focus on what is really happening behind the curtain at company X. When you are done, you will more than likely discover one or more of their Achilles' heels.

In this learning process going from David to Goliath, figure out how you should stand out and how you can differentiate your products or services from the others. Marketers call this positioning — I call it picking your spot. Example: if the competitor claims to be able to custom-make its widget for a customer in 30 days, the "David" position could be to promote that its product is ready for immediate delivery because it is pre-custom designed for industry X. You package the message that hits the target's needs. If your nemesis many times your size promotes its 24/7 call center, you can position that your company assigns to every client a living, breathing personal service rep who has a beeper and even a first and last name. In every situation there is almost always more than one key positioning opportunity and possibility.

Once you have the answer, it is time to become the mouse that roars. Target your positioning statement where you will get the biggest bang for the buck. It's the 80/20 rule — 80 percent of the business comes from 20 percent of the customers. Small marketing budgets can go a long way producing big results when a laser rifle approach is employed. Another example: if you are trying to reach left-handed, freckled-faced accountants, don't spend big money buying a 30 second TV spot on the Super Bowl to reach tens of millions of people, most of whom don't even have an interest in what you are pitching. Instead run your ad in the Left-handed, Freckled-faced Accountants' Almanac.

Finally, be sure that everybody on your team is tuned in and turned on. Some of the biggest positioning failures occur because management didn't send the "message" to the troops before the big idea is launched. To succeed, an organization must deliver on the promise. Every single person in the organization, institution, company needs not only to hear the message from the top, but also understand it and buy into it and then live by it.

Plan your launch, pay attention to every last detail and listen for the fat lady of success to sing, savoring the thought that the board of directors in Goliath's Ivory Tower is no doubt telling its people that you are smarter, stronger, better than they will ever be. Remember, many a battle can be won with a well-aimed sling shot.

Know when to spar and when to strike

An important lesson to preserve time, energy and sanity

This column was originally published in August 2006

"Youth is a wonderful thing. What a crime to waste it on children."

This quote from George Bernard Shaw could be used with a bit of literary license to describe the inexperienced manager's early naive miss-steps and the value of a little "seasoning." Most of us started our careers with determination. A new and young manager launching a career typically undertakes everything and anything with the same unbridled and dogged enthusiasm, without filtering for the importance factor. Much like young love, it's exciting, but many times ephemeral as the new manager learns the hard lesson that not everything can be a cause celebre and a number one priority. Most importantly, not every battle is even worth fighting. One of the more meaningful lessons a new manager learns in the first few years is: "Knowing when to spar and when to strike."

In this same vein, one must learn that in the rough and tumble corporate/organizational world, getting in the last word in a business debate and proving one's point just for the sake of being right are not always really worth the effort invested. These are sure ways to dissipate one's energy and simply prematurely burn out.

The trick to producing, succeeding and excelling is not to succumb to futile exercises that don't provide an adequate pay back. Sure, most everyone wants to be right and is reticent to back down from a point of view or position which may be laudable and possibly even correct. Before, however, going into battle this simple question must be asked: "To accomplish the objective, or to prove a point, what is

343

the investment in time and energy?" And always consider how much "personal currency" one will have to use to accomplish the goal. This is another reason to also count to 10 before charging ahead.

This may seem mercenary, but after surviving the first 10 years of my career and moving through the maturation process, aka "growing up," I seldom did or said anything unless I knew what was in it for either my company, my cause or me. Sounds Machiavellian but it's a pragmatic approach that avoids superfluous effort . We all have limited mental and physical resources so why waste them on those issues that at the end of the day will do no good and no one will remember anyway?

I don't know many people who would decide to go on a vacation, wake up the next morning, jump in the car and drive away without knowing where they were heading. The same applies to putting money in a bank account; one should always know the interest rate that will be earned. These analogies apply to a business project, initiative, or a debate with a boss, board of directors, peers or subordinates … know the pay back!

Just like working out or lifting weights, sometimes it's healthy and even fun to go through the mental gymnastics of a "friendly discussion." If you're doing it for sport, go for it! However, realize what your motivation is and then enjoy the process, win, lose or draw if that is how you choose to spend your time.

Business transactions, service initiatives and product launches should employ these same ground rules as personal efforts. Many companies have gotten caught up in the chase for the sake of the chase. Wall Street is littered with what at first blush looked like the "dream come true" merger or acquisition. A company goes down the road of the chase, and the contest of who wins begins to overshadow what the deal will produce in long-term benefits. The statistics on deals that actually work as planned are startling. According to a number of experts on the subject, in the U.S. of all business combinations only 25 percent ultimately produced results as originally promised, be it bottom or top line, or other transaction "boast and brag" synergies of market share gain, customer benefits of efficiency. What happened? More likely than not in a number of instances one side got sucked into a battle that wasn't worth winning. The rationale becomes that so much time, effort, and don't forget ego, were invested that the buyer didn't want to back down even though in the buyers' heart of hearts they knew that something just wasn't right. Experience shows that some of the best deals are the ones executives walk away from when they cease to make sense. The headline announcing the big acquisition makes for great reading in the morning paper but remember that same paper with the banner headline will wrap that night's garbage and the glory of the deal will soon bow to shareholders' demanding, "show us the money."

For a more in-depth study on this subject, which can be understood in 3 minutes and 19 seconds, while you tap your foot, I direct you to one of my true business heroes, Kenny Rogers. This legendary composer sang the famous song "The Gambler" which tells it like it is: "You need to know when to hold 'em, know when to fold 'em, when to walk away, when to run." Remember getting there is just the first phase of the real battle.

Which comes first: proclaiming 'game on,' or being 'on your game'?
To succeed, the sequence is the key

This column was originally published in December 2011

A popular phrase today that we hear, read and view online is "game on." These two words typically signify that the time for talking is done and the time for action is now. It's used frequently in competitive encounters, everywhere from the gridiron to the corporate boardroom. I like the phrase because it's catchy and short and implies that one is taking off the gloves to move forward. However, these are just empty words unless they're backed up by effective action and positive results.

For decades — no make that centuries — a variety of gauntlets, both words and objectives, has been thrown down with friend and foe alike to raise the testosterone levels of the combatants. It could be two prizefighters in the center ring who are given their final instructions and then bump boxing gloves or a company's splashy rah-rah sales team video of competitors' products being blown up to symbolize how the new corporate marketing campaign will devastate the other guy.

The problem with phrases, clever clichés and "boast and brag" prognostications is that they mean zilch unless there's a plan to accomplish the feat. That's where being "on your game" in business separates the men from the boys, and the women from the girls. Only hip-shooting leaders would ever think of jumping the gun by proclaiming: "Today, we're going to conquer the world," without first devising a strategy for the team to execute in order to accomplish the objective. Doing this requires a methodical approach before it's "game on."

There are few substitutes, except for perhaps unadulterated luck, for winning without planning, strategizing, training and continuing to fine-tune the integral pieces and parts of the task.

Too many organizations, however, make hollow statements, both publicly and internally, in attempts to fire up the troops to eke out a few extra dollars in sales. Summarily announcing "game on" to your team can cause a great deal of angst and result in serious shortcomings or even total failure if it's not backed by substance.

All too often, leaders assert a battle cry without providing a thorough explanation of the whys and wherefores of the ultimate objective. If this key omission is made, those who have to follow quickly get lost because the goal is blurry, and they either stray from the course or become totally confused. Quickly the team chalks up the boss's assertions extolling the company to reach new heights as just another example of the CEO's having a big hat but no cattle — in direct reference to the rancher who talks a good game but is missing the most important ingredient, the cows.

Engaging in any competition, including business, takes someone to lead and that someone is also responsible for ensuring that all of the required boxes have been checked before proceeding, which includes having a backup plan to make modifications on the fly if any elements of the strategy are not jelling. Good management means understanding how to mitigate risk and quickly discover alternatives.

Not only must a plan be created but all of the essential accouterments must also be provided with appropriate resources, including capital, to achieve the objective topping the list. We can all learn from Apple, a company with the world's largest market capitalization, about how to launch great products not just once but time and time again. Two obvious examples: the iPhone and iPad. Well before Apple even hinted about their existence, it spent years and huge amounts of money not only creating the products but also crafting/branding the messaging to help ensure success.

Apple is the master of starting with a whisper and building to a shout. First there are industry stories about what might be coming, followed by many different "teasers" directed at suppliers to whet their appetites, to consumers to build anticipation and, yes, to competitors to instill a bit of fear. When everything is in place, then it's time for the big announcement that the new product will change the world.

Your organization can employ these same Apple tactics, fueled by a strong dose of perseverance and a liberal amount of perspiration. This all adds up to being "on your game" well before you proclaim it's "game on" because, to succeed, you can't have one without the other.

The other guys
down the street
Who are they, and what can they do for your company?

This column was originally published in October 2011

The other guys down the street, across town or in another state are ubiquitously referred to in boardrooms and management meetings in public companies, private businesses, nonprofit institutions and locker rooms from coast to coast.

So who are these other guys? They are the competition. I'm involved with a number of companies and sit on boards of directors for both corporate and nonprofit institutions. Virtually without exception, at every meeting the other guys surface not once or twice but three or more times without fail. What is even more unusual is that no one ever dares to actually mention the other organization by name. It's as if one is watching a Harry Potter movie in which everyone fearfully refers to the story's antagonist and evil-doer Voldemort as "He who shall not be named."

Something about not uttering the name of the other guys makes them less credible and renders them not quite as powerful or threatening. It's probably much like whistling in the dark; if we hear ourselves whistling, we won't hear the scary sounds, and therefore, there is nothing to fear.

As a business leader, how can you use these other guys or the people down the street to marshal your team, taking them to new heights? In my office for 15 years, I had two baseball caps mounted on the wall emblazoned with each of my two biggest competitors' logos. Each hat also had an arrow running through one side to the

349

other. This display sent a strong message to every visitor that I was focused on "my" own other guys.

Let's face it, competition, as unpleasant as it may be at times, is not only here to stay but also forces your company to strive to be better, provide greater value to your customers or constituents and basically continuously rise to the occasion.

The other guys can be very useful as a benchmark to measure your organization against on just about every metric. I've always felt that a hidden advantage of competition is that everyone needs someone to blame for something and you're much better off having your team blame the other guys for their intermittent woes then blaming you, which proves that in every bad situation there is always some good for someone.

Smart operators know more about the other guys in many respects than they know about themselves. There must be a biological factor in business that makes management secretly think that the competition is smarter, more efficient and does a lot more things right than they do. What most companies don't realize is that the other guys across town are probably sitting in their conference room talking about you and how smart your company is, of course without saying your name, and how you always do it better and that they need to get their act together before you eat their lunch. It is almost ironic because the competition, in many cases, makes a company much better than it would have been otherwise and serves as a catalyst to take that extra step. Leaders deep down inside should be thankful for the impetus that these other guys provide their company or institution.

Those rare organizations that don't worry about the guys down the street are probably the companies that just don't get it and think they're invincible. Inevitably they trip over their own hubris and take a bad, sometimes, fatal fall.

Give me a good fight any time, a tough competitor and someone I can use to rally the troops against, driving them further and faster, based on their competitive need to beat the other guys and prove their self-worth. An added benefit of competition is it also tends to keep a company's ego in check, because just when one company thinks it found the greatest widget of all time, another company comes down the pike that one-ups it.

As much as we hate to admit it, those guys down the street, across town or in the next state keep our blood boiling and energize our creativity. At the end of the day, we are probably better off fighting the competition, lest we start fighting even more with ourselves internally. Because of a worthy opponent, the customer wins, employees stay on their game, and it certainly makes life interesting. That's what the other guys can do for you; all you have to do is learn how to use them to your best advantage.

How to "package yourself" to send the right message

You have less than four seconds to make your first impression

This column was originally published in November 2007

Companies spend hundreds of thousands, if not millions, of dollars to make that right first impression communicating who they are and what they stand for. Before a box of cereal reaches the grocery shelf, scores of "experts" have been involved with deciding what that particular shade of pink on the front of the box might mean to the buyer. Does it stand for warm and fuzzy or wimpy and weak? One of key answers depends on who is the customer: man, woman or child.

With all of this money being invested in the packaging of the package, it is startling to realize how little thought, time and effort are spent on packaging the "packager," defined as the person who is presenting the products, goods or services to the perspective buyer.

Business has evolved over the years in terms of expectations of how associates dress in the workplace. I prefer to call it "packaging the person." From the mid 1960s through the 1980s, business attire for men meant a suit, tie and any color shirt as long as it was white. There were exceptions at the fast track, bleeding-edge companies, which probably allowed pale blue shirts as well. For women it was heels, hose, and dresses just below the knee length or mid-calf unless, of course, one worked for an avant-garde organization. Then the skirt length moved above the knee and the top blouse button could go unfastened to signal utter and unabashed confidence.

The mid 1990s, or thereabouts, ushered in the new Silicone Valley dress code which was defined as "whatever floated your boat." To exude coolness and confidence the extreme power players dressed in the new ultra casual business look which meant wrinkly khakis and t-shirts with provocative message or two-word expletives emblazoned on the shirt, the more outrageous the better. Shoes were optional. Anyone wearing socks was immediately labeled a nerd. This look spread from Northern California's Valley of high technology to Wall Street's Lower Manhattan faster than the CDC's (Center for Disease Control) worst expectations of what might happen someday with the dreaded bird flu.

Then one day some executives must have mused, "Hey, business is soft, earnings are in the dumper, and production is down. It must be the way our people dress." These geniuses probably never thought the cause could be bad financing, poor quality and dumb management decisions. On the heels of this epiphany came the "Dot-Com Crash." This time in reverse geographic sequence Wall Street types were issued mandates that wrinkled khakis and t-shirts were now appropriate only for cleaning the garage, not schmoozing customers. As they say, "what comes around goes around."

So what is the right look for your organization? The decision must be predicated on what you're pitching and how you want to package yourself and your team to make that right first impression. Before you utter, your obligatory "nice to meet you" the customer has already formed an impression not only of you and/or your representatives but also of the organization. The first key to the haberdashery puzzle is whether one is the buyer or seller. The buyer usually has the edge and can dress as he chooses — often extremely informally. The savvy buyer understands, however, that conveying an image of power and authority might eventually help tip the scale when the negotiating process commences.

If you want to create an image of decisiveness, intellect and expertise, it's hard to beat the traditional business look with all its restrictive accouterments, including that noose around your neck. This is particularly apropos when selling abstracts and intangible services when, in fact, brainpower is the product. If you're selling the very cool and very chic iPhone, then a black turtleneck and jeans work just fine, thank you very much, Steve Jobs.

When we started my company, not only did we not have much money, but we also worked out of an office where the rent was a $1 a square foot and we were probably overpaying. No doubt, the impression from this corporate headquarters was "nouveau poor." Attempting to overcome this deficiency on the first day, I wore my best business suit, white shirt and rep tie. The other six people who joined me in this startup appeared à la Silicone Valley in jeans, golf shirts and flip-flops. As I welcomed the team for our first meeting, I ignored superficial appearances and cut to the chase about what we had to do and by when, before the money ran out. A funny thing happened on the second day; a couple of the folks showed up dressed-to-win in their Sunday best and then a few days thereafter the balance chose to adopt "our corporate look." What they realized, as I did, was that if nothing else at least we had to look the part. We had to show others that we were the real deal, knew our stuff and had it together. Therefore, we packaged ourselves accordingly. As vendors started to visit our "world headquarters," which on a good day did have running water, they arrived mirroring our unspoken, unwritten dress code.

The trick is to set standards and know when it is appropriate for traditional business garb vs. a casual look. Instead of "Business Attire" or "Business Casual," your dress code should be known as "Business Ready" so that the total package reflects the contents, and you maximize your four-second opportunity to make the best first impression.

Warning: Satisfaction can lead to complacency

If you are content, you aren't doing your job right

This column was originally published in January 2010

Every company's mission statement should contain what the Federal Drug Administration calls a "black-box warning." This is similar to what appears on each pack of cigarettes and on numerous medications approved by the FDA. For companies, a comparable admonishment should be: "Complacency is a silent value destroyer that can cause your business to fall behind competitors." Remember you are in a race that has no finish line.

Most companies promote the promise of complete satisfaction to their customers, which is a good thing. However, fostering a state of satisfaction and contentment within your corporate culture is not. Am I promoting that all business leaders become malcontents? Yes, pretty much. To do otherwise can stifle innovation. You can bet that as sure as there are little green apples, there are others, right this minute, thinking about how they can do what you do better, faster and cheaper.

Forget for a moment that it's politically correct to assert that competition is good. Frankly, as a CEO, I never once recall jumping out of bed in the morning and screaming, "Yippee, maybe today I'll get a new competitor!" Yes, competition makes us all better but not without considerable pain — both economical and emotional. That's why the best of the best leaders suffer from various degrees of "F of F," or Fear of Failure. F of F is one of the strongest drivers known to man to spur improvement. Every time you think you have it knocked, lo and behold, some competitor that was lurking in the shadows seems to appear almost out of nowhere with a different twist or turn of your contraption or business that makes your heart skip a beat. And that skip ain't caused by love or happiness.

What's a CEO to do?

For survival, you must confront the potential of a new interloper head on. It is altogether fitting that your team pauses to smell the roses by celebrating a success. If you don't, your troops will rightfully perceive you as an ungrateful curmudgeon or an unrelenting taskmaster — although there probably is some underlying truth in these assumptions.

A quick series of attaboys and toasting a win are always appreciated by those involved. However, as soon as the party glasses are cleared from the table, it's time to start planning your next iteration. This is just a simple matter of survival of the fittest. I'm frequently asked, "What are you going to do now that the big job is done?" My response is always, "If I'm doing my job efficiently, I'll never be done." Just look around and you will find examples of too many great ideas that were translated into a finished "must-have" product, only to, in short order, wilt and die on the vine. Does anyone remember Polaroid Instant Cameras, Sony Betamax Recorders or Microsoft's WebTV? All were initially heralded as the next best thing to sliced bread, only to fall from grace when the next generation was introduced — by a shrewd and heartless competitor.

How do you keep your organization energized knowing that once they're done creating they'll have to do it all over again and then again and again? One effective method is to have more than one team ready in the wings to begin working on the same product or project. When team A is done, the next new and improved version becomes the job of team B. While team B picks up the gauntlet, the original team starts on something completely different. team A is satisfied by its accomplishments and can savor the moment while team members gain enthusiasm for their next undertaking. team B, meanwhile, is motivated to top its predecessor with improvements that the first group may not have even envisioned. Competition within your own organization sure beats the competition that comes from outside.

As the leader, your job is to be not only the chief cook and bottle washer but also the head pot stirrer, always prodding the search for the unexplored or the unimagined. Some cynics may call you a malcontent but so be it, because if you're not, you are almost guaranteed to be called much worse — a has-been.

How to get past the toughest gatekeepers
Lessons every executive must teach

This column was originally published in June 2008

In the typical company, about 80 percent of business decisions are made by only 20 percent of its employees. Before your team members can get to a "yes" for an order or deal, they must first navigate past the gatekeeper to reach the decision-maker with the big pen.

Most companies spend their efforts training salespeople how to sell but neglect to teach them how to get in front of the manager who can give the nod.

As the CEO of a *Fortune* 500 company, I was always impressed and, at times, even amused by the renegade peddler who made his or her way across the desk from me for a one-on-one session. I would wonder if this person was the no-account brother-in-law of my gatekeeper, had incriminating photos or perhaps was a bona fide seller who had convinced my assistant that he was offering something that could make a difference.

So what's the combination to unlock that formidable door? First, make sure your people are targeting the right person. Translation: Find out who in the company calls the shots on what your organization is trying to sell and, equally important, who is this honcho's trusted assistant.

Sometimes, reaching the higher-up is easier if one initially starts a step lower. Increase the odds for success by writing and/or calling the target's assistant, addressing him or her by name. Always remember an administrative assistant has real clout and must be treated accordingly.

Unless the salesperson is lucky, the initial call or note will probably not get the job done. Instead, teach your people how to stand out in the crowd. Start with a letter to the assistant and follow up with a phone call two or three days later, but no longer, or the note will be long forgotten. Any combination of phone calls, emails or personal handwritten notes can be effective in breaking through the clutter that bombards an overworked assistant.

Bear in mind that assistants aren't obstructionists. It's just their job to block time-wasters. The worst nightmare for any gatekeeper is being rebuked by the boss asking, "Why did you let that turkey in?" One must always provide meaningful rationale for the proposed tête-à-tête with the leader.

I vividly recall around the spring of 2000 when my assistant suddenly started telling me "wonderful things" about the state of Pennsylvania. Turns out that Tom Ridge, the then-governor of the Keystone state, learned that I would be making a decision on where to locate a new mega-sized distribution center that would employ hundreds of people.

Instead of sending me the usual propaganda, he chose to call my assistant, introduce himself and explain why Pennsylvania would be the right site for us. My assistant later "confessed" that she had several calls and a note of thanks from the governor, who subsequently became the country's first security czar. Although she never admitted it, I suspect the assistant provided the governor tidbits of useful insights about the other states with which Pennsylvania was competing.

It sure doesn't hurt, either, as was the case with Gov. Ridge, to convince this right-hand person she would be fulfilling her mission by getting him through to me because, in fact, Pennsylvania really was the best location.

Things to avoid include calling and saying, "I'm from the IRS," or implying that it's a "sensitive personal matter," which might get one through to the boss but also result in having the phone slammed down in the caller's ear within three seconds.

Also, never, ever bully the gatekeeper with threats, such as, "Do you know who I am?" This tactic is guaranteed to put the pursuer at the top of a "black list" — which can prove more difficult to get off than Homeland Security's "No Fly list."

For those who ultimately reach the sacred ivory tower and are successful, it's wise to give the gatekeeper credit for having had the smarts to let them in, which is exactly what Ridge did. Teach your team members that the velvet-glove approach can spare them the wasted energy from huffing and puffing and trying to blow the door down.

P.S. Yes, Pennsylvania won the competition to become the site of the new facility.

Epilogue

I hope you enjoyed "Tips from the Top" and found at least a few ideas you can put to immediate use in your own world. While the book focuses on business topics, many long-time readers of my *Smart Business* columns have commented that they found many of the themes I have written about just as applicable to dealing with not only their work, but their life and family, and how to get things done. Taking some of the common-sense thoughts I have strived to weave into my narratives, readers have also told me they have applied them to solving a wide variety of uses and capitalizing on all types of opportunities that have come their way.

Another handy method for using this book is to look for topics that might reaffirm a course of action you're considering or, when you have a few extra minutes, simply troll for new ideas.

I plan to continue writing my monthly *Smart Business* columns until someone cries "Uncle" — either my publisher or readers. I encourage you to read the new monthly columns for *Smart Business* by going online to www.sbnonline.com and typing Michael Feuer in the search bar.

As a bonus to those who have purchased this book, you can receive my monthly email version of future columns by simply sending an email to: **Free_columns@mfeuer.com**. In the subject line type: Free column subscription and your email address.

We hope you enjoy reading Tips from the Top columns each month in the future.